# Grounded Theory

# Grounded Theory

## A Practical Guide for Management, Business and Market Researchers

# Christina Goulding

SAGE Publications
London • Thousand Oaks • New Delhi

ISBN 0-7619-6682-X (hbk)
ISBN 0-7619-6683-8 (pbk)
© Christina Goulding 2002
First published 2002
Reprinted 2005

SAGE Publications Ltd
1 Oliver's Yard
55 City Road
London EC1Y 1SP

SAGE Publications Inc
2455 Teller Road
Thousand Oaks
California 91320

SAGE Publications India Pvt Ltd
B–42 Panchsheel Enclave
PO Box 4109
New Delhi 110 017

**British Library Cataloguing in Publication data**
A catalogue record for this book is available from the British Library

**Library of Congress Control Number: 2001135911**

*Printed on paper from sustainable sources*

Typeset by SIVA Math Setters, Chennai, India
Printed and bound in Great Britain by
Athenaeum Press Limited, Gateshead, Tyne & Wear

# Contents

# Acknowledgement

Thanks to Frances, Patrick and Henry

# Illustrations

## Tables

## Figures

# Preface

The primary audience that this book is aimed at is the increasing number of students pursuing taught Master's degrees, higher degrees by research, namely MPhils and PhDs, academics interested in qualitative methodologies, and practitioners who hold an open mind with regard to methodological theory meeting practice. This book will be of value to students on most MA, MBA and MSc programmes which have both a methodology component and the requirement that the student completes a dissertation. From personal experience of teaching Master's-level research courses, PhD methodology programmes, and involvement in supervising MPhil and PhD students, there is a certain amount of *naïveté*, followed by shock, when students, particularly in the management sciences, realise that research involves analysis of philosophy, epistemologies, particular principles and an evaluation of self in the role of researcher. However, given that many Master's programmes are now operated on a semester basis, there is little time for the depth of reading required to assimilate the full range of methodologies, let alone reflect meaningfully on their critics and counter critics.

In addition to postgraduate and research students, with the spectre of research assessment exercises hanging over institutions of higher education more staff than ever are being encouraged down the research road. Journal editors and reviewers are becoming increasingly discriminative and fastidious over methodological procedures and applications, which it appears are fast becoming the main criteria for publication. However, many academics, for example those trained primarily in the positivist approach to research, may not be totally familiar with the area of qualitative enquiry and may need an easy-to-access summary of what is available to them before making a choice. It is hoped that this book will be of value in terms of providing an overview of the key principles associated with qualitative research and in particular those concerned with grounded theory, a methodology that is growing in popularity within the fields of organisational and consumer research.

# Introduction

The main intention of this book is to take the initial frustration out of grappling with some complicated, sometimes confusing and often conflicting texts, journal papers and research reports in order to gain an insight into a particular methodology. The focus of this book is upon one such methodology, grounded theory, an approach which has grown in popularity across a number of disciplines and found its way in recent years into the literature on marketing and management research. The key objectives of the text are to locate the methodology in relation to the changes that have occurred within the field of management, and in particular the area of consumer behaviour with regard to the interpretivist influence on generating knowledge. The book should be of interest to researchers in the field of organisational studies and consumer research where the emphasis is on behaviour. It may be argued that, ultimately, management is about people: it is about communicating, leadership, relationships and culture. Indeed, one of the original authors of the methodology, Anselm Strauss, whilst generally regarded as a sociologist interested in health and coping strategies, contributed significantly to the work on organisational culture through his work on negotiated orders. Consequently, grounded theory is a methodology suited to interaction and, given this emphasis on behaviour, a comparable discipline is that of consumer behaviour, which in recent years has seen a shift away from its focus on positivism and measurement to an appreciation of experiences and meaning, with insights derived from qualitative approaches.

The aim therefore is to offer examples of grounded theory in practice by drawing upon work from both organisational and consumer research. In addition to describing the philosophy and principles associated with the methodology, each conceptual chapter is accompanied by student exercises which allow for critical reflection, and in the case of Chapter 3, data from the author's own research into consumer behaviour are provided to allow students to 'get a feel' for handling interview transcripts.

The text is divided into three sections. The first examines the philosophical principles and procedures of qualitative research and aims to locate and describe grounded theory within the general paradigm of qualitative enquiry. The second section offers an illustration of applying grounded theory, while section three provides a critical review of the methodology in the form of 'some concluding remarks'.

Essentially, the book aims to strike a balance between the theoretical principles behind the methodology, its application, and the problems associated with putting it into practice. The book draws upon the work of a number of authors to illustrate the range of research contexts for which grounded theory is applicable and includes an in-depth case study which charts the process of using grounded theory from the identification of a problem, through to the development of core categories and their integration with the literature.

However, it would be foolish to begin by claiming that there are no good books on grounded theory. To start with there is the classic by Glaser and Strauss (1967), *The Discovery of Grounded Theory*, which lays down the reasons behind the development of the method and details the procedures for applying it. This was followed by Glaser's (1978) *Theoretical Sensitivity*, which elaborated on the nature of theory and in particular the issue of letting theory emerge from the data. In 1990, Strauss and Corbin published the often quoted *Basics of Qualitative Research: Grounded Theory, Procedures and Techniques*. This book marked a split between the two original authors with regard to the principles associated with the methodology and was vociferously criticised by Glaser in his (1992) publication *Basics of Grounded Theory Analysis: Emergence v Forcing*. Consequently it is clear that grounded theory has an established history and that full intellectual ownership of the methodology belongs to the two original authors, Barney Glaser and Anselm Strauss. However, outside of disciplines where the method is heavily used, such as sociology and health sciences, little attention has been paid to the differences in how the method is conceptualised. Furthermore, all the texts mentioned were written by sociologists for sociologists, and whilst there has been a diffusion in the use of the methodology across a variety of disciplines since its inception, the tendency within business and management studies has been to focus primarily on the Strauss and Corbin adaptation to the relative exclusion of Glaser's version. This text aims to strike a balance and evaluates the merits and weaknesses associated with the two approaches.

With regard to structure, the opening chapter is mainly concerned with providing context in terms of the evolution of qualitative methodologies. It begins by outlining the growing use of qualitative research in both academic and practitioner circles and then proceeds to discuss four different approaches to generating knowledge. No book on research methods would be complete without making some reference to the principles of positivism, which still remains the dominant paradigm within the field of organisational and consumer research. Consequently an overview of the philosophies and practices associated with the positivist school are presented before proceeding to contrast them with interpretivist methods of enquiry. This section is followed by a summary of two widely used qualitative methodologies, phenomenology and ethnography, before concluding the chapter with a brief discussion of postmodern perspectives on research in the social sciences. Essentially Chapter 1 attempts to demonstrate the fact that qualitative research is varied in philosophy and practice, and acts as the foundation for differentiation between those methodologies described and grounded theory, which forms the focus of the chapters which follow.

Chapter 2 introduces the qualitative methodology known as grounded theory. Its origins are traced by outlining the nature of symbolic inter-actionism, a perspective which influenced the orientation of the two origina-tors of grounded theory. The development of the method as first presented in *The Discovery of Grounded Theory* (1967) is next reviewed, with a brief overview of the fundamental principles which underpin the methodology. In order to aid comprehension and distinguish the approach from other qualitative perspectives, some of the similarities and differences are explained. These are followed by a definition of theory and the levels of theoretical generalisation. A further factor which is becoming increasingly important when determining the choice of method is the fact that grounded theory has split into at least two camps, each associated with one of the two original authors. This divide between the 'Glaserian' method and the 'Strauss and Corbin' version is summarised in order to provide early guidance for researchers who are new to the method. In recent years we have witnessed the diffusion of the methodology into a range of disci-plines including management. Consequently some examples of the use of grounded theory within the general management sphere are given in order to demonstrate the scope and potential of its application outside of sociology and health studies, the fields most commonly associated with grounded theory. The chapter concludes with an example of cultural and cross-cultural research and addresses some of the potential problems which may be encountered when applying grounded theory.

After having described the origins, divergence in thought, and diffusion across a range of disciplines, Chapter 3 aims to provide an understanding of the early stages associated with the identification of an area of interest and some important questions associated with this stage. The practicali-ties of the process, for example what kind of data are appropriate for grounded theory research, the distinctive nature of theoretical sampling and the use of constant comparison of data as a technique for developing theory from the start of the research are next described before concluding with an explanation of 'when to stop' collecting data and when to consult the literature to enhance theoretical sensitivity. In effect Chapter 3 deals with early decisions, methodological distinctions and procedures for col-lecting data.

Chapter 4 examines the process of handling the data and the various stages associated with abstraction and interpretation. It begins with a description of the most elemental stage in the interpretive endeavour, that of open coding, and proceeds to discuss the more abstract and theoreti-cal stages of the research. In this section the focus is on the nature of axial coding and the identification of relationships across concepts which have emerged from the data as having meaning for the phenomenon under study. Dimensionalisation of concepts into properties forms the basis for the subsequent discussion which also provides an overview of the work of Schatzman who developed the concept of dimensional analysis as an alternative form of grounded theory. This may provide food for thought for researchers considering using grounded theory, but who may be unsure of the version that will have the best fit to their preferred way of working. The section on dimensional analysis is followed by a brief summary of theoretical coding using grounded theory, with a particular emphasis on analytical frameworks, the concept of basic social process, and the conditional matrix. At the pinnacle of theoretical coding are core categories. These are higher order categories which represent the developed theory. The nature and explanatory power of core categories is discussed before attention is turned to the writing process and the challenges faced by researchers when presenting their theoretical interpretations. The chapter concludes with a brief discussion of computer-assisted interpretation and its potential and possible shortcomings in relation to grounded theory analysis.

Chapter 5 represents the first part of an in-depth illustrative case that demonstrates the process of putting grounded theory into practice. Essentially this chapter is about process, emergence and abstraction in the context of analysing the consumption behaviours of visitors to heritage sites and should be of assistance to those unfamiliar with methods of handling inductively derived data. Whilst there are many papers which describe and explain what grounded theory is and how to use it, one of the most common requests of the two original authors (Glaser and Strauss, 1967) is for illustrations of the process to show how theories are developed (Strauss and Corbin, 1994). An obvious response to this is to direct enquiries to published reports, papers or theses. However, as with any methodology, within the final body of the work the actual processes of coding, reduction and concept development become subsumed and invisible in the final interpretation and presentation of the analysis. Therefore, the main aim of this chapter is to demonstrate the application of the method by drawing upon examples from the author's research into consumer behaviour and the meanings derived from visiting heritage sites.

This chapter is split into a number of sections which chart the process of collecting and analysing grounded theory data. To begin with, a brief discussion of the issues and debates surrounding heritage consumption which led to an interest in the topic and subsequent research questions is presented in order to locate the research and give a sense of the rationale for conducting the enquiry. The location of the study and the process of collecting and analysing the data are next discussed in order to give a picture of the theory-building process.

The rest of the chapter is concerned with the various stages of developing the theory. It begins with an example of an interview transcript and presents a memo that accompanied the early analysis. This is followed by a line-by-line analysis in order to demonstrate how one concept was developed. By way of illustration, the process of abstraction is discussed in relation to the development of the concept of nostalgia, the properties of this concept, and, finally, its dimensions. The other concepts which emerged are then described to give a sense of the developing theory. After this a brief explanation of the three core categories is offered and in order to show the process a diagram detailing the concepts which were the foundations for the categories is presented. The chapter concludes by outlining the concepts which formed the starting point for theoretical abstraction and interpretation.

Chapter 6 continues the process of developing theory by re-sorting the data into concepts that have meaning and significance to each other. The key behavioural influences are compared, contrasted and located under unifying categories which were the result of reduction and re-sorting. These behavioural types which constitute the core categories are located, contextualised and evaluated in the literature which informed the theoretical development.

Whilst Chapters 5 and 6 set out the details of theory building within a specific context, Chapter 7, the concluding chapter, discusses some of the decisions and specific problems associated with the process of data collection, analysis and interpretation. The chapter attempts to spell out and pull together some of the main dangers or potential problems most commonly associated with grounded theory. It begins by stating that grounded theory is risky. This is followed by a discussion of the divergence in thought of the two original authors, and a requirement that any researchers considering using the method should base their choice on an understanding of the key issues which define and divide the two quite distinct approaches. Some of the main criticisms of the empirical literature published as grounded theory studies in the field of management are next outlined by drawing a distinction between what is termed 'full' and 'partial' grounded theory. Problems with contemporary interpretation are further explained by considering the implications of rewriting the method and the importation of 'non'-grounded theory rules for judging the credibility of grounded theory research. The discussion then focuses on two specific issues which have been the subject of some controversy and misunderstanding: namely, the overemphasis on induction, which is one of the main reasons many reject using the method, and the problem of premature closure. The chapter draws to a close by revisiting the key stages involved in grounded theory research and addresses the role of the researcher in the process.

# Part One

## PHILOSOPHY, PRINCIPLES AND PROCEDURES

# 1

# The Qualitative Turn in Management Research

## Introduction

The last decade has witnessed several shifts in emphasis among teachers and researchers when dealing with research methodology. First, method has given way to a discussion of methodology. Second, the pre-eminence and predominance of quantitative methodology has been replaced by an emphasis on qualitative methodology in British sociology. Third, stages of social investigation have been replaced with the idea of research as a social process. (Bryman and Burgess, 1994: 1)

Whilst Bryman and Burgess mention the paradigmatic shift in thinking within the field of sociology, this change in thought has spread beyond the immediate field of the humanities and is evinced in the growing number of publications based upon qualitative research evolving from the disciplines of business and management. Even the realm of marketing research, once so heavily reliant on the survey instrument as the main source of data collection, is starting to place greater emphasis on understanding consumer behaviour through qualitative insights, rather than rushing to measure and predict actions before such insights are established. Furthermore, these developments are not purely confined to the domain of academia, but have started to enter the world of commercial research. Shankar and Goulding (2000) note that the Market Research Society commissioned Robson and Hedges (1993) to research the issue of the analysis and interpretation of qualitative research. They found that clients on the whole ignored the issue of analysis and interpretation, as they felt this was the domain of the researcher. Glen (1999) further reinforced this point, viewing analysis and interpretation as a 'black box', with the data being the input and insights into the research problem the output. Interestingly, there is some evidence that managers are more likely to trust the findings derived from qualitative research more so than the findings of large-scale quantitative surveys, mainly as a result of the vividness of the data (Shankar and Goulding, 2000).

## Qualitative Research in the Commercial World

On the surface, therefore, it would appear that how researchers arrive at their conclusions is not too important for clients so long as they get some insights (Shankar and Goulding, 2000). The researchers' experience, methods and ultimately 'value-adding' abilities are often more important than the theoretical basis upon which their insights are based. However, not all practitioners operate in this way. Semiotic Solutions, for example, is a company which specialises in cultural qualitative research, drawing upon techniques borrowed from linguistic philosophy, cultural anthropology and the systematic study of signs and codes. Its findings have formed the basis for many national and international television commercials, as in the case of the British Telecom 'It's good to talk' campaign (Valentine and Evans, 1993; Alexander et al., 1995). Additionally, Semiotic Solutions has been responsible for image and brand changes for organisations as large as Tesco and Coca-Cola. The company's success in promoting itself lies largely in the fact that it locates its insights in theory, it is explicit about it, and it communicates this to its prospective clients (Valentine and Evans, 1993). A sound theoretical basis upon which to base interpretations can therefore give a practitioner credibility in the rhetorical battle to convince clients of the usefulness of qualitative insights (Shankar and Goulding, 2000). Nonetheless, companies such as Semiotic Solutions are the exception rather than the rule and it is within the academic domain that the philosophical and theoretical debates are receiving the greatest attention.

## Academic Divisions in Thought and Practice

Whilst there may be a paradigmatic shift within the field of management studies, it is still in its infancy with many publications continuing to reflect the positivist tenets of enquiry (Hirschman, 1993). Furthermore, it still appears to be a necessary requirement for those engaged in qualitative research that they defend their choice of methodology by first providing a rationale for not using the logical deductive and objective approaches most commonly associated with the scientific canons of positivism. The reverse, however, does not appear to be true. On examination of research publications derived from a positivist or, more commonly, a quantifiable perspective, scant, if any, attention is paid to justifying the use of such a framework in the light of other possible qualitative methodologies. To some degree this is due to the fact that the rules and procedures for establishing knowledge within the positivist framework are less diverse than interpretive methodologies. There are also many cases where accusations of methodological muddling have been made regarding the procedures and epistemological claims (Baker et al., 1992; Stern, 1994; Goulding, 1999a) of the end product. Consequently, owing to the nature of qualitative research, its processes, procedures, goals, claims and diversity of philosophical and intellectual underpinnings, some justification and clarification are often called for. Furthermore, this justification should be based on a demonstrated understanding of what each method involves. Dreher (1994: 293) sums it up in her essay on evaluating qualitative research from the reviewer's perspective, in the statement that:

The single most important element in constructing a research design is the consistency of the method with the research questions being asked. Providing a rationale for using a specific method should not be a treatise on the relative merits of phenomenology or logical positivism, but rather the clearest explanation possible for why the proposed strategy has the potential for answering the specific research question ... this explanation should be grounded in an analysis of the existing research literature.

Although this book is concerned with detailing one specific methodology, that of grounded theory, it is necessary to first outline the philosophical orientations of research methods in general in order to anchor them within the domain of qualitative enquiry. The aim of this chapter, therefore, is to outline briefly the differences in possible approaches to the study of organisational or consumer behaviour, by providing a summary of positivism which is then contrasted with two popular qualitative methodologies, phenomenology and ethnography, before the other extreme in the spectrum, postmodernism is discussed.

## The Positivist Paradigm

### Paradigms in Conflict

From a review of the literature it is quite clear that this book could be devoted to analysing the ongoing debates surrounding positivism versus humanistic methods of enquiry. The field is riddled with opponents levying attacks against advocates of the opposing tradition. On the one hand, many positivists perceive qualitative research to be exploratory, filled with conjecture, unscientific, value laden and a distortion of the canons of 'good' science. For example, Miles and Huberman (1994: 49) refer to a tongue-in-cheek quote from Gherardis and Turner (1987):

The message ... is that quantitative work is courageous, hard biting, hard work. Collecting hard data means making hard decisions, taking no nonsense, hardening one's heart to weaklings, building on a hard core of material, using hard words to press on to hard won results which often carry with them promises of hard cash for future research and career prospects. By contrast soft data [are] weak, unstable, impressible, squashy and sensual. The softies, weaklings or ninnies who carry it out have too much of a soft spot for counter-argument for them to be taken seriously, they reveal the soft underbelly of the social science enterprise, are likely to soft soap those who listen to them. They are too soft hearted, pitying and even foolish to be taken seriously, so that it is only right that they should be employed on soft money.

On the other hand, humanists or interpretive researchers argue that positivism in the social sciences is pseudo-scientific, inflexible, myopic, mechanistic, outdated and limited to the realm of testing existing theories at the expense of new theory development. This debate is as widespread within the field of management, and consumer behaviour in particular, as it is in any of the humanities. Many of these arguments, however, are based on misconceptions, misinterpretations and a certain degree of mistrust regarding the nature and philosophies of the other. Both fields have their different schools of thought, methodologies and intellectual foundations. It is not enough to reject positivism based on the premise of quantification, the use of questionnaires and statistical analysis. This is not necessarily positivism. To reject the paradigm on these grounds alone without exploring its meaning would be to progress from a starting point of half-hearted understanding and appreciation.

### Positivism: Philosophical Foundations

One widely cited author on the subject, Shelby Hunt (1991), recognises this fundamental divide between proponents of the two conflicting schools of thought, and proposes that the debate has largely been poorly informed about the origins and beliefs of an early group of philosophers known as logical positivists. This group of German philosophers (the Vienna Circle) working in the 1920s and 1930s developed a perspective which was highly influenced by the work of Mach, from whom they drew their conviction that science should avoid metaphysical concepts and rely only on observables; from Hume they developed the belief that inductive reasoning is impermissible and only conclusions derived from deduction and direct observational experience could be labelled 'certainties'; and from Wittgenstein they constructed their 'verifiability principle' which required that only statements that could be shown to be true or false could be treated as having cognitive meaning.

Thompson (1993) points to the further influences of the seventeenth-century philosophers Descartes and Compte. For Descartes, mathematics reflected the divine perfection of God's worldly creations. Consequently, understandings that could be expressed in terms of this language provided an indubitable knowledge of the divine natural order. Compte formally adopted the term 'positivism' to describe his methodological procedures for attaining 'positive' knowledge of theory-neutral empirical facts. For Compte, mathematics constituted a supra-human language of description and by using mathematics as the sole method for attaining facts, the realm of scientific knowledge would be purged of culturally bound assumptions and beliefs (Thompson, 1993). Hunt (1991) proceeds to argue that taken on face value, these underlying conditions of positivism have been the source of much criticism and have served to discredit the paradigm. He highlights three elements of positivism in particular that have instigated much debate: the notion of causality, the machine metaphor, and the concept of 'reality'.

With regard to causality he refers to the accusation that the positivist approach emphasises causal explanation due to the assumption that 'real causes' exist, which is an axiom of positivist thinking. In this light Wittgenstein's construal of 'acausalism' means that there can be no question of, for example, invoking a memory as a cause of behaviour. Hunt disputes this accusation as ahistorical and pre-Humean in thinking. He maintains that 'the positivists rejected causality because they viewed "cause" as an unobservable, metaphysical concept that violated their Humean scepticism' (p. 34).

The second misconception centres around the idea of determinism and the machine metaphor, a framework for constructing the world view as mechanistic in which reality is perceived as a machine-like event determined by forces and constraints. Hunt suggests that rather than accept this view, the positivists aimed to develop an alternative by creating one that replaced the machine metaphor with one that was indeterministic and probabilistic.

The third area of debate concerns the ontological interpretation of reality and the concept of reification. In relation to this, critics claim that: 'The positivists tend to take a realist position and assume that a single objective reality exists independently of what individuals perceive ... in contrast interpretivists deny that one real world exists: that is, reality is essentially mental and perceived' (Hunt 1991: 35). With regard to reification, there is the accusation that positivists 'reify' subjective states and treat them like objects. However, Hunt again disputes this point referring to the fact that the positivists embraced a minimal reality known as 'empirical realism' and that those influenced by the work of Mach and Hume viewed unobservables as metaphysical concepts to be strictly avoided rather than attempt to make them concrete.

## The Positivist/Interpretivist Debate

### Science v Humanism

Even when considering positivism in a dispassionate light it is hard to ignore the overtones of the physical sciences, which brings into play the question of treating human social behaviour in such a detached and 'logical' manner. Even if the objective is not to identify 'cause' and 'effect' as if it occurs in a test tube, it is hard to deny the metaphysical, the intangible and the irrational as aspects of the complex, interactional and sometimes conflicting influences that constitute human behaviour. Nevertheless, the paradigm remains saturated with the language and logic of the physical sciences, almost as if the physical sciences have the exclusive premium on credibility. Atkinson and Hammersley (1995) refer to the characteristics of the physical sciences which are mirrored in the positivist paradigm. These include a common logic with the physical sciences reflected in the experimental and quantifiable variables which can be manipulated to identify relationships, as the model for social research and the establishment of universal laws. These universal laws, or the 'covering law' model, are characteristic of explanations of events derived from deduction and statements of regular relationships between variables which hold constant across all relevant circumstances. According to Bryman (1984: 77);

> Quantitative methodology is routinely depicted as an approach to the conduct of social research which implies a natural science, and in particular a positivist, approach to social phenomena. The paraphernalia of positivism are characterized typically in the methodological literature as exhibiting a preoccupation with occupational definitions, objectivity, replicability, causality and the like. The social survey is typically seen as the preferred instrument within this tradition because it can apparently be readily adapted to such concerns. Through questionnaire items concepts can be operationalized; objectivity is maintained by the distance between observer and observed along with the possibility of external checks upon one's questionnaire; replication can be carried out by employing the same research instrument in another context; and the problem of causality has been eased by the emergence of path analysis and related regression techniques to which surveys are well suited.

Atkinson and Hammersley (1995) further highlight that in addition to methodologies, the neutral language of the natural sciences is a feature of positivism. Priority is attributed to directly observable phenomena and the intangible or metaphysical are treated as speculation and as such considered to be 'unscientific'. Within this framework there is little room for theoretical assumptions or flexibility, as standardised procedures for data collection are judged to be the only sound base upon which to build. The question of how theoretical ideas are generated remains largely outside of the realm of 'scientific' method, with the emphasis placed on testing and measuring existing theories. From this perspective, only through the physical or statistical control of variables and their rigorous measurement is science able to produce a body of knowledge whose validity is conclusive, replacing the myths and 'dogma' of common sense. This is a view, however, that is increasingly challenged. Essentially, there is the need to recognise that the landscape of possibilities for conducting research into a wide array of exciting and insightful phenomena is rich in opportunities, and that to

> propose that the hallmark of scientific knowledge is its empirical testability is to settle for far less than we should demand of such an important enterprise as science ... the requirement of empirical testability is notoriously ambiguous within the recognised sciences [yet] it is a criterion that is allegedly met by patently 'non-scientific' disciplines. Thus empirical testability and inter subjective certification are far weaker criteria than we have been led to believe by contemporary positivists. (Anderson, 1986: 156)

Hirschman (1993), whose research is in the field of consumer behaviour and marketing, conducted a historical review of papers published in the *Journal of Consumer Research*, the leading journal in the field. Her analysis revealed a great imbalance between quantitative and qualitative publications, and that by far the most prominent theme in both the 1980s and early 1990s was the use of quantitative models to construct and test consumer behaviour theories. In her critique she proposed that positivism is a masculine and gendered ideology and argued that such a masculine drive towards quantification decontextualises entities and constructs artificial linkages between them on the basis of 'worth' or 'utility'. In this context she maintained that quantification may be perceived as contributing to the process of alienation in modern society, particularly when consumers feel that they have been reduced to mere statistics. She further stressed the cold and inhuman theme of the 'people as machines' metaphor derived primarily from cognitive psychology which depicts consumers as computer-like information processors. In line with this analogy she discussed the fact that such methods of conceptualising behaviour were detached from emotional life, the particulars of time and place, and from personal quirks and interests.

Wallendorf and Brucks (1993) on a similar theme argued for the use of researcher introspection as a method of producing material to provide the empirical grounding for theory-building effort. These approaches vary from the researcher's personal introspection, the introspection of others, interactive introspection (between the researcher and the respondent), synthetic introspection (researcher's life history and experience used as criteria for evaluating the reports of others) and finally reflexivity, the adoption of an analytical stance. Gould (1995) on a somewhat more critical note expanded this view of introspection so that it might be seen as an ongoing process of tracking, experiencing and reflecting on one's own thoughts, mental images, feelings, sensations and behaviours. Using this perspective, introspection could act as an internal method of focusing perceptual awareness along with extrospection, which is a focus on the external world.

### Is there a Place for Both?

Nonetheless, we need to recognise that both positions have their strengths and weaknesses, and their place in the research process, whether used alone or as complementary tools for generating valid and valuable knowledge. Bryman (1984) suggested that the linking of more abstract philosophical issues with questions of research practice offers a more sophisticated way of treating the comparability of different methods of investigation than a direct juxtaposition in terms of relative superiority. Anderson (1986: 159) summarised some of the key issues that need to inform paradigm and methodological choice in an attempt to broaden the acceptability of a diverse array of methods and philosophies as 'good science'. These include:

1 A recognition that scientific methods underdetermine theory choice and scientific goals underdetermine methods. That is to say, methods do not uniquely pick out particular theories, and scientific goals may be achieved via alternative methods.

2  Falsification is not a workable methodology for the social sciences.
3  Empirical tests are not intersubjectively certifiable in any strong sense.
4  Social scientific constructs may be more profitably characterised as researchers' artefacts than as reified 'unobservables'.
5  The content of social scientific knowledge is impacted by social, historical and economic factors.
6  There are many alternative ways of constructing and justifying knowledge in the social sciences.
7  While there exists no privileged epistemological platform from which to assess competing knowledge claims, relative judgements can be made between competing programmes on the basis of social and cognitive aims, metaphysical beliefs and preferred methodologies.

In the midst of the controversy over methodological superiority, it would not seem inappropriate to argue, as do Atkinson and Hammersley (1995), that the first requirement of social science is fidelity to the phenomena under study, not to any set of methodological principles, regardless of how strongly supported by philosophical arguments. On a similar theme, Sandelowski suggests that 'we refute the art in our science when we forget that rules of method serve us, but only to a certain point, after which they may enslave us' (1994: 56). However, on the question of building knowledge, it is clear that there are strict divides between the principles, practices and claims established through the utilisation of positivist and humanist methods. According to May (1994) rules regarding knowing are clearer in the positivist paradigm where findings are a direct product of the observable processes of science, and as such knowledge claims are attributed to verification and replication. The internal processes of arriving at this knowledge, however, are ignored. This is in direct contrast with the principles of qualitative researchers who often have to proceed with 'gut' feeling. This in turn has attracted criticism from positivist researchers who deny the role of instinct, and is defended, in turn, often by an overcompensation and presentation of detailed explanations of implementation and explication of method (May, 1994). Nonetheless, this is often the result of the nature of the process, the requirement for flexibility and theoretical emergence, and self-reflexivity, which are often integral to the experience.

Bryman (1984) suggests that the qualitative researcher embarks on a journey of discovery rather than one of verification. Such research is likely to stimulate new leads and avenues of further research that the quantitative researcher is likely to come across. He continues, however, with the observation that, because qualitative research is often viewed as exploratory, it is designated a much lower rung on the epistemological ladder. However, Bryman proposes that more recent writing on methodology which emphasises epistemological distinctions is less likely to exhibit a propensity to accept a secondary role in the research process. Essentially, it is necessary to understand that quantitative and qualitative research are epistemologically distinct: they offer alternative *modus operandi* for conducting social research.

Nonetheless, it has to be recognised that the positivistic paradigm still dominates much research. However, since the emergence of interpretive approaches we have witnessed a 'spirited debate' (Hunt, 1991) between its proponents and opponents (see, for example, Hunt, 1991; Calder and Tybout, 1987; Anderson, 1986). However, in spite of these philosophical disagreements, the efforts of vanguard researchers have allowed the subsequent development of a variety of innovative interpretive research techniques. What we have seen is the continued enrichment of management-related subjects by researchers drawing from developments in other academic disciplines. For example, the philosophy and methods of existential phenomenology (Thompson et al., 1989), post-structuralism (Thompson and Hirschman, 1995; Holt, 1997), postmodernism (Firat and Venkatesh, 1995), introspection (Gould, 1991, Brown and Reid, 1997), semiotics (Mick, 1986), critical theory (Murray and Ozanne, 1991) and literary theory (Stern, 1989), to name but a few, have all been used in recent times (Shankar and Goulding, 2000).

Shankar and Goulding go on to argue that it is possible that it is this very explosion of different interpretive approaches that is in part responsible for the lack of acceptance of interpretive techniques *per se*. There is no one accepted method; but then, there never can be. Interpretive research methods are thus prone to be criticised because they uphold variations of a relativistic ontology of multiple, individually constructed but socially and culturally constrained, realities. If reality is constructed then it follows that we are active and implicated in that process. This is in marked contrast to the positivistic ontology which suggests there is a single reality 'out there'. Furthermore, because there is a single reality out there, it is also axiomatic within positivism that the researcher is independent of that reality. Controversy within positivistic research is thus mainly reduced to methodological issues (sampling accuracy, reliability and validity of measures, generalizability, etc.) For interpretive researchers it is not quite so simple. They have to entertain complex philosophical debates about what constitutes reality, argue against relativistic criticisms (Anderson, 1986), debate epistemological questions about the relationship between the knower and what can be known, before even getting to methodological issues. It is hardly surprising that most management research is positivistic in nature. Basically it is 'easier' to do (Shankar and Goulding, 2000)!

## Common Criticisms of Qualitative Research

It is probably worth, at this stage, briefly reiterating some of the main criticisms of qualitative research, before moving on to discuss individual approaches and procedures. According to Borman and Preissle-Goez (1986), most often critics of qualitative research operate from the positivist tradition that has dominated social scientific enquiry this century. From this perspective, qualitative research is criticised for not being something it never intended to be in the first place. According to Morse et al. (1998), a common criticism of qualitative research is that it goes nowhere. This is taken to mean that it does not usually fit with the current agenda for practical, managerial, applied and outcome-driven research. However, this accusation needs to be re-examined and the value of qualitative research reassessed. As mentioned in the introduction to this chapter, companies have developed highly successful campaigns based on qualitatively derived data. This disputes the notion that such research generates theory for theory's sake. On the contrary, '*qualitatively derived theory is a refined and tightened view of real-world experiences*' (Morse et al., 1998: 336).

### The Researcher as the Research Instrument

A further bone of contention is that with qualitative research, the researcher is pre-eminently the research tool. Therefore, because all data are filtered through the eyes of the data collector the findings are often considered to be subjective, intuitive and value laden. However, this is a rather condescending view of the researcher. Personal discipline assists qualitative researchers in avoiding excessive subjectivity. Furthermore, it is widely accepted that qualitative researchers should adopt a rigorous and self-conscious examination for bias at each stage of the research process. There is also the requirement that the researcher checks for negative incidents in the data and accounts for occurrences that do not fit the emerging story. Moreover, qualitative researchers also make use of external referees such as other fieldworkers, academics and the informants themselves, in order to check the accuracy of their interpretation. They also check indirectly through the use of similar or related literature which enables them to provide a comparative picture (Borman and Preissle-Goez, 1986).

### Description or Science?

Another charge against qualitative research is that it is novelistic, entertaining and descriptive, but it is not rigorous and falls short at explaining why things happen. This, however, is an unwarranted criticism and relates more to poor examples of flat descriptions which do not allow for the conceptual linkages of incidents and lack any kind of socio-historical context as an explanatory framework. Studies that lack these characteristics are open to attack, and are not demonstrative of the analytical strengths of the paradigm (Borman et al., 1993).

Finally, qualitative research has been accused of having no hard and fast rules of procedure, largely because methods for data collection and samples are not always identified in advance. Furthermore, variables are not always measurable or defined in operational terms. However, reports of well-executed qualitative research often focus on the flexible, evolutionary, and recursive nature of the investigation:

> the emphasis of the paradigm is upon remaining sensitive to the data and to input from the field. When initial questions of procedure appear to clash with incoming information, the paradigm permits researchers to abandon unworkable lines of enquiry and reformulate new ones that have a better fit. The resulting nested working hypotheses help guide a course of enquiry that leads toward results that closely adhere to the phenomenon and have great authenticity. Rather than simply being an ill-thought *ad hoc* operation, the looseness that characterises qualitative research is one of its defining features and greatest strengths: It permits the researcher to correct mistakes. (Borman and Preissle-Goez, 1986: 52)

## A Qualitative Approach

According to Morse (1994) the process of qualitative research relies on inference, insight, logic and luck, and eventually with hard work and creativity the results emerge as a coherent whole. However, some of the key issues that need to be addressed include:

1   An explanation of what was done and how conclusions were reached. This may lead to accusations of overemphasis on method and process, but without this knowledge the soundness or credibility of the findings may be called into question.
2   There have been few attempts to untangle methodological ambiguities, and disagreement among methodologists regarding procedure and protocol still persist.
3   These ambiguities are further exacerbated by differences in terminology. Confusion can occur when using references from different methodologies, and again needs clarification. Furthermore, a common criticism of qualitative research is that it is judged in the same manner as positivist research because it uses the same language, namely the language of the laboratory. This is one area that has attracted accusations against methodologies such as grounded theory: its use of positivist language results in it being misconceived as emulating its procedures. This is a falsity and has led to calls for the development of a specific language in order to allay these misconceptions and embed the practice firmly where it belongs, in the domain of humanistic qualitative research.
4   One further problem in the use of qualitative research is inadequate conceptualisation and understanding of the canons of a given perspective. This has been found to impact on process and findings, or has resulted in the 'mixing' of methods which have different philosophical

foundations (Baker et al., 1992; Stern, 1994; Wells, 1995; Skodal-Wilson and Ambler-Hutchinson, 1996; Goulding, 1999a). There are many qualitative methodologies, including ethnography, phenomenology, hermeneutics, ethnoscience, discourse analysis, conceptual description, ethnomethodology, thematic analysis and constructivism. All have their own philosophies and strategies, but a degree of overlap exists with regard to the data that are collected and used, usually interviews and observations. However, the main problem occurs when the canons of a method are compromised through intentional or unintentional 'muddling' (Skodal-Wilson and Ambler-Hutchinson, 1996). Stern (1994) discusses research that claims to have developed a grounded theory analysis, but explanations of behaviour and theoretical constructs are attributed to the use of an ethnographic framework. Similar problems may occur when a report is presented in terms of percentages based on content analysis and as such falls outside of the arena of interpretive research.

### The Role of Theory

Before any discussion of specific methodologies is offered, there is one common aim of most qualitative methods which needs to be made clear, and that is the role of theory. Whereas positivist research is largely concerned with theory testing, much qualitative work has as its objective the building or development of new theory. This is a critical distinction between the two approaches and according to Morse (1994) challenges the qualitative researcher to push further and take risks in order to contribute. Miles and Huberman (1994: 91) distinguish between different types of theory which include:

1   Implicit theory – This is based upon preconceptions, biases and values which lead us to refer to situations under study as, for example, 'broken homes', thus implying that they are imperfect or damaged.
2   Explicit theory – This is usually a set of concepts which indicate, for example, a hierarchy or a network of propositions. Examples may include 'innovation adoption' or 'culture'.
3   Syntagmatic or process-oriented theory – These are usually the detailed results of a study of process over time of a specific case.
4   Paradigmatic theory – This usually involves using a variable-oriented approach that deals with the relationship among clearly defined concepts. Miles and Huberman give the example of a study of adolescent decisions to attend college by looking at the relationship among variables such as socio-economic class, parental expectations, school grades and peer support.

However, Morse (1994) points to the fact that the neglect or inability of qualitative researchers to make explicit the cognitive struggle of theory construction has led to the belief that qualitative research is 'easy' or 'unscientific', an accusation which she strongly denies:

> Data analysis requires astute observation, questioning, relentless search for answers and active recall. It is a process of piecing together data, of making the invisible obvious, of recognising significance from insignificance, of linking seemingly unrelated facts logically, of fitting categories one with another and of attributing consequence to antecedents. (Morse, 1994: 25)

She draws attention to a number of cognitive processes that are a further common feature of qualitative research and include:

1 Comprehending – The need to learn about the setting in order to distinguish the norm from the exception.
2 Synthesising – The collection of 'stories' and the identification of critical junctures, variations and patterns of alternative stories, during which categories are sorted by commonalties based on segments of transcripts or notes compiled from transcripts.
3 Theorising – The final solution of the theory that provides the best comprehensive, coherent and simplest model for linking diverse and unrelated facts in a useful and pragmatic way. It is a way of revealing the obvious, the implicit, the unrecognised and the unknown. Theorising is the process of constructing alternative explanations until a best fit that explains the data most simply is obtained. This involves asking questions of the data that will create links to established theory.
4 Recontextualisation – The development of the emerging theory so that it is applicable to other settings and populations to which the research may be applied. Here, established theory plays a crucial role by providing a context in which a researcher's model links the new findings with established knowledge. Ultimately, the goal is to be able to place the results in the context of established knowledge and to claim new contributions.

Having looked at the common aim of theory construction through qualitative research, the next sections look at two methodologies, phenomenology and ethnography, in order to illustrate the subtle, but significant, differences in principles and procedures, before discussing the postmodern perspective.

## Phenomenology

### Phenomenology in Management Research

Phenomenology, as both a philosophy and a methodology, has been used in organisational and consumer research in order to develop an understanding of complex issues that may not be immediately implicit in surface responses. For example, Letiche (2000) discussed the underlying philosophies, their various interpretations, and the possible application of phenomenology within organisations, particularly with regard to management change. Boje (2000) extended this by applying phenomenology (in his case, phenomenol complexity theory) within the context of the Disney Corporation in order to investigate change and the management of change. The study raised questions regarding accepted management theories and models and offered a fresh perspective on organisational behaviour. Thompson et al. (1990) on the other hand used a phenomenological framework to penetrate and understand the lived experience of married female consumers, a study which revealed the importance of intangible experiences such as the role of fantasy, imagination and escape in relation to consumption. Also working within the field of consumer behaviour, Goulding et al. (forthcoming) adopted phenomenology to investigate the meaning of the 'rave' experience in relation to consumption and contemporary youth culture. This study examined the importance of symbols, codes, the creation of new communities, and, like Thompson et al., the importance of fantasy and escape. However, whilst these studies provide examples of phenomenology in practice, it is necessary to understand the origins and particular techniques associated with the methodology in order to distinguish it from other forms of qualitative enquiry.

### The Origins of Phenomenology

Phenomenology has a long, controversial and often confusing history within the social sciences (Rhesrick and Taylor, 1995), and, depending upon one's epistemological and ontological position, it is either conceptualised as a philosophy, for those who adhere to the thinking of Husserl (1962) and Heidegger (1962), or a methodology, for those who adopt the position put forward by Schutz (1967). Whilst Husserl's intention was to develop a schema for describing and classifying subjective experiences of what he termed the life world (Langenbach, 1995), Schutz (1967) developed the approach as a method which incorporated details of experience often at the level of mundane everyday life (Costelloe, 1996). The life world is defined as the world in which we, as human beings among fellow human beings, experience culture and society, take a stand with regard to their objects, are influenced by them, and act upon them (Schutz, 1966). Grekova (1996) distinguishes between the life world and the social world, proposing that the life world consists of formal structures about which we are less implicitly aware, while the social world relates to everyday familiar actions and experiences. Essentially, the goal of phenomenology is to enlarge and deepen understanding of the range of immediate experiences (Spiegelberg, 1982). Merleau-Ponty (1962: vii) suggests that the results of phenomenological enquiry should be '*a direct description of our experience without taking account of its psychological origin'*. Phenomenology is a critical reflection upon conscious experience, rather than subconscious motivation, and is designed to uncover the essential invariant features of that experience (Jopling, 1996). It has also been heralded as a critique of the positivist position which views social reality as a system without any respect for the grassroots of everyday interests (Srubar, 1998). Accordingly, the aim of the researcher is to construct a model of the sector of the social world within which only those events and behaviours which are of interest to the problem under study take place (Costelloe, 1996).

## Phenomenology as a Methodology

Schutz proposed that individuals approach the life world with a stock of knowledge made up of common-sense constructs and categories that are essentially social in action. These stocks of knowledge produce familiarity, but they are always incomplete and open ended. Naming requires the interpretative application of a category to the concrete particulars of a situation (Holstein and Gubrium, 1994). Language is the central medium for transmitting meaning and as such provides a methodological orientation for a phenomenology of social life which is concerned with the relation between language use and the objects of experience. The meaning of a word is taken to be what it references, corresponds with, or stands for in the real world. This is based on the premise that the essential task of language is to convey information and describe 'reality'. It is also assumed that there is a degree of commonalty in that others experience the world in fundamentally the same way, intersubjectively sharing the same meaning. The basic assumption is that a person's life is a socially constructed totality in which experiences interrelate coherently and meaningfully. With regard to the process of enquiry, the phenomonologist has only one legitimate source of data and that is the views and experiences of the participants themselves. Furthermore, participants are selected only if they have lived the experience under study. Sampling is therefore purposive and prescribed from the start and the main instrument of data collection is the interview.

> In social research the language of conversation, including that of the interview, remains one of the most important tools of social analysis, a means whereby insight is gained into everyday life, as well as the social and cultural dimensions of our own and other societies. (Bloch, 1996: 323)

## Interpretation of Findings

As a means of interpretation, Thompson (1997), in his analysis of consumer experiences, advocates part to whole analysis of participant accounts by proceeding through an interactive process. This involves reading texts (interview transcripts) in full, in order to first gain a sense of the whole picture. After several readings of the text, the next stage is hermeneutic endeavour (Thompson et al., 1990) or intertextuality (Thompson, 1997), whereby patterns and differences are sought across transcripts. This strategy of interpretation must broaden the analysis to include a wider range of considerations, which helps the researcher arrive at a holistic interpretation. There must also be recognition that the final explanation represents a fusion of horizons between the interpreter's frame of reference and the texts being interpreted (Thompson, 1997). With regard to the application of phenomenology as a method, Morse (1994) summarises the process in relation to four of the constants of qualitative research mentioned previously: comprehension, synthesising, theorising and recontextualisation.

In terms of comprehension, the phenomenologist attains this by first reflecting on his/her own experiences. The next stage is to enter into a dialogue with others to gain experiential descriptions, after which transcripts are examined and key words highlighted. Phrases are sought that will provide or enhance an understanding of the experience and literature is used for further experiential descriptions and compatibility with the findings of the research.

Synthesising involves merging the data and applying thematic analysis in order to identify common 'structures' of the experience. These structures provide the researcher with an understanding of the world which contributes towards the development of theory. On the question of theory Morse (1994) suggests that phenomenologists do not label themselves as theorists in the strictest sense, rather linkages from the data to theory are based on reflections of theoretical literature. Recontextualisation comes from writing and rewriting, which as a practice sensitises the researcher and provides new insights. This increases the level of abstraction by moving from the 'particular' sphere to a 'universal' sphere where themes are readily comprehensible to the humans which they seek to describe.

Nonetheless, it stands to reason that individual situations, circumstances and perceptions will differ. However, whilst acknowledging this, it is also important to recognise that it is the similarities in the way in which experiences are meaningfully shared that form the basis of interpretation (Thompson et al., 1990). Thompson et al. also offer the analogy of a melody when conceptualising such phenomenological themes:

> The perception of a melody does not depend on any specific set of notes. What is critical is the organisation of notes related to each other ... the notes of a song can be transposed into a different octave, yet the same melody will be experienced. (1990: 352)

## Misconceptions and Misuse

However, there are a number of misconceptions and *ad hoc* interpretations of phenomenology to be found in the literature. Firstly, the philosophy that underpins phenomenology is often misused to refer to the qualitative paradigm as a whole. This is not the case. Phenomenologists seek guidance from existential philosophers in the interpretation of their data. Through careful study of individuals they hope to discover the deeper meaning of the 'lived' experience in terms of the individual's relationship with time, space and personal history (Stern, 1994). The collection and analysis of data using this methodology are also specifically prescribed. Phenomenology demands that intense reflection is an integral part of the process, but, above all, the primacy of the subjective experience is felt to be crucial. Analysis is conducted by scrutinising the text for meaning 'units' which describe the central aspects of the experience. These are then synthesised to provide a general description of the 'whole'. In order to highlight the differences in practices and procedures, an overview of ethnography is presented next.

## Ethnography

### The Origins of Ethnography

Ethnographic enquiry is usually concerned with matters of culture, power and sometimes conflict. As such, it is often associated with critical theory (Muecke, 1994). Consequently, consideration has to be given to the fit between the research questions and the appropriateness of the methodology (Hirschman, 1985). Whilst ethnography developed as a method from cultural anthropology, with its focus on small-scale societies, the original central concept remains paramount today; that is, a concern with the nature, construction and maintenance of culture. Ethnographies are always informed by this concept as ethnographers aim to look beyond what people say to understand the shared system of meanings we call 'culture'.

### Ethnography in Management Research

The idea of culture is one which permeates much of the literature on organisations and ethnography has a history in the literature on organisational culture and behaviour. For example, Watson (1994, 1996) conducted an ethnographic study in a manufacturing and development plant. The central focus of the work was the everyday thinking of the subjects and the meanings and processes through which members of particular groups make sense of their world. Watson used participant observation, the primary method associated with ethnography, to study how managers think. This involved spending twelve months as part of the management team, adopting in the process a number of responsibilities. In terms of findings, the research revealed a frequent gap between what managers say and what they actually do. Adopting a similar approach, A. Brown's (1998) investigation of narrative, politics and legitimacy with regard to IT implementation involved researcher immersion in a 'stream of organisational events' in an effort to generate an ethnographic account of the phenomenon. The thick description of the events observed and an analysis of group narratives demonstrated how a system of technical surveillance, designed to routinise and formalise aspects of a social system, was undermined and subverted by the efforts of individuals acting to protect their task discretion and autonomy. Ethnography is also starting to be used in studies of consumption. For example, Schouten and McAlexander (1995) published the results of a three-year ethnographic investigation into the consumption patterns and related subcultural activities of the new bikers in the USA, while Ritson and Elliott (1999) reported the findings of an ethnographic study of adolescents' response to advertising. Both of these papers were published in the *Journal of Consumer Research*, the premier journal in the field, proving that good, rigorous qualitative research is now accepted and is taken seriously. Moreover, whilst these four studies were diverse in terms of context and objectives, they were all concerned with culture, interaction and behaviour. Similarly, the methods used drew on a set body of techniques common to most ethnographic studies.

### Identifying an Appropriate Ethnography

It is important for the researcher considering the use of ethnography to understand the various types of investigation that may potentially form the framework for analysis. Ethnography can be any full or partial description of a group (ethno–folk, graphy–description), as a means of identifying common threads, whether these be religion, social relationships or management style. Ethnographies may be cross-sectional, such as Goffman's (1961) study of asylums which looked at a cross-section of 'total' institutions (Fine and Martin, 1990), or ethnohistorical, which describes the cultural reality of the present as the historical result of events in the past. They may be classified on the basis of spatial or geographic dimensions, by language, by theory, or in any number of diverse ways; there are few limitations to the cultural contexts to which they can be applied (Boyle, 1994).

### Ethnography as a Methodology

Boyle (1994) describes how the product of ethnography may be processual, which describes some aspect of the social experience, or 'classical' or 'holistic' ethnography which focuses on entire social groups and includes descriptions of complete cultural systems and interactive processes. Conversely, the ethnography may be particularistic, which is the study of any social 'unit' or isolatable human group. This form of ethnography involving fewer participants than normal is sometimes described as micro ethnography, but the need to describe and explain holistically remains constant. There are many variations of ethnography, but Boyle lists three characteristics that are common to all. These are:

1 It is holistic and contextual in nature.
2 It is reflexive in character.
3 It always involves the use of emic (outsider perspective) and etic (insider view) data.

Holistic and contextual approaches involve placing observations into a larger perspective where people's behaviour can be understood in the context of meaning and purpose. Its objective is to move beyond description in an attempt to understand why behaviour takes place and under what conditions. Another key component is that of participatory observation, which should combine participation in the lives of those studied while maintaining a professional distance. Participatory observation involves immersion in the culture or way of life of a group, and long-term residence with the group under study, as in the case of Watson (1996), is often necessary to learn about the group's basic beliefs, hopes and expectations (Boyle, 1994). Lowe et al. (2000) offered an interesting example of participant observation and 'shadowing' in their comparative study of British, Mexican and Japanese front-line management and supervision in a Japanese-owned electronics firm. The study involved the collection of data in three different locations and included the analysis of secondary data such as documentary evidence of labour relations, organisational structures, wage rates and appraisal systems. They also interviewed a range of employees including management, personnel staff and supervisors. In addition to this they utilised observational analysis in the form of shadowing supervisors in their daily routine in order to develop a diary of a typical work period. Their general conclusions were that Japanese systems of supervision were transferable to alien contexts.

## Ethnographic Process: Data Collection

As can probably be gathered, ethnography is labour intensive and always involves prolonged direct contact with group members in an effort to look for rounded, holistic explanations. The hallmark of ethnography is fieldwork – working with people in their natural settings. The voices of participants are an important source of data and should be allowed to be heard in the written end product which should be a coherent, fluent and readable narrative (Boyle, 1994; Muecke, 1994). This poses two obvious problems:

1 The researcher must have some basic understanding of the culture and norms of behaviour of the particular society/culture under study, especially if he/she is to gain access to informants who will provide the richness of first-hand accounts.
2 The researcher must be fluent in the language of those studied in order to ensure accurate translation of informant's words. Words may take on a different meaning when translated literally by an outsider, and other considerations need to be given to the cultural significance of non-verbal communication.

In part, the location of studies is often dictated by these concerns. For example, Goulding and Domic's (1999) study of heritage consumption in Croatia required that the researcher responsible for the collection of data was not only fluent in the language, but also familiar with cultural nuances and the implied meaning of non-verbal communication. Whilst some would argue that 'familiarity' flies in the face of the principles of ethnography and its concern with 'alien' cultures (Chock, 1986), the practicalities of the situation are usually the overriding factor. Furthermore, the reflexive nature of ethnography is a characteristic which implies that the researcher is part of the world that is under study and is consequently affected by it (Boyle, 1994). In a catch-22 situation, this view has resulted in criticisms of 'value-laden' interpretations (Borman Preissle-Goez, 1986). However, the interpreter does not take the data on face value but considers them as a field of inferences in which hypothetical patterns can be identified and their validity tested. This usually entails a long and discursive process of data interpretation, reasoning and consideration of the fit to related studies (Agar, 1983; Borman Preissle-Goez, 1986).

Unlike phenomenology, which allows only the voices of the informants to form the theory, with ethnography, insider and outsider views combine to provide deeper insights than would be possible by the 'native' alone. This two-sided view produces a third dimension that rounds off the ethnographic picture which is a theoretical explanation of the phenomena under study. The emic perspective is at the heart of ethnography, while the etic perspective is the researcher's abstractions or scientific explanations of reality (Boyle, 1994). Boyle further suggests that, although ethnographies vary, most combine some element of etic and emic analysis, although the emphasis may differ according to the philosophy of the researcher.

### Analysing Ethnographic Data

With regard to the analysis of ethnographic data, this involves the search for patterns, and ideas that will help explain the existence of these patterns, taking into consideration emic and etic interpretations. This is frequently done through the application of content analysis, a technique for making inferences from text data. Each word or phrase in a text is categorised by applying labels that reflect concepts such as aggression, denial and so forth inherent within it. Some counting may be done (but not always), and some researchers use factor analysis, although this runs the risk of substituting numbers for rich description and it is rare to see this in an ethnographic study. More often than not, the ethnographer identifies categories and instances within the data by desegregating the text (notes) into a series of fragments which are then regrouped under a set of thematic headings.

Morse (1994a) summarises the process employed by ethnographers, again as a series of stages, as follows.

In the first stage comprehension is attained through the data collection process. To begin with observations are unfocused. Data collection proceeds slowly but gradually becomes more specific and the research questions more defined. Unlike the phenomenologist, the ethnographer may use unstructured interviews to supplement observations in addition to data obtained from other sources, such as the minutes of meetings, records, maps and so on, to provide additional knowledge. Comprehension is thought to be complete when the researcher can describe the events, incidents and exceptions from an emic perspective, although the danger of 'going native' (adopting the beliefs and values of the group under study) is one to guard against as to do so would be to bias the interpretation.

The second stage, synthesis, involves coding and content analysis where the data are pooled and the constructed categories are linked. Often, however, ethnographic analysis is not developed beyond the level of 'thick description', presented as informants' stories and case studies. Furthermore, the analytical phase of theorising is seldom separated from the descriptive discourse and treated as a separate level with a distinct purpose.

### Ethnography, the Role of Theory and Ethical Considerations

With regard to theory, ethnography is embedded in cultural theory and the establishment of macro/micro, or etic/emic, distinctions are ultimately linked to established theory. Finally, recontextualisation is achieved by forcing the theory to a level of abstraction, the degree of which determines the generalisability of the theory.

However, according to Atkinson and Hammersley (1994, 1995) the degree to which ethnography is conducted in its 'truest' form is sometimes controversial. To some it constitutes a philosophical paradigm to which one makes a total commitment, for others it designates a method that one uses where and when appropriate. Furthermore they propose that the nature of participatory observation is something that has attracted criticism on ethical grounds and it is argued that the following should be made explicit:

1   Whether the researcher is known to be a researcher by those studied.
2   How much, and what, is known by the participants about the research.
3   What sort of activities are and are not engaged in by the researcher.
4   What the orientation of the researcher is and how involved he/she is in the situation.

While these factors are not necessarily unique to ethnography, the matter of involvement and participation brings them very much to the fore. A further bone of contention stems from those who adopt a critical stance towards ethnography. Critical ethnography, comprising largely feminist and postmodernist perspectives, is thought to present an impressionistic collage, an image that represents only a 'slice' of time and context and therefore challenges the claims of holistic interpretations (Muecke, 1994). On this note attention turns to the final section of this chapter, which to date has focused on examples of philosophy and practice in relation to generating knowledge. Given the nature of the subject matter, it would be difficult to ignore the current trend in postmodern thinking and the controversies and contributions arising from this position.

## Postmodern Approaches to Research

This chapter started by outlining the tenets associated with positivism, a paradigm that conforms to the canons of natural science principles and procedures. It seems fitting, therefore, to finish by considering the reverse of the coin, the antithesis of positivism, by presenting a brief discussion of postmodernism in relation to social research. The concept of postmodernism itself is an amorphous and contentious issue over which there is little cohesion or consensus regarding definitions, origins and applications. According to Denzin (1993) it is a 'slippery term with no clear referents' (p. 507). Firat and Venkatesh (1995) argue for the term 'postmodernisms' to be used in order to reflect the pluralistic essence of this intellectual movement. Lash (1990) maintains that it is often the subject of aesthetic and moral discourse but seldom serious systematic sociological analysis. He further claims that any real value to be gained from the concept can only be obtained by applying it to the realm of culture rather than interpreting it as a defining societal condition such as capitalism. Connor (1995: 184) proposes that in the realm of popular culture:

> the post modern condition is not a set of symptoms that are simply present in a body of sociological textual evidence, but a complex effect of the relationship between social practice and the theory that organises, interprets and legitimises its form.

The idea of postmodernism rests on the proposition that we have entered a new phase or epoch, a post-industrial age characterised by schizophrenic modes of space and time. It is a concept that distinguishes between evolutionary stages and thresholds which mark each particular new era. As such, modernity, as much as feudalism, is a cultural construct based on specific conditions with a historical limit (Foster, 1990). However, Turner (1993) asks the question: are the major changes in the social structure and culture of modern society profound enough to constitute the crossing of a historical fissure on the same magnitude as the transition from feudalism to capitalism?

### Philosophical Foundations of Postmodernism

Whichever perspective is adopted, 'late' modernism, or 'post' modernism, the philosophical roots lie in the post-structuralist rejection and denial of the possibility of absolute 'truths', a questioning of Western metaphysics with its perceived aim of defining, naming and knowing the world. One common property of postmodernism is the claim that if modernity had a particular essence, it was a belief in rational advancement through increments of perpetual improvement, the foundations of which lay in the age of 'enlightenment', the Renaissance with its shift from the mythical superstitious framework of the pre-enlightened period (Walsh, 1992). Modernism saw the development of meta-narratives, statements which implied rigid objectivism and an ultimate thorough analysis of the world from a 'scientific' and rational perspective (Lyotard, 1984). Darwin, Marx and Freud are all symbolic of the 'modern' era with their attempts to explain social phenomena empirically through a general theory of universals. Vattimo (1992) suggests that the main aim of modernity was to present a society that was 'transparent' to its members as structured and understandable. This, he suggests, is impossible in reality as all structures are chaotic and confusing.

The concept of postmodernism is possibly most manifest in its architecture, an attack on the modernist high-rise architecture of the 1960s which brought destruction to communities and the concept of neighbourhood (Haraven and Langenbach, 1981) with its imposition of high-rise 'utopian' tower blocks. This took the form of postmodern aesthetic populism, or the mixing of different periods and historical styles into a form of bricolage (Jameson, 1990). Jameson argues that postmodernism emerged as a specific reaction against established forms of high modernism such as the work of Proust, Joyce, Elliot, Pound and Turner which conquered the universities and art galleries. These styles, formerly thought to be subversive and shocking, were felt to be 'establishment' and dead – reified monuments that offered nothing new. Such movements coupled with advances in the arts and sciences, divisions between 'high' and 'lumpen' art and development through industrialisation, characterise the modern age.

### Postmodernism: A Critical Perspective on Management Theory

Nonetheless, whilst postmodern theories provide insightful explanations of cultural phenomena, they have also proved useful in terms of offering a critical perspective on orthodox management theory. For example, Hassard (1993, 1994) provides a useful perspective from a postmodern position on the sociology of organisations. Cutler (2000) on the other hand analyses the nature of the 'cynical manager', whilst S. Brown (1995, 1998) examines the concept of postmodern marketing in two volumes dedicated to this critical perspective. Feldman's (1998) paper is a very useful explication of the basic propositions of postmodernism and the limitations inherent in its principles in relation to the organisation and particularly business ethics. These are, however, only examples of the work in the field. There is a large and growing literature evolving from the disciplines of management, organisation and consumer studies. This work is continuing to fuel the debate surrounding both the existence of postmodernism and its value as a philosophy and methodological framework.

### Postmodernism and the Role of Theory

One of the key factors that distinguishes positivism, and indeed interpretivism, from postmodernism is the nature of theory. According to Annells (1996: 389):

> Positivism and postpositivist approaches to theory construction have been, and continue to be, a focus of postmodernist challenge. Specifically challenged is the notion that that the enquirer can stand removed from text during the enquiry process and objectively capture 'truth' for encapsulation in a theory aiming for prediction and control. (Annells, 1996: 389)

Annells goes on to argue that:

> For postmodernism, theory construction is a dubious activity and especially problematic in the relationship to legitimate when qualitative research evaluation criteria are merely reclothed or reconceptualised positivist notions of reliability, validity, and generalizability. Postmodern researchers are not concerned about the 'truth' of their research product but rather the pragmatic applicability of their results. (1996: 391)

Indeed postmodernism does appear to offer an alternative view of the social world and it is possibly a matter of philosophy and the nature of knowledge claims that distinguishes the paradigm from other perspectives. There are many critics of postmodernism who see it as anti-establishment, anarchic, nihilistic, openly antagonistic and fatalistic, and as such condemn it outright. Its image is possibly not helped by the fact that there are also those of a postmodern persuasion who do adopt this extremist position and decry any attempts at scientific discovery. As Marcuse (1994) points out, there is currently a widespread reaction to the years of postmodern debate that might best be characterised as ambivalent rejection. Most of those who have been influenced by it now hold postmodernism apart, as an object of reference, used by unspecified others. Nonetheless, it appears to remain a subject of fascination for any who have explored and debated its propositions.

Rule (1995) argues that postmodernism appeals to those distrustful of natural science models of enquiry who are attracted to literary and interpretive approaches to the study of social order. Postmodernists hold that modernism and its accompanying doctrines have become too narrow, dogmatic and unidimensional in their philosophy. Accordingly, modernism is incapable of tapping into the richness of human experience, regards the social order as transparent, and deals only with surface realities and simple solutions. Modernism has come to represent a limiting view of the world as merely a cognitive agent (Firat and Venkatesh, 1995). Harvey (1992) proposes that societal changes are so great that we cannot hope to articulate them fully. This aspect of postmodernism is one that acts as a guiding principle for the activities of the deconstructionists with their suspicion of any narrative that aspires to coherence or bears any resemblance to meta-theory (Harvey, 1992; Feldman, 1998). Nevertheless, in this drive to challenge all basic propositions, knowledge is reduced to a collection of dislocated 'signifiers' in a freewheeling denial of the complexities of the world (Harvey, 1992: 350). Such an approach:

> rejects the enlightenment tradition, challenging global all encompassing world views. It reduces Marxism, Christianity and capitalism to the same order, dismissing them as logo centric, transcendental, totalising meta narratives that anticipate all questions and provide predetermined answers ... All such systems rest on assumptions no more certain than witchcraft and superstition. (Rosenau, 1992: 6).

However, while this is an extremist view, it is not necessarily a solid constant of postmodernism. According to Firat and Venkatesh (1995: 240):

> modernism has marginalised the life world. The post modern quest is therefore to 're-enchant' human life and liberate the consumer from a repressive rational scheme ... modernism reduces the world into simple dichotomous categories of producer/consumer, male/female and so on. Postmodernism regards these dichotomies as unsuccessful historical attempts to legitimise partial truths.

Holbrook and Hirschman (1993) articulate the importance of postmodern interpretivist approaches to the study of consumer behaviour, and point to the need to remind business scholars that those engaged in the humanities are human, and those engaged in the social sciences are social.

Central to postmodern thinking are the influences of culture, language, aesthetics, narratives, symbolic modes and literary expressions. All of these are considered secondary to economy, science, analytical constructs and concrete objectifications by those who hold a modernist position. With regard to process, modernism concerns itself with progression, order and harmony, processes that are considered illusionary by postmodernists who hold that the micro practices of everyday life, discontinuities, pluralities, change and instabilities better define the human condition. Furthermore, postmodernism rejects rigid interdisciplinary boundaries and is eclectic in thought and practice. It accepts the possibility that several theories which may conflict can still have a legitimate place in social discourse. In sum, postmodernists view all knowledge as a construction of one sort or another, and the product of language and discourse. As such they contend there can be no 'ultimate' truth (Firat and Venkatesh, 1995).

## Criticisms of Postmodernism

However, in reaction to this view Parker (1995) proposes that postmodernism is dangerous and no project can be best served by giving up on all notions of truth and progress. Furthermore, he claims, we do not need the label of postmodernism to be humble about truth claims. Today it is generally accepted that we cannot 'know' all that there is to know, and we cannot predict with absolute accuracy. However, postmodernism is premised on continually exposing contradictions at the heart of meta-narratives, and he asks the question: where does this take us? According to his interpretation, the postmodern perspective is limited to an analysis of language, metaphor and discourse as the constructs that shape our world, and these in themselves have their limitations.

Rule (1995) suggests that the problem with adopting postmodernism as an approach is that it leaves little room for the systematic study of social life as there are no rules or norms to guide enquiry, no overall validity, no basis for truth and no causality or responsibility. As such, 'sceptical' postmodernists abandon the mission of research as a futile exercise (Rosenau, 1992). Norse (1991), on the other hand, maintains that postmodernists use theory as a pretext for avoiding any serious engagement with real-world historical events. However, those who reject such an extremist philosophy, 'affirmative' postmodernists (Rosenau, 1992), still hold out hope for a framework for the analysis of political doctrine, and social values. Thompson (1993) adheres to this latter position, proposing that while:

> modernists have always been suspicious of 'interpretation' postmodernists have been equally suspicious of claims to 'objective' truth because they often betray an implicit failure to recognise the socio-cultural underpinnings of scientific understanding. Accordingly, the postmodern concern is not whether theoretical concepts refer to reality, rather it is how theoretical narratives frame understandings and the socio-cultural effects that derive from these narratives. (p. 332)

Firat and Venkatesh (1995) argue that the true nature of postmodernism is the construction of a cultural and philosophical space that is both human and sensible. It is a space that is local and particular rather than universal, acknowledges subject-centred experiences, multitudes of 'truths', and attributes equal status to the role of narratives, discourse and aesthetic and cultural concerns. For example, Harvey (1992) maintains that space and time are basic categories of human experience, yet we rarely debate their meaning. We record the passage of time in hours, minutes, months and years, as if everything has its place upon a single objective time scale. Space gets treated like a fact of nature with common-sense everyday meaning. It has direction, area, shape, pattern, volume and distance. However, space is a subjective experience that can take us into the realms of perception, imagination, fiction and fantasy which produce mental spaces and maps as so many mirages of the supposedly 'real' thing.

### The Fear of Postmodernism

According to Thompson (1993), such alternatives to the established paradigms of viewing and analysing the world constitute a threat to the order of logo-centric rationality, and its procedures for establishing truth. The result of this is a fear that such alternatives will somehow induce the demise of meaning, knowledge, morality and science. Writing on the subject of consumer research Firat and Venkatesh (1995) argue that such fears are based on unwarranted alarmism. They sum it up concisely in their defence of such accusations:

> Postmodernists do not advocate the abandonment of 'scientific' procedures, nothing in postmodernism suggests such a move. Postmodernism simply argues that scientific knowledge should not relentlessly peruse universal knowledge. Translated into the field of consumer research, it means that we must opt for multiple theories of consumer behaviour rather than a single theory that silences all other theories. In addition, we should expand the notion of what a theory is to accommodate different kinds of conjecture and not get bogged down in the correspondence theory of truth ... the joys of doing research must be found not in the pursuit of a holy grail of singular knowledge but in capturing many exploratory moments. Postmodernism is not post science, only post universal science. (p. 260)

## Summary

This chapter has attempted to explain and distinguish between four different approaches to building knowledge in the social sphere. It began with an overview of positivism and then proceeded to compare and contrast its philosophy and principles with the interpretivist school of thought. This was illustrated by offering the examples of two approaches, phenomenology and ethnography. In the final section the concept of postmodernism was discussed in order to highlight the fact that there is no such thing as a simple juxtaposition between quantitative and qualitative methodologies, rather there is a need to understand the guiding ideologies which ultimately reflect the objectives, the context and the claims of the research. One thing that should be clear is that choosing a methodology is a time-consuming, personal and reflective process. It requires an evaluation of self in terms of convictions, beliefs and interests. It means being honest about these beliefs, about what you know, and what you think you can know, and demands commitment to the process once a decision has been made. According to Stern (1994) methods are personal, people think differently and have their own way of getting to some type of truth. Knafl (1994) proposes that this is something that is seldom discussed; namely, the fit between the method and the person, between their style of working, who they are and how they think. Guba and Lincoln (1994: 107–9) summarise the process as a series of questions that the researcher should address in relation to his/her own personal philosophy.

1 The paradigm question – What is the basic belief system or world view that defines the nature of the world, the individual's place within it and the range of possible relationships to that world?
2 The ontological question – What is the form and nature of reality, and, therefore, what is there that can be 'known' about it?
3 The epistemological question – What is the relationship between the researcher as the would-be 'knower' and what can be 'known'? This has strong implications for the fourth question.
4 The methodological question – How can the enquirer go about finding out what he/she believes can be known?

Annells (1996; 379) sums up the process in her comment that:

> the research question is somewhat dependent on the 'worldview' of the researcher. Although the research focus may emerge from a variety of sources, the actual formation of the question arises from the researcher's notions about the nature of reality, the relationship between the knower and what can be known, and how best to discover reality. Thus the selection of method can best be viewed as arising from the basic philosophical beliefs about enquiry as held by the researcher.

Any research is part of an integrated process. It involves the researcher, his/her beliefs and experiences, the co-operation of all involved, the implementation of a chosen methodology, and the realisation that what is discovered is one perspective and a reflection of a process. Very few researchers would be naïve enough to claim that their research provides a definitive explanation of the problem. It is well accepted today that no method allows the researcher access to a font of indisputable truths. Whichever method is adopted the findings will only be one perspective drawn from a range of possibilities. However, Spiggle (1994), in her essay which discusses the trend away from positivism to interpretivism, makes the point that in many cases qualitative researchers stop short at the descriptive level rather than lift the analysis to the level of abstraction and explanation.

One possible approach, suggested by Spiggle in order to move beyond description, is the application of grounded theory. Grounded theory is a method that aims to penetrate the phenomena, by moving through various levels of theory building, from description through abstraction to conceptual categorisation, in order to probe underlying conditions, consequences and actions (Glaser and Strauss, 1967). Grounded theory is a qualitative methodology, but while it retains many similarities with other qualitative techniques such as those outlined in this chapter, it has a set of distinct procedures, which if followed correctly force the researcher to aim at the level of abstract theorising. Having outlined the basic tenets of qualitative research in this chapter, these differences should become apparent as the reader explores the remainder of this book.

---

### Student exercises

1  In no more than 1,000 words, critically evaluate the strengths and weaknesses of the positivist approach to conducting research and the interpretivist perspective.
2  You have been given a research brief to investigate the nature of employee stress in an IT organisation with a particular emphasis on shop-floor workers.

   (a)  You are to design a preliminary research proposal focusing on your sample.
   (b)  You are to detail the method(s) you would use.
   (c)  You are to justify your choice.
   (d)  Consider carefully whether you aim to measure stress or investigate its cause, or both!

3  Taking the four questions

   Paradigm
   Ontology
   Epistemology
   Methodology

   answer them in relation to your own beliefs, perspective and preferred method of working.

# 2

## Grounded Theory

Evolutionary Developments
and Fundamental Processes

### Introduction

This chapter introduces the qualitative methodology known as grounded theory. However, to enable the reader to understand the reasons for, and influences on its development, its origins are traced in order to contextualise and locate its guiding principles within contemporary qualitative research. Consequently, as with the methodological positions discussed in Chapter 1, the opening discussion focuses on the roots of the methodology by outlining the nature of symbolic interactionism, a perspective which influenced the orientation of the two originators of grounded theory, Barney Glaser and Anselm Strauss. The development of the method as first presented in their book *The Discovery of Grounded Theory* (1967), which still remains the primary point of reference for students of the method, is reviewed next, with a brief overview of the fundamental principles which underpin the methodology. In order to aid comprehension and distinguish the approach from other qualitative perspectives, some of the similarities and differences are explained. These are followed by a definition of theory and the levels of theoretical generalisation. A further factor which is becoming increasingly important when determining the choice of method is the fact that grounded theory has split into at least two camps, each associated with one of the two original authors. This divide between the 'Glaserian' method and the 'Strauss and Corbin' version is summarised in order to provide early guidance for researchers who are new to the method, along with indicators of appropriate reading relevant to the respective positions. It must also be acknowledged that grounded theory was developed by sociologists for sociologists, and as such much of the subsequent literature is located in sociological studies. However, according to the basic principles grounded theory is transcendent in terms of its application. In recent years we have witnessed the diffusion of the methodology into a range of disciplines including management. Consequently some examples of the use of grounded theory within the general management sphere are given in order to demonstrate the scope and potential of its application outside of sociology and health studies, the fields most commonly associated with grounded theory.

## The Influence of Symbolic Interactionism

The roots of grounded theory can be traced back to a movement known as symbolic interactionism, the origins of which lie in the work of Charles Cooley (1864–1929) and George Herbert Mead (1863–1931). The concern of these scholars was to avoid the polarities of psychologism and sociologism. Psychologism is a view predicated on the assumption that social behaviour is explicable in genetic terms and by logical or neurological processes. Sociologism is the opposed theory which looks at personal conduct as if it were in some way programmed by societal norms (Blumer, 1969). According to this paradigm, individuals engage in a world which requires reflexive interaction as opposed to environmental response. They are purposive in their actions and will act and react to environmental cues, objects and others, according to the meaning these hold for them. These meanings evolve from social interaction which is itself symbolic because of the interpretations attached to the various forms of communication such as gestures, and the significance of objects. These meanings are modified, suspended or regrouped in the light of changing situations (Schwandt, 1994).

Methodologically, the researcher is required to enter the worlds of those under study in order to observe the subject's environment and the interactions and interpretations that occur. The researcher engaged in symbolic interaction is expected to interpret actions, transcend rich description and develop a theory which incorporates concepts of 'self, language, social setting and social object' (Schwandt, 1994: 124). The developed theory should be presented in a form that creates an eidetic picture, and enduring examples can be found in the work of such scholars as Erving Goffman (1959, 1961, 1970).

Symbolic interactionism is both a theory of human behaviour and an approach to enquiry about human conduct and group behaviour. A principal tenet is that humans come to understand collective social definitions through the socialisation process. The notion of symbols is intrinsic to this perspective and social life is expressed through such symbols which include the most powerful of all, that of language. The classic symbolic interactionism is a micro-sociological theory, as it does not deal with the larger questions regarding the shape of society. Rather, it focuses on the nature of the individual in society and the relationships between individual perceptions, collective action and society (Annells, 1996).

Most symbolic interactionsist approaches within sociology are heavily influenced by critical perspectives. Lowenberg (1993) argues that even before critical perspectives such as critical feminism and postmodernist approaches, traditional symbolic interactionism utilised participant observation to identify power imbalances. The research itself usually takes the form of field studies in which the researcher observes, records and analyses data obtained in a natural setting. However, historically, although the final product was a theoretical explanation of the events, little reference was made to the analytical process used to derive the theoretical explanation (Robrecht, 1995).

## The Origins of Grounded Theory

Using the principles of symbolic interactionism as a basic foundation, two American scholars, Glaser and Strauss, set out to develop a more defined and systematic procedure for collecting and analysing qualitative data. The method they developed was labelled 'grounded theory' to reflect the source of the developed theory which is ultimately grounded in the behaviour, words and actions of those under study. Glaser, in the late 1950s, trained at Columbia University which had a strong tradition of formal theorising, verification and quantitative methods. His main influences were Paul Lazerfield, Paul Merton, Hans Zetterberg, Herbert Hyman and Hannah Selvin. Strauss, on the other hand, studied at the University of Chicago which had a reputation for critical and qualitative approaches such as observation, intensive interviewing and pragmatic theorising (Locke, 1996). However, they both shared a belief in the following:

- the need to get out in the field if one wants to understand what is going on
- the importance of theory grounded in reality
- the nature of experience in the field for the subjects and researcher as continually evolving
- the active role of persons in shaping the worlds they live in through the process of symbolic interaction
- an emphasis on change and process and the variability and complexity of life, and
- the interrelationship between meaning in the perception of subjects and their action. (Glaser, 1992: 16)

Interestingly, Strauss's early studies started in pre-med school. He then changed to psychology and sociology from which he chose to focus on sociology. Arising from this Baszanger (1998) notes how the theme of identity is one which has dominated much of the work of the pioneers of grounded theory. For example, the notion of identity permeates much of the work of Strauss and was used to inform such concepts as social worlds and negotiated order. In Strauss's work there is a recurring emphasis on histories, social situations, and identities developed through interaction. Consequently, meanings are culturally created and mediated and all the interpretations take root in social worlds or communities. However, it is also recognised that individuals participate simultaneously in several communities or worlds and are also responsible for their construction. Hence identities must be seen as multiple, processual and dialogic (Baszanger, 1998). For Strauss, the focus of attention was on active individuals responding creatively to the events which they encounter. These responses, whether individual or group, could only be analysed in terms of sets of prior conditions which themselves influence the present. The present consequences of an action become, in turn, the prior conditions for actions yet to come (Baszanger, 1998). This perspective on behaviour remains a guiding principle behind the methodology that was subsequently developed.

The two respective authors devised the methodology now known as grounded theory while researching the experiences of chronically ill patients. It was constructed as a means of systematically collecting data which could be interpreted and developed through a process which offered clear and precise guidelines for the verification and validation of findings. Such a procedure was deemed necessary given the climate which prevailed. The 'academy' at the time, the 1950s and 1960s, for the most part regarded qualitative research as subjective, unsystematic and, above all, unscientific, and as such unworthy of serious recognition. Thus a method which could track, check and validate the development of theory from a qualitative perspective was deemed both timely and necessary (Goulding, 1998). The richness of grounded theory research is still attributed to the fact that grounded theory is Glaser and Strauss's version of the broader sociological schools of both ethnography and symbolic interactionism (Lowenberg, 1993).

## Glaser and Strauss: The Discovery of Grounded Theory

Grounded theory, in contrast to theory obtained by logico-deductive methods, is theory grounded in data which have been systematically obtained through 'social' research. The development of grounded theory was an attempt to avoid highly abstract sociology and was part of an important growth in qualitative analysis in the 1960s and 1970s. The main thrust of this movement was to bridge the gap between theoretically 'uninformed' empirical research and empirically 'uninformed' theory by grounding theory in data. It was part of a reaction against extreme empiricism, or 'Grand Theory', a term coined by Mills (1959) to refer pejoratively to sociological theories couched at a very abstract conceptual level. Mills similarly criticised abstracted empiricism or the process of accumulating quantitative data for its own sake. It may be argued that like many qualitative methodologies, the role of grounded theory was, and is, the careful and systematic study of the relationship of the individual's experience to society and to history (Goulding, 1998).

Grounded theory was first presented by Glaser and Strauss in their book *The Discovery of Grounded Theory*. The text provided a strong intellectual rationale for using qualitative research to develop theoretical analysis. It was largely a protest against a methodological climate in which the role of qualitative research was viewed as preliminary to the 'real' methodologies of quantitative research (Charmaz, 1983). A further aim of the book was to encourage new and creative research and was a reaction against what the authors viewed as a rather passive acceptance that all the 'great' theories had been discovered (Marx, Freud, Durkheim, etc.) and that the role of research lay in testing these theories through quantitative 'scientific' procedures. Part of the rationale proposed by Glaser and Strauss was that within the field of sociology there was too great an emphasis on the verification of theory and a resultant:

> de-emphasis on the prior step of discovering what concepts and hypotheses are relevant for the area one wished to research ... in social research generating theory goes hand in hand with verifying it; but many sociologists have diverted from this truism in their zeal to test either existing theories or a theory that they have barely started to generate. (Glaser and Strauss, 1967: 1–2).

Grounded theory therefore was intended as a methodology for developing theory that is grounded in data which are systematically gathered and analysed. The theory evolves during the research process itself and is a product of continuous interplay between analysis and data collection (Glaser and Strauss, 1967; Glaser, 1978; Charmaz, 1983; Strauss, 1987; Strauss and Corbin, 1990, 1994). It requires the recognition that enquiry is always context bound and facts should be viewed as both theory laden and value laden. Knowledge is seen as actively constructed with meanings of existence only relevant to an experiential world. Therefore the focus is on how people behave within an individual and social context (O'Callaghan, 1996). Essentially, the methodology is most commonly used to generate theory where little is already known, or to provide a fresh slant on existing knowledge. With grounded theory the researcher must work in the actual environments in which the actions take place, in natural situations, in order to analytically relate informants' perspectives to the environments through which they emerge (Baszanger, 1998: 354).

### Basic Principles

In principle, the naturalist as a researcher will not presuppose more than the basic rudiments of social order and social value. Rather, the naturalist should maximise the possibilities of discovering these as they emerge from the data (Baszanger, 1998). However, this has often been interpreted as a requirement that the researcher enter the field with a completely blank canvas to work from. Glaser (1978) discusses the role of extant theory and its importance in sensitising the researcher to the conceptual significance of emerging concepts and categories. From this perspective knowledge and theory are used as if they were another informant, for without this grounding in existing knowledge, pattern recognition would be limited to the obvious and the superficial, depriving the analyst of the conceptual leverage from which to commence theorising. This is an important point and one that must be stressed early on, as the ultimate goal of the grounded theory researcher is to develop theory which goes beyond thick description. According to the original guidelines (Glaser and Strauss, 1968: 3), the developed theory should:

1 enable prediction and explanation of behaviour
2 be useful in theoretical advances in sociology
3 be applicable in practice
4 provide a perspective on behaviour
5 guide and provide a style for research on particular areas of behaviour
6 provide clear enough categories and hypotheses so that crucial ones can be verified in present and future research.

## Some Similarities and Differences between Grounded Theory and Other Qualitative Approaches

### Similarites

Grounded theory is a qualitative methodology, and as such it shares a number of characteristics with other qualitative methodologies such as those discussed in Chapter 1. For example, according to Strauss and Corbin (1994), qualitative researchers have refined the usual scientific canons of research for the purpose of studying behaviour. However, at this point it is worth noting that even today, all too often qualitative research is assessed as being valid according to quasi-positivistic criteria. Given the paradigm dominance of positivism within the field of management this is hardly surprising. For example, Shankar and Goulding (2001) suggest that qualitative marketing research has tended to adopt Lincoln and Guba's (1985: 289) parallel criteria for assessing the 'trustworthiness' of qualitative insights. Consequently, internal validity is replaced with credibility, external validity with transferability, reliability with dependability, and objectivity with confirmability. Such criteria and language for judging the worth and credibility of qualitative studies can, and do, lead to confusion over the aims of the research, the process followed and the contribution of the end product.

According to Strauss and Corbin (1994), theory is not the formulation of some discovered aspect of a pre-existing reality 'out there'. Such a belief is more congruent with positivist research. On the contrary, truth is enacted and theories are interpretations made from given perspectives. Consequently, it is important to recognise that interpretations are temporally constrained. They should always be seen as provisional and subject to future elaboration, and it should be recognised that they are limited in time; they may become outdated or in need of qualification. Furthermore, Rennie (1998) points out that solutions to problems may be pluralistic. Problems have many facets, and therefore commonality in judgement often comes from scrutiny by a community of enquirers and/or the informants themselves who are sometimes asked if explanations offered accurately describe their experiences. This is sometimes referred to as member checking or auditing.

Additionally, with regard to providing evidence to support the validity of the theory, interpretations must, or should, include the perspectives and voices of those studied. As the researcher proceeds with a piece of work, he/she should pass through a number of stages, each of which, in principle, should add to and refine the theory. In the early stages of data collection, interpretation may consist of, for example, interview transcripts and descriptions of events occurring within the data. As patterns are noted and relationships tentatively identified, the next stage is one of abstraction, through to conceptual identification, and finally theorising. However, the theory should be supported by extracts from interviews, or recordings of observations, which show the fit between conceptual abstraction and reality. This in turn has implications for the kind of data that are collected and how the theory is presented.

With most forms of qualitative research, the sources of data are usually the same. These are most commonly interviews and observations. However, this is where grounded theory starts to differ from other methodologies such as phenomenology, which allows only the words and actions of the informants as a source of data. Grounded theory allows for a much wider range of data, including company reports, secondary data and even statistics, providing the information has relevance and fit to the study. Indeed Glaser and Strauss (1968: 185–220) devote a whole chapter to the theoretical elaboration of quantitative data.

### Differences

Having stated that there are similarities across qualitative methodologies, it also needs to be noted that there are also some fundamental differences. With grounded theory the emphasis is upon theory development and building. For example, Spiggle (1994) advocates the application of grounded theory to the study of consumer behaviour for this very reason. Her argument is that most qualitative researchers shy away from identifying causal links, often stopping short of making conceptual links that result in an integrated structure. Furthermore they seldom provide the setting for identified patterns or themes. In short, 'qualitative researchers do not typically think in causal terms' (Spiggle, 1994: 495).

Grounded theory also has a built-in mandate to strive towards verification through the process of category saturation. This involves staying in the field until no further evidence emerges. Verification is done throughout the course of the research project, rather than assuming that verification is only possible through follow-up quantitative data. This is a subject of some conflict between Glaser and Strauss. Corbin (1998) describes how Glaser believes that verification belongs to quantitative researchers and for grounded theorists the fit between the theory and reality should be sufficient for practical action. According to Glaser, it is the purely inductive which leads only to theory, not its verification (Corbin, 1998). Nonetheless, it may be strongly argued that grounded theory is also validational owing to the symbiosis of induction and abduction during constant comparison of data (Rennie, 1998).

One essential feature of the methodology is that the developed theory should be true to the data – it should be parsimonious. This is a point of departure between Glaser, who argues that the theory should only explain the phenomenon under study, and Strauss, who insists on excessive use of coding matrices to conceptualise beyond the immediate field of study. Furthermore, the developed theory should have conceptual density and meaningful variation which should go beyond thick description. With many qualitative studies, the intended end result is a form of thick description, as in the case of ethnography and phenomenology. Such studies are indeed valuable, but they are also different: they have different aims and objectives to grounded theory research. On this note it is important to clarify what is meant by a theory.

## The Nature and Role of Theory

According to Strauss and Corbin (1994) a theory is a set of relationships that offer a plausible explanation of the phenomenon under study. Morse (1994: 25–6) extends this interpretation by proposing that:

> a theory provides the best comprehensive, coherent and simplest model for linking diverse and unrelated facts in a useful and pragmatic way. It is a way of revealing the obvious, the implicit, the unrecognized and the unknown. Theorizing is the process of constructing alternative explanations until a "best fit" that explains the data most simply is obtained. This involves asking questions of the data that will create links to established theory.

Strauss and Corbin (1990) suggest that a theory has a number of characteristics. To begin with it should be a plausible statement of a series of relationships across concepts and sets of concepts which can be traced back to the data. This plausibility becomes strengthened through continued research. Furthermore, a theory should be conceptually dense. It should include many conceptual relationships presented in a discursive form which is embedded in conceptual writing. Theoretical conceptualisation means that grounded theory researchers are interested in patterns of action and interaction among various types of social units or actors. They are less concerned with theory which centres on the individual. As such, process is a central feature of the theory. Finally, theories should be seen as fluid, owing to the fact that they should embrace the interactions of multiple actors, and emphasise temporality and process (Strauss and Corbin, 1990).

### Levels of Theory Building

Glaser and Strauss differentiate between two major types of theory, substantive and formal. Substantive theory is developed from work in a specific area, such as a particular type of organisation. A substantive theory does not attempt to explain outside of the immediate field of study. The theory should remain parsimonious: that is, it should not try to generalise with explanations of situations for which there are no data.

> A theory at such a conceptual level, however, may have important general implications and relevance, and become almost automatically a springboard or stepping stone to the development of a grounded formal theory. (Glaser and Strauss, 1968: 79)

A formal theory, on the other hand, has explanatory power across a range of situations. For example, it may be a theory of organisational culture that is applicable across organisations rather than specific to a particular type. Formal theory is usually the end product of longitudinal research, normally on the part of a team of researchers engaged in the collection of data across a range of situations and locations. Consequently, owing to the time, expense and high levels of abstraction, most researchers tend to avoid constructing formal theory, preferring to remain at the substantive level.

## Grounded Theory: A Method in Transition

Whilst there are different approaches and aims regarding the development of theory, these also need to be understood in terms of the changes that have taken place with regard to the methodology itself. Essentially there has been a split between how the two original authors conceptualise and operationalise the method, which has resulted in two versions being used. Some of these differences will be discussed throughout the text, but at this point it is worth noting that there are also a number of constants which are used regardless of the version adopted. These include the constant comparison of data to develop concepts and categories; the gradually abstraction of data from the descriptive level to higher order theoretical categories, or one all-encompassing supreme category that forms the basis for the explanation; the use of theoretical sampling as opposed to purposive sampling; the writing of theoretical memos which help track the process and provide a sense of reorientation; and the saturation of data which requires the researcher to stay in the field until no new evidence emerges (Rennie, 1998). A further proposition stated in the original text was that the theory should be readily understandable to sociologists of any viewpoint and that it should 'fit' the situation being researched. By 'fit' it is meant that the categories developed must be applicable to, and indicated by, the data. These categories should also 'work', defined as 'they must be relevant to, and be able to explain the behaviour under study' (Glaser and Strauss, 1968: 3).

There appears to be agreement that since its inception, grounded theory has undergone many major transformations that have distanced it from its symbolic interactionist roots with its emphasis on behaviour grounded in social and symbolic actions. According to Skodal Wilson and Ambler Hutchinson (1996), researchers in disciplines such as nursing, where the method is widely used, are now obliged to specify whether the grounded theory approach they employed is the original 1967 Glaser and Strauss version, the 1990 Strauss and Corbin rendition, or the 1978 or 1992 Glaser interpretation. This is largely the result of the two original authors reaching a diacritical juncture over the aims, principles and procedures associated with the implementation of the method. This bifurcation was largely marked by Strauss and Corbin's 1990 publication of *Basics of Qualitative Research: Grounded Theory, Procedures and Techniques*, which provoked accusations of distortion and infidelity to the central objectives of parsimony and theoretical emergence (Glaser, 1992). In the face of this, grounded theory has split into two camps, each subtly distinguished by its own ideographic procedures. On the one hand, Glaser stresses the interpretive, contextual and emergent nature of theory development, while, on the other, the late Strauss appeared to have emphasised highly complex and systematic coding techniques (Goulding, 1999a). In particular, Strauss and Corbin (1990) exemplified this rupture with their presentation of multiple coding procedures such as open, axial and selective coding, and techniques of comparison that are now used to advance analysis by the intentional manipulation of data in a variety of ways (Kools et al., 1996). This overemphasis on the mechanics of the research has been criticised for reducing the degree of theoretical sensitivity and insightful meaning (Glaser, 1992). For example, Stern (1994) argues that Strauss, as he examines the data, stops at each word to ask 'what if?' Glaser keeps his attention focused on the data and asks 'what do we have here?' Strauss brings to bear every possible contingency that could relate to the data whether it appears or not, while Glaser lets the data tell their own story.

A comparison of the original *Discovery of Grounded Theory* with Glaser's 1978 *Theoretical Sensitivity* and Strauss and Corbin's 1990 *Basics of Qualitative Research* demonstrates the subtle but distinct differences in perceptions of the method between the authors since its inception. Not only are there differences in style and terminology, but Strauss and Corbin's version of the method has been reworked to incorporate a strict and complex process of systematic coding. Glaser's reaction to these developments was vociferously documented in his publication *Basics of Grounded Theory Analysis* (Glaser, 1992) which is a critique of Strauss and Corbin's popular and widely used 1990 work. Pages 1–2 detail letters from Glaser to Strauss imploring him to withdraw his text for revision on the basis that what it contained was a methodology, but it was not grounded theory. He stated that in fact it ignored up to 90 per cent of the original ideas and proceeded with the accusation that:

> Strauss's book is without conscience, bordering on immorality … producing simply what qualitative researchers have been doing for sixty years or more: forced, full conceptual description. (Glaser, 1992: 3)

Other grounded theory researchers have reiterated this, arguing that Strauss has modified his description of grounded theory from its original concept of emergence to a densely codified operation. To Glaser, the Straussarian school represents an erosion of grounded theory (Stern, 1994). However, these discrepancies came as something of a surprise to Strauss and Corbin, who saw it more as a difference in writing style and interpretation. Nonetheless, the two men had not worked together for more than twenty years and both had developed different research and teaching careers (Corbin, 1998). Whilst not wishing to enter into a discussion about the differences inherent in the two approaches before explaining the nature of grounded theory, it is important to note that it is now generally accepted that at least two versions do exist. Consequently, care should be taken to decide which method best suits the researcher's personality and preferred modes of working, before embarking on the research.

## A Method for Sociologists or Adoption in the Field of Management

As may be inferred already from the previous discussion, grounded theory was originally developed as a methodology for sociologists. However, as a general methodology it has been adopted within the disciplines of psychology, anthropology, nursing, social work, education and more recently management. This has meant the adaptation of the method in ways that may not be completely congruent with all of the original principles. As with any general methodology, grounded theory's actual use in practice has varied widely with the specifics of the area under study, its purpose and its focus. This does not mean that its central elements are altering, only that additional ideas and concepts suggested by new intellectual movements are entering analytically as conditions into grounded theory studies (Strauss and Corbin, 1994). Most texts and articles on the subject advocate reading the original *Discovery* as a starting point. Whilst it may have dated somewhat since its publication, the guiding principles and procedures are explained in detail and endure as the essential guidelines for applying the method. According to Lowenberg (1993: 62):

> Social scientists have been moving in a diametrically opposed direction. Particularly in sociology and anthropology, but also in a broad range of social sciences and humanities ... the interpretive research approaches have not only gained broader acceptance, but also have moved in more radical and less structured directions.

Both theory and research in the social sciences are increasingly emphasising everyday life experience. Not only are more disciplines embracing interpretive approaches, but they are doing so within a collaborative, interdisciplinary framework (Lowenberg, 1993) and this is also the case within the fields of organisational and consumer behaviour. One often overlooked fact is that Strauss has contributed significantly to work on organisation culture. Baszanger (1998) describes in some detail this contribution. In their work on negotiation and social worlds Strauss and his collaborators developed a different approach to what is more generally known as the sociology of organizations and their interpretation owes much to the symbolic interactionist philosophy. For example:

> organizations are not seen as formations structured by unequivocal standardized rules. Individual and collective reflections and dialogue are necessary not only to modify the rules but also to maintain and reproduce them. The very existence of organizations depends on their continuous reconstitution in action. Their aims and strategies can be debated, and the agreements arrived at can take on varied forms, including the intentional or tolerated coexistence of many different goals. Each agreement is transient and conditional. The actors themselves have theories arising from their daily experience, concerning the nature, scope, and possible success of the negotiation process.

Baszanger goes on to say that:

> Strauss proposes a paradigm of negotiations, a grid for analysing negotiation processes, and applies it to a wide range of case studies ... He starts, as in his analysis of work, from the negotiation itself and the secondary sources (e.g., bargaining, obtaining gratification, paying debts, and negotiating agreements), interactions, types of actors, their strategies and tactics, and then proceeds to examine the consequences. (Baszanger, 1998: 367)

Unlike many traditional organisational studies, Strauss did not start with the proposition of a formal division of labour, nor the allocation of tasks. On the contrary, his main focus and central argument concerned the primacy of the work itself. By analysing not only occupations or organisational structures, but also the work itself, concepts such as mistakes at work, group work, and work with customers and clients came to be seen in a different light (Baszanger, 1998).

Apart from the work of Strauss, there is growing recognition within the field of management that alternative perspectives on experience are needed. For example, Calloway and Ariav (1995) argue that there is a growing sense in the management information systems (MIS) research community that new ways of discovering knowledge are needed and qualitative approaches to MIS research seem to offer some possibilities. This point is reinforced by Seeley and Targett (1997) and King (1996), who argue the case for interpretive case research as a complement to positivist thinking by bringing to light the human and organisational issues which strongly influence systems development practice. Other research in the field, for example A. Brown's (1995) study of the political processes through which legitimacy was sought for a large IT system by its sponsors, further underlines the growing acceptance and use of grounded theory research in the field of managing understanding.

TABLE 2.1 *Examples of grounded theory in management research*

| Example | References |
| --- | --- |
| Senior executives and IT | Seeley and Targett (1997) |
| Systems development | King (1996), Calloway and Ariav (1995) |
| Managing understanding in organisations | Brown (1994, 1995) |
| Organisational culture | Turner (1981, 1988) |
| Staff perspectives on work | Clegg et al. (1996) Nuefeldt et al. (1996) |
| Retailer response to manufacturers' low-cost programmes | Manning et al. (1998) |
| Rural women entrepreneurs | Egan (1997) McKinley-Wright (1995) |
| Competitive strategy and manufacturing process technology | Schroeder and Congden (1995) |
| Building co-operation in competitive industries | Browning et al. (1995) |
| Consumer behaviour | Houston and Venkatesh (1996) Goulding (1999b, 1999c, 2000b, 2000c) |
| Advertising and mass media | Hirschman and Thompson (1997) |
| Marketing | Burchill and Fine (1997) De la Cuesta (1994) Beard (1989) |
| Career development | Sperber-Richie et al. (1997) |
| Electronic data interchange | Crook and Kumar (1998) |
| Leadership in organisations | Parry (1998) Hunt and Ropo (1995) |
| Strategic alliances | Lang (1996) |
| Ideal business images for women | Kimle and Damhost (1997) |
| Tourist behaviour | Riley (1995, 1996) |
| The information-seeking patterns of academics | Ellis (1993), Ellis et al. (1993) Cole (1997) |
| Employment outcomes | Mullins and Roessier (1998) |

In particular it is an approach which allows the researcher to look beyond the surface, to embrace issues of myth making and power (Brown, 1994), and to explore the symbolic (A. Brown, 1995). Table 2.1 is intended to give a snapshot of the diffusion of grounded theory in management research, and the nature of the issues explored using its principles.

As can be seen from this snapshot, grounded theory is being used to explore a wide range of management issues. Ultimately, in many ways management is about people, their behaviour, relationships and communication. This may involve using grounded theory in leadership studies, as in the case of Parry (1998) and Hunt and Ropo (1995), or the management of self-identity at work (Kimle and Damhost, 1997). Management is also about markets and developing and maintaining an understanding of the behaviours of those markets, as in the case of Hirschman and Thompson's (1997) grounded theory study of consumer response to advertising messages.

Additionally, grounded theory has been used to explore cultural issues in relation to organisations (Turner, 1981, 1988), consumption behaviours (Houston and Venkatesh, 1996) consumer experiences (Goulding, 1999b, 1999c, 2000b, 2000c), and tourist behaviour (Riley, 1995, 1996). In contrast, competitive strategy and manufacturing processes have been looked at using grounded theory, as have strategic alliances (Lang, 1996). These situations merely serve to demonstrate the transcending nature of grounded theory and its potential for application in the field of management research. There is of course another issue that should be addressed, which has implications for both the selection of an area of study and the methods chosen for investigation. This is the area of cultural research, particularly if it involves investigating non-familiar cultures (for an excellent example of the process of developing grounded theory in a non-familiar culture see Turner's [1994] account of patterns of crisis behaviour).

Traditionally, cultural research has been dominated by ethnographers. However, there has been an increase in recent years in the publication of cultural analysis of work settings, and more recently within the literature on marketing. Naturally enough, this raises issues about interpretation and the need to understand cultural nuances, and even begs the question: should we be trying to conduct cross-cultural research at all without some first-hand appreciation of the particular culture we wish to investigate? According to Barnes (1996: 430) the danger with qualitative methods that do not make culture explicit is that culture can become transparent or lost in the pages of observations, interviews and analyses of social processes.

## Grounded Theory and Cross-Cultural Research

Increasingly, the critical role of language is seen as problematic and the nature of the context as constituitive of meaning has caused concern for those involved in qualitative research (Lowenberg, 1993). There is some debate as to whether the researcher should conduct the research if he/she does not share the same language as those being researched. For example, should the researcher analyse transcribed scripts and field notes based on interviews constructed and translated by someone else? With the exception of Barnes (1996) these issues have been largely ignored in the literature on grounded theory, but they do, however, need to be addressed as the following extract illustrates:

> An important linguistic question when doing qualitative research with respondents from a culture(s) different from that of the researcher is the possibility of using translated texts for analysis. It is generally acknowledged that translators actually interpret, rather than translate literally, constantly making judgements about what the respondent meant to say and what the researcher meant to ask. A language barrier between researcher and respondent disarms a researcher's ability to assess meanings, intent, emotions, and reactions and creates a state of dependency on the interpreter or translator. (Barnes, 1996: 433)

Culture conditions the use and meaning of language. Language describes the boundaries and perspectives of a cultural system and reflects how social life is represented within that culture. Different cultures use words, narratives and explanations differently according to the understandings shared by members of a particular cultural group. Different cultures supply different verbal interpretations of reality and thought. Physical gestures, postural attitudes and distance from the respondent to the interviewer are all organised in pattern sets, such as words and sentences (Barnes, 1996).

Consequently, a researcher using interpretive methods should construct his/her analysis in reference to the respondent's cultural orientation. The researcher should be sensitive to the kinds of questions asked and the techniques employed for conducting interviews. Barnes (1996) suggests that it would be helpful for grounded theory researchers to have experience of the culture of the respondents, either by living or working in their culture prior to investigation. They should be attentive to their beliefs, customs, habits and cultural context. Without sufficient cultural experience an interpretation may not be culturally relevant and may create description rather than interpretation.

> Although not frequently reported in grounded theory studies a multicultural study should emphasize the collection, recording, and analysis of data in the context in which it was collected, including the space, actors, time, and feelings of the context. (Barnes, 1996: 439)

However, this may not always be enough. There are times when the researcher has to stand back from the problem and thoroughly assess the situation. For instance, the example of research into consumer experiences and interpretations of historical representations in Croatia mentioned in Chapter 1 was originally designed with the idea of using grounded theory. However, after a short time in the field it became clear that the central issues that were emerging from the data did not lend themselves to the grounded theory paradigm. The research needed to be reassessed and relocated within a more critical perspective. As a result of this an ethnographic framework of analysis was adopted in order to situate the concepts of language, power, control and culture within the historical and political literature pertaining to the complexities of that particular country. However, because grounded theory did not work in this case, there are situations where it has proved suitable. For example, Houston and Venkatesh (1996) offer an illustration of researching an unfamiliar culture using grounded theory and the importance of looking beyond language to gain an understanding of particular behaviours.

### Grounded Theory and Culture: An Example

Houston and Venkatesh (1996) undertook a study of the consumption patterns of Asian immigrants to the USA based on the rationale that whilst the Asian population represent a significant group of consumers, relatively little attention has been paid to influences on their consumption patterns. Therefore grounded theory, with its emphasis on inductive theory development, was considered an appropriate methodology for the study. The authors spent eight months in the field collecting data and made use of source documents such as field notes, interview transcripts, focus group data, and the concurrent integration of secondary, interdisciplinary literature as new concepts were developed and refined.

Their findings centred around the relationship between three concepts:

1   Cultural health beliefs – These concerned attitudes towards conventional and alternative methods of treatment and health practices and indicated a predisposition towards culturally determined practices (vapour cupping to suck out poisonous air and so forth).
2   Cultural values systems – These revealed differences in such factors as time orientation which had obvious implications for health scheduling. They also highlighted problems of communication and the low utilisation of services. These were linked to the third concept:
3   Cultural differences in the consumer/provider relationship – This concept identified the need to develop trust, break down cultural barriers, and look beyond language as communication to consider non-verbal cues.

The findings had practical implications for health care managers. They pointed to a lack of awareness on the part of the establishment regarding the importance of cultural factors in the way people define themselves, the way they seek help, and the way they present problems and respond to treatment. They also offered an explanation of reasons behind the low utilisation of health care, the high rates of emergency room usage and the lack of pre-natal care. The results of the research offered opportunities for developing clearer communication and greater efficiency.

Their research provides an example of the merging of disciplinary boundaries such as sociology, consumer behaviour and marketing, and is indicative of the current interdisciplinary thinking within the general field of management.

## Summary

This chapter has attempted to differentiate grounded theory from other qualitative methodologies, particularly with respect to the nature of theory and the process of developing or inductively building theory. It has largely been concerned with the evolutionary developments and diffusion of grounded theory research, the splintering or fragmentation of the methodology, and its growing application in the field of management research. The next chapter focuses more on process and the fundamental principles associated with generating theory through the collection of various types of data.

---

### Student exercises

1 Compare and contrast the basic philosophy and principles associated with grounded theory with those approaches described in Chapter 1, namely:

   Phenomenology
   Ethnography
   Postmodern perspectives

2 What do you feel are the main strengths and weaknesses of grounded theory in comparison to phenomenology, ethnography and postmodern approaches?

3 In order to gain an appreciation of grounded theory in practice, students should obtain a sample of papers from those listed in Table 2.1 (Examples of grounded theory in management research) and then carry out the following:

   (a) Conduct a comparative analysis of which version of the method was used (i.e. the 1967 original, Glaser's (1978) *Theoretical Sensitivity*, or Strauss and Corbin's (1990) version).
   (b) Analyse how the method was used (what was the *process* of grounding theory in the data?)
   (c) Which grounded theory principles were applied (i.e. theoretical sampling)? What coding procedures were used? Did the author(s) reach saturation? How did they justify this?
   (d) Was the process of how the theory emerged made explicit?

# 3

## Getting Started

### Data Collection and Sampling

#### Introduction

Since a description of the origins, divergence in thought and diffusion across a range of disciplines was given in Chapter 2, the purpose of this chapter is to provide an understanding of the early stages associated with the identification of an area of interest and some important questions that may arise from this stage. The practicalities of the process, for example the kind of data appropriate for grounded theory research, the distinctive nature of theoretical sampling and the use of constant comparison of data as a technique for developing theory from the start of the research, are next described before concluding with an explanation of when to stop collecting data and when to consult the literature to enhance theoretical sensitivity. In effect this chapter deals with early decisions, methodological distinctions and procedures for collecting data.

#### The Identification of an Area of Interest and Data Collection

Despite conflicting perceptions over methodological transgressions and implementation, there remains a set of fundamental nomothetic principles associated with the method (Goulding, 1999a). Initially, as with any piece of research, the process starts with an interest in an area one wishes to explore further. Usually researchers adopt grounded theory when the topic of interest has been relatively ignored in the literature or has been given only superficial attention. Consequently, the researcher's mission is to build his/her own theory from the ground. However, most researchers will have their own disciplinary background which will provide a perspective from which to investigate the problem. Nobody starts with a totally blank sheet. A sociologist will be influenced by a body of sociological thought, a psychologist will perceive the general phenomenon from a cognitive, behavioural or social perspective, and a business academic may bring to bear organisational, marketing, economic or systems concepts which have structured the analysis of managerial behaviour. These theories provide sensitivity and focus which aid the interpretation of data collected during the research process. The difficulty in applying grounded theory comes when the area of interest has a long, credible and empirically based literature. Grounded theory may still be used, but work in the immediate area should be avoided so as not to prejudice or influence the perceptions of the researcher.

Here the danger lies in entering the field with a prior disposition, whether conscious of it or not, of testing such existing work rather than developing uncoloured insights specifically pertinent to the area of study. In order to avoid this, it is generally suggested that the researcher enters the field at a very early stage and collects data in whatever form appropriate. Unlike other qualitative methodologies which acknowledge only one source of data, for example the words of those under study as in the case of phenomenology, grounded theory research may be based on single or multiple sources of data. These might include secondary data, life histories, interviews, introspection, observations and memos.

## Sources of Data

Glaser (1978) discusses the adaptability of the method, proposing that:

> Grounded theory method although uniquely suited to fieldwork and qualitative data, can be easily used as a general method of analysis with any form of data collection: survey, experiment, case study. Further, it can combine and integrate them. It transcends specific data collection methods. (Glaser, 1978: 6)

Grounded theory is transcending in the sense that it conceptualises the data, thus raising the level of thought about the data to a higher level. It also transcends by inclusion and integration at a higher level previous descriptions and theories about an area and uses them to create a dense integrated theory of greater scope. One of the key aspects of grounded theory is the generation of 'good ideas' (Glaser, 1978). As already stated, grounded theory may include data collected from a wide range of sources, and as with any other qualitative research may include the use of secondary data to give context and factual substance to the analysis.

## Secondary Analysis of Qualitative Data

Secondary analysis involves the use of data that have been gathered for a previous research study. However, the interpretation and use of secondary data has received limited coverage in the literature. Szabo and Strang (1997) suggest that this is largely due to perceptions that research is only 'real' if it involves original data collection. Nonetheless, there are instances when lack of resources, time or problems with gaining access to individuals may necessitate the examination and inclusion of secondary data as the main source of information. Szabo and Strang (1997) suggest that apart from the obvious cost-effectiveness and convenience, there are a number of advantages to using secondary data. Namely, that while it removes the steps of sampling and data collection, more effort is placed on other elements of the research process such as analysis and interpretation of findings. Furthermore, secondary analysts have the opportunity to view the data from a different perspective to the original researcher, which may open up new conceptual interpretations. Turner's (1994) analysis of patterns of crisis behaviour during a fire at the Summerland Leisure Centre on the Isle of Man in 1973 acts as a good illustration of this.

Turner began by examining documentary accounts provided by the public inquiry into the fire. He then proceeded to label cards with the titles of categories which had been identified in the official documents. This was done by scrutinising the reports, paragraph by paragraph, with the aim of developing a theory of disaster prediction:

> I then recorded each name or concept label on the top of a 5 inch by 8 inch file card, together with a note of the source paragraph, and added further paragraph references to the card as I encountered additional instances of the concept identified. (p. 198)

During the course of the analysis, 182 cards were produced which had to be 'sorted and juggled into a theoretical model' (p. 198). The process involved the search for general definitions for categories and the identification of causal links. By incorporating data from previous disasters with the Summerland incident, the core of the emergent theory was refined. The emergent concepts included:

- Reliance on informal networks to communicate about ill-structured problems.
- The waiving of regulations.
- Ineffective safety procedures.
- The use of ambivalent statements which apparently resolve differing views of complex problems.
- Idealistic and unrealistic normative views of a problem area by top management.
- Limited range of action and responsibility for individuals whose organisational position and organisational behaviour are influenced by institutional bias.

In addition to having theoretical significance, the findings of this study also had policy implications for the prediction and management of disasters.

A further example of using secondary data as the primary source of information is the case of a researcher who was engaged in a grounded theory study of language ability in relationship marketing as a factor influencing the success of small and medium-sized enterprises in overseas markets. In this instance the researcher had difficulty in gaining access to a wide spectrum of companies. However, he was granted access to data collected over a period of time by the Department of Trade and Industry. The data concerned companies which had won awards for excellence and been analysed for the factors involved in success. Raw data, both quantitative and qualitative, were made available and the principles associated with grounded theory (open and selective coding, constant comparison, dimensionalisation, concept development and category identification) were employed to form an interpretation of those data.

However, this particular researcher encountered a number of problems similar to those noted by Szabo and Strang (1997). Basically these centre around the fact that there are limitations to what can be achieved through the use of secondary data. First, there is the lack of control in generating the data to be used for the study. Problems may include the fact that the researcher is unable to ask questions that come to mind when, for example, listening to a taped interview. There is also no opportunity to conduct second or third interviews for elaboration, clarification and penetration of particular issues which may emerge as important. Consequently, theoretical sampling is only possible within the confines of the data set (Szabo and Strang, 1997). This may limit the degree to which the researcher can truly claim saturation. It is therefore necessary that the original data set is large enough to allow for the process of constant comparison and theoretical sampling if the results are to be recognised as a product of grounded theory.

### Using Life Histories as Data

There are many ways of collecting data and the range is not limited to those described in this book, which deals with the most commonly used methods. One of these is the collection of life histories or diaries which have been constructed by participants and which provide insights into a 'slice of life'. Clondinin and Connelly (1994) discuss the use of getting informants to construct annals of their lives or part of their lives. This allows the researcher to gain a sense of the whole of an individual's life as described from his/her point of view. They suggest that after the informant has constructed the document he/she should be asked to tell stories, describe chronological events and elaborate on major junctures. A particularly powerful way to track and reflect on experiences is to ask informants to keep a journal or a diary which may then be analysed both from the perspective of the writer and the researcher. One example of this approach used in a grounded theory study is McKinley-Wright's (1995) investigation of rural women's work experiences. In this study women were asked to provide reflective life history projects. These were semi-structured reminiscences which covered the entire life course of the informants. Descriptions were developed of the way women engaged in formal (paid), informal (market work) and home-based work and from these descriptions the most salient properties were identified, grouped and dimensionalised in order to show the intensity or the importance of the actions. The analysis focused on the consequences of the work experience and the coping strategies developed by the women. The analysis identified three important dimensions of a continuum model of work based on economic benefits, location and time control characteristics. These tended to funnel women into multiple work strategies where they combined several labour options to maximise economic benefits. The findings of this research had practical implications in that it cast doubt on some social policies regarding child care and care of the elderly. However, whilst life histories are a useful method, it is not always practical to expect informants to co-operate fully, or even be relevant to the research problem. By far the most common source of data used in grounded theory and qualitative research in general is interviews.

### Interviews

As in many forms of qualitative research, interview data are usually favoured as a means of illustrating findings and supporting the developed theory. According to (Bloch, 1996: 323):

> in social research the language of conversation, including that of the interview, remains one of the most important tools of social analysis, a means whereby insight is gained into everyday life, as well as the social and cultural dimensions of our own and other societies.

Interviews may take many forms: they may be structured, unstructured, group, face to face or conducted over the telephone. With grounded theory the most common form of interview is the face-to-face unstructured or, more realistically, semi-structured, open-ended, ethnographic, in-depth conversational interview. This is favoured because it has the potential to generate rich and detailed accounts of the individual's experience. It should also be flexible enough to allow the discussion to lead into areas which may not have been considered prior to the interview but which may be potentially relevant to the study. However, interviews are not always easy to conduct and require a certain amount of skill and usually a great deal of practice. Fontana and Frey (1994) offer a summary of the key considerations associated with interviewing which include:

- *Accessing the setting* – Gaining entry into an organisation and permission to talk to employees, management or customers may not always be straightforward. Access needs to be granted before the interviews can take place and this can take time, particularly if the researcher has to go through a number of different channels or layers to receive permission.
- *Understanding the language and culture of the respondents* – This is an issue that has been discussed in Chapter 2. Of course it is not always relevant, but, for example, when the research is of a cross-cultural or multicultural nature it becomes of prime concern.
- *Deciding on how to present oneself* – This naturally begs the question: how much detail is revealed about the nature of the research to the

informants? It tends to influence the nature of the relationship between the researcher and the researched. Other considerations, such as whether the researcher presents him/herself as an academic, a 'learner' or a fellow worker, need to be thought through carefully beforehand as the method of presentation may dictate the openness of the responses given.

- *Locating an informant* – It can be very useful and time saving if the researcher can identity a key informant who can not only provide information, but also introduce others who are willing to talk and share experiences. The idea of key informants is particularly valuable during the early stages of grounded theory research when sampling is open and data collection is conducted with the objective of generating ideas for more focused work.

- *Gaining trust* – This is important for any interview situation, but particularly if the research is of a sensitive or very personal nature, or if there is any fear that the information may be used against the individual supplying the detail. Trust and confidentiality need to be established right from the very start as it is virtually impossible to develop them late in the research when attitudes are already formed.

- *Establishing rapport* – As with the issue of trust, it is unlikely that the informant will be forthcoming with information if no sense of rapport or affiliation exists. Consequently an obvious academic position or even an overfamiliarity with the informant may detract from the quality of the data. Fontana and Frey (1994) point to the fact that there will of course be times when it is impossible to establish a rapport, or be able to trust that what is being said is accurate and truthful. This supports the proposition that the researcher should stay in the field, interviewing as many as it takes to saturate the data, which is a feature of theoretical sampling.

In addition to these factors, which are mainly concerned with the collection of data, there are also 'types' of interview data which are worth mentioning as they may provide some guidance when interpreting, labelling or comparing transcripts.

Haslam (1999), in his research into personal legitimising in the context of small consultancy firms, adopted the Glaser model of theory building. His thesis provides a good example of handling interview data based on Glaser's description of five different types of data: baseline, interpreted, properline, vague and conceptual. The following is drawn from Haslam's (1999) work in order to illustrate the nuances between the various forms of data:

- *Baseline* – Baseline is factual and may be used as a reference point. Haslam includes the following extract from an interview with one consultant which was conducted over lunch:

  KGL talked about her fee earning ability since joining the firm. She said, where she worked previously, a good consultant could invoice £220k per year. Between June and December she invoiced £170k.

Here there is little to be interpreted; it is just a clear factual statement regarding potential and actual earnings of a consultant.

- *Interpreted* – The second form of data is known as interpreted. Essentially, this is because it represents participant's interpretations of their behaviour or experience. For example:

> *Interviewer:* How did they [the consulting firm] get on internally [with the client on an assignment]?
>
> *Respondent:* The team I was working with last year, very well. BB [managing partner] has very little exposure to the business now, he's had one meeting with me and the Group Chief Executive, which I would say didn't go down as well as we'd hoped. TC [senior consultant and project manager of the assignment] had a pretty direct style which our group executive liked. BB is quite reserved so there wasn't any chemistry there that existed before, but they are very different individuals.

Haslam discusses how the respondent was interpreting the affinity between her firm and a client's organisation as a factor of the personality fit between the two heads of the two organisations. He also describes how he was able to check this by talking to the two heads who were the subject of this conjecture to see if their interpretations matched the respondent's.

- *Properline* – This form of information involves people choosing expressions to support a particular line: For example:

> TS talked about the firm being 'completely postmodern'. TS had attended the staff meeting a few days previously where the managing director had spoken about the firm as 'postmodern' in its approach. I looked for TS to expand on what he meant by postmodern and he spoke about the split of the firm into two separate businesses, and their intention to get rid of all bureaucracy and red tape.

Haslam interpreted TS's use of postmodern as a properline view on how the firm operated. This led him to investigate further whether the term really did reflect the style of work, and also what activities were classified as postmodern.

- *Vague* – Vague data, on the other hand, are imprecise. They may simply require further investigation, or may be deliberately vague in order to conceal an aspect of behaviour. Haslam illustrates the evasiveness of the respondent in one particular instance:

> *Interviewer:* What do you use them for?
>
> *Respondent:* Lots of culture stuff, just lots and lots of stuff. And we'd also used them to give psychological support to people within the company. That's an area I obviously don't want to talk much about.

- *Conceptual* – Conceptual data are the fifth form of data type and usually involve an ungrounded opinion or hypothesis, as in the following extract from an interview about the future of the company:

  *Interviewer:* I'll go on and ask the question about the picture of the future and how marketing fits.

  *Respondent:* And the view that I was just thinking about – the cultural elements of this business that attract people and keep people. There is space for you to do what you want here. And it may be, that people become too self indulgent in doing what they want to do.

  In his analysis Haslam discusses the way in which the respondent introduces the concept of 'becoming self-indulgent' and how she articulated the outcome as a process, suggesting that one of the causes was the freedom for staff within the firm.

This categorisation of the different data types is useful for developing initial codes. However, with grounded theory, the idea is to look for patterns and reoccurring events in the data through comparing data against each other. Consequently, it is important to recognise that it is the similarities in the way in which experiences are meaningfully shared and expressed that form the basis of interpretation (Thompson et al., 1990). As mentioned earlier, there are a number of considerations which may affect the outcome of the interview, such as presentation, trust and rapport, and the degree of honesty which exists. It is sometimes suggested that in order to minimise the possibility of corrupt data, the same informant be interviewed at least twice or, failing this, engage others to assess the paucity of the responses.

## Introspection

On a different but related theme is the role of introspection in the process. Introspection has been the cause of some controversy between the two original authors particularly with regard to the notion of introspection and personal experiences. This debate is not limited to the application of grounded theory and is worth some attention. According to Corbin (1998), early on in the research project meanings may be obscure, particularly the meaning or relationship between early emerging themes. Consequently, we should be able to draw upon prior knowledge and experience in order to stimulate comparisons in the data:

the researcher can get – and cultivate – crucial insights not only during his research (and from his research) but from his own personal experiences prior to or outside it. ... such insights need not come from one's own experience but can

> be taken from others. In this case the burden is on the sociologist to convert these borrowed experiences into his own insights. (Glaser and Strauss, 1968: 252)

Nonetheless, there are a number of 'types' of introspection other than just self-reflection on experience. The following is taken from Shankar et al.'s (2001) discussion of introspection in the research process in order to clarify its meaning and place.

Introspection is the examination of one's own mental and emotional processes. During the research conversation the researcher draws on these pre-understandings to interpret the participant's emerging story. During a research conversation inconsistencies in this story may become obvious to the researcher. The role of the researcher is to interpret these inconsistencies. These interpretations are then offered to the participant, reflected on by both researcher and participant, and revised during the conversation until consensus is achieved between them. Interpretation is always an ongoing event. Typically in interpretive research, an interpretation is normally arrived at after the interview process. Interpretation may be shown to the original participant for subsequent corroboration or member checking (Shankar and Goulding, 2000).

Shankar and Goulding propose that such a technique has four major implications for interviewing. Firstly, the task of the researcher is very onerous and so more than one interview may be necessary to allow space for both researcher and participant to reflect. Secondly, this process is best suited to interviewing techniques like the long interview (McCracken, 1988). Long interviews can last for four hours or more and will often involve more than one interview. Thirdly, the technique requires that a good deal of trust and rapport exists between researcher and participant so that the interpretation–reinterpretation process becomes 'power neutral'. Finally, such a technique requires both researcher and participant to exhibit a high degree of self-reflexivity. Nonetheless, despite these difficulties, Rennie (1998: 109) suggests that grounded theory's innovation is its ability to work with:

> the subjectivity and reflexivity of both the subject being addressed and the researcher doing the addressing. The theories it produces are about the meaning of experience – they are 'emic' as much as 'etic' and it is very difficult to preserve the subjectivity by appealing to the objectivism of the natural science methodology.

This captures the essence of introspection as a two-way process. However, Rennie goes on to warn against pure reflection and personal introspection as the sole source of data, by noting that the:

> problem with introspection and self experience as a source of data is that it's against the symbiosis of abduction (hypothesising) and induction (testing of these hypotheses). It is a way of developing conceptualisations that are insufficiently grounded. (p. 113)

## Observational Data

Another method of collecting data, and one which is often used to complement interviews and sometimes introspective accounts, is that of observation. According to Grove and Fiske (1992) observational methods refer to data-gathering techniques that focus on 'experience' by providing 'real'-world impressions in authentic surroundings. These observations can be either mechanical, through the use of videos, or human. However, in keeping with most writers on the subject, Adler and Adler (1994) suggest that the hallmark of observation is its non-intrusive nature which minimises any interference in the behaviour of those observed, neither manipulating nor stimulating them. Observation of behaviour also locates the researcher within the context under investigation, a point which Belk et al. (1989: 1) propose leads to:

> highly charged encounters suffused with meaning. Because these incidences are directly experienced by the researcher, the significance of the phenomenon is more fully appreciated.

We all use observational techniques as part of everyday life. They are a way of constructing meaning and attributing 'sense' to interactions and actions, but as human beings we do not, or cannot, internalise the whole range of activities occurring in the social world around us. This 'selectivity' has filtered through as one criticism of the method and is one reason that mechanical observations are sometimes considered more reliable. They also provide a record which may be used as evidence when presenting the data. On the other hand, there are ethical issues raised by covertly recording the behaviour of individuals without their knowledge or consent. This is not an easy problem to overcome as awareness on the part of the observed inevitably alters that behaviour and ultimately the outcome of the research. Other problems documented by Adler and Adler (1994) include questions of validity, for example there are no informant's quotes to confirm findings, and there are also issues of reliability such as the degree of 'chance' occurrences versus 'real' behaviour. Furthermore, it needs to be recognised that the problem with observational understanding is its inability to open up the meaning of an individual's lived experience for the observing individual (Costelloe, 1996). In isolation observations do little to explain what is happening and why individuals act in particular ways. In order to overcome some of these fundamental problems Adler and Adler (1994) suggest the use of multiple observations, the search for negative cases to enhance validity, and the repetition of observations across various conditions and places to strengthen reliability.

## The Use of Memos

One of the problems with observational data is conveying the story or events to the reader in a manner that is believable and a true reflection of the process. With grounded theory, another central part of the method is the use of memos throughout the research journey. Memos can be used with observational data, or with any form of data. These memos are vital as they provide a bank of ideas which can be revisited. They help map out the emerging theory, and are used to identify concepts and their properties Essentially memos are ideas which have been noted during the data collection process and which help to reorient the researcher at a later date. However, ideas can also occur away from the data and should be written down as the ideas strike. Glaser (1978) provides some useful guidance in relation to producing memos and using them to underpin theory. He suggests that memos are a core stage in the process, and without using them theoretically to write up ideas, the researcher is not in fact doing grounded theory.

We can ask ourselves: what do memos look like? Essentially they can be a few lines or several pages long. According to Glaser (1978), the researcher should write freely and take chances with ideas. In the initial stages, memos should be run 'open' without claims to fit. Fit can be established through the sorting of memos at a later stage. Without memos there would be no ideas. Memos help to generate relationships, abstract integrative frameworks and more general problems. They are also an excellent source of direction for future theoretical sampling (Glaser, 1978).

In terms of using them to aid in the interpretation of data and theoretical formulations, during the sorting process memos may be cut up and sorted comparatively on the basis of reoccurring concepts. Each memo should be introduced by a title or a caption, which is usually a category or a concept. Any other concepts or properties which appear in the memo should also be highlighted and their relationship discussed. This will allow the researcher to sort for evidence of these concepts in further memos. Glaser recommends that in order to maximise the use of memos, memos and data should be kept separate. Essentially they are ideas and descriptions, and consequently it is suggested that data should be kept out of memos, except in some cases where the former can be used to illustrate a particular case, or to refer the reader to particular field notes. Moreover, using memos as data is part of the process of abstraction, and therefore, when writing memos, ideas should be expressed in conceptual terms, not necessarily in people terms. Memos should be a consistent part of the process and should be generated simultaneously throughout the sampling and data collection stages. Drawing on their own experiences and the work of Glaser (1978) and Strauss and Corbin (1990), Miles and Huberman (1994: 74) offer a good checklist of advice on using memos, which include:

a) Always give priority to memoing. When an idea strikes, STOP what ever else you are doing and write the memo. Your audience is yourself. Get it down. Don't worry about prose elegance or even grammar. Include your musings of all sorts, even the fuzzy and foggy ones. Give yourself the freedom to think. Don't self censor.

b)  Memoing should begin as soon as the first field data start coming in, and usually should continue right up the production of the final report.
c)  Keep memos "sortable." Caption them by basic concept and mark or under-line other concepts discussed in the text of the memo.
d)  Once again, memos are about ideas. Simply recounting data examples is not enough. By the same token, memos are not chiefly about people or events or interactions; these are all used as indicators for an analysis that is set in a conceptual frame.
e)  Don't standardize memo formats or types, especially in a multi-researcher study. Memoing styles are distinctive, and memo types are as various as the imagination can reach.
f)  Memo writing is fun. And it often provides sharp, sunlit moments of clarity or insight – little conceptual epiphanies.

Memos therefore are an integral part of doing grounded theory research. Another key aspect of grounded theory is that of theoretical sampling, which differentiates it from other qualitative techniques in the sense that it is guided by the developing theory rather than being predetermined. The next section looks at the nature of theoretical sampling in order to clarify this fundamental feature of grounded theory research.

### Sampling in Qualitative Research

It is fair to say that sampling has a profound effect on the quality of the research, regardless of what methodological perspective and approach the researcher adopts. However, in the literature, there appears to be some con-fusion as to the nature of sampling in qualitative research. To a degree, this confusion is the result of differences over sampling terminology and precise procedures for collecting data. Drawing on the work of respected qualita-tive researchers, Coyle (1997: 627) offers an insight into the variations on sampling in qualitative research. These are summarised in Table 3.1 in order to show the diversity in terms of terminology which could potentially lead to confusion and ambiguity in the sampling stages of the research.

### Theoretical Sampling

With grounded theory sampling is directed by theory. It is an ongoing part of the process of data collection and analysis which in turn directs the researcher to further samples. Some might argue that all sampling in quali-tative research is to a degree selective. However, while a qualitative project may contain both purposeful and theoretical sampling, purposeful sampling is not always theoretical. Theoretical sampling is the purposeful selection of a sample according to the developing categories and emerging theory (Coyle, 1997). Glaser argues that purposeful sampling refers to the calculated

TABLE 3.1 *Types of qualitative sampling*

| | |
|---|---|
| Theoretical sampling (Strauss and Corbin, 1990) | Open sampling<br>Relational sampling<br>Discriminate sampling |
| All sampling is purposeful – fifteen strategies (Patton, 1990) | Extreme or deviant case sampling<br>Intensity sampling<br>Maximum variation sampling<br>Homogeneous sampling<br>Typical case sampling<br>Stratified purposeful sampling<br>Critical case sampling<br>Snowball or chain sampling<br>Criterion sampling<br>Theory-based or operational construct sampling<br>Confirming and disconfirming cases<br>Opportunistic sampling<br>Purposeful random sampling<br>Sampling politically important cases<br>Convenience sampling |
| Four types (Morse, 1991) | Purposeful sample<br>Nominated sample<br>Volunteer sample<br>Total population sample |
| Two types (Sandelowski et al., 1992) | Selective sampling<br>Theoretical sampling |
| All sampling is purposeful – three kinds (Sandelowski, 1995) | Maximum variation<br>Phenomenal variation<br>Theoretical variation |

decision to sample a specific locale according to a preconceived but reasonable set of dimensions (time, space, identity or power) which are worked out in advance of the study. The analyst who uses theoretical sampling cannot know in advance what to sample for and where it will lead (Glaser, 1992; Coyle, 1997). With grounded theory, groups are chosen when they are needed rather than before the research. Initially, the researcher will go to the most obvious places and the most likely informants in search of information. However, as concepts are identified and the theory starts to develop, further individuals, situations and places may need to be incorporated in order to strengthen the findings. This is known as theoretical sampling which is:

> the process of data collection for generating theory whereby the analyst jointly collects, codes and analyses the data and decides what data to collect next and where to find it, in order to develop the theory as it emerges. This process of data collection is 'controlled' by the emerging theory. (Glaser, 1978: 36)

Grounded theory is about the simultaneous collection and analysis of data. If following the guidelines correctly, the researcher will start to generate codes within days of entering the field. The data are then analysed in order to see where to sample next. Groups are then selected for their relevance for furthering the development of emerging categories and concepts. The researcher must then calculate where the next theoretical question will lead, and where a given order of events is likely to take place (Glaser and Strauss, 1968). Glaser and Strauss suggest that sampling should be centred around groups. The researcher should systematically start sampling in groups that give data on each possible direction. The process starts with open coding of the data, which leads to sampling in all directions until the discovery of core variables which are found to reoccur consistently in the data. When this stage is reached sampling then becomes selective and focuses on the issues which are central to the emerging theory. According to Glaser (1978), the researcher must be prepared to stay 'open' to the possibility of new directions, and should be prepared to change, for example, interview style, place and interviewees in order to follow up new ideas. The researcher must also be open to the idea of modification, and look for patterns in what is not said, as well as what is. Only when there are no new patterns, or possible concepts, emerging from the data, should the researcher leave the field. In other words, when the data are saturated:

> the general procedure of theoretical sampling is to elicit codes from the raw data from the start of data collection through constant comparative analysis as the data pour in. Then one uses the codes to direct further data collection, from which the codes are further developed theoretically, with properties and theoretically coded connections with other categories until each category is saturated. Theoretical sampling on any category ceases when it is saturated, elaborated and integrated into the emerging theory. (Glaser, 1992: 102).

The process of theoretical sampling is, in effect, based on a happy marriage of induction and deduction. According to Glaser (1978: 38), deductive work in grounded theory is used to derive from induced codes or conceptual guides where to go next for which comparable group, in order to sample for more data to generate theory. Deduction is used in the service of further induction and derivations are the codes generated from comparing data. One of the main benefits of theoretical sampling is that it allows for flexibility during the research process. It provides the researcher with the opportunity to change the emphasis early on so that the data gathered are a reflection of what is occurring in the field rather than speculation about what should have been observed (Coyle, 1997; Glaser, 1978, Strauss and Corbin, 1990).

### Constant Comparison

In addition to theoretical sampling, a fundamental feature of grounded theory is the application of the 'constant' comparative method. Comparative analysis is a general method, like statistical experiments, and like other methods it can be used for social units of any size (Glaser and Strauss, 1968). As the name implies, constant comparison involves comparing like with like, to look for emerging patterns and themes.

> Comparison explores differences and similarities across incidents within the data currently collected and provides guidelines for collecting additional data. ... Analysis explicitly compares each incident in the data with other incidents appearing to belong to the same category, exploring their similarities and differences. (Spiggle, 1994: 493–4)

This process facilitates the identification of concepts. Concepts are a progression from merely describing what is happening in the data, which is a feature of open coding, to explaining the relationship between and across incidents. Incidents in the data need to be checked against each other in order to validate interpretation (Corbin, 1998). By comparing where the facts are similar or different, we can generate properties of categories that increase the categories' generality and explanatory powers (Glaser and Strauss, 1968: 24). Evidence is used as a test of emergent hypotheses, and the most effective way of achieving this is through comparative data. According to Corbin (1998), in order to test emerging hypotheses, relationship statements are made at the abstract level, not from raw data, but from concepts. This requires a different, more sophisticated, coding technique which is commonly referred to as 'axial coding' and involves the process of abstraction onto a theoretical level (Glaser and Strauss, 1967). Once it is safe to go outside the data for comparisons with other data, for example anecdotes or stories told by informants, the interpretation may begin to take on various perspectives which were not arrived at through systematic research, but which may be helpful. This class of comparison is called experiential incidents (Glaser, 1978).

Just as theoretical sampling is sampling directed by the theoretical relevance of the information gathered from particular groups, group comparisons or the comparison of data, are also theoretical. Conceptual ideas are developed by comparing diverse or similar evidence which indicates the same conceptual category. It is also important, however, to note the extent to which the properties of particular concepts are varied by diverse conditions (Glaser and Strauss, 1968). According to Glaser and Strauss (1967), the researcher needs to generate conceptual properties or categories from evidence. This evidence should then be used to illustrate the emergent concepts or theoretical abstractions about what is going on. By comparing where the facts are similar or different, we can generate properties or categories that increase the categories' explanatory power.

### Reaching Saturation: What is it?

The researcher must also ensure that constant comparison is an ongoing feature of the process. Theoretical sampling should direct the researcher to further individuals, situations, contexts and locations and the theory should only be presented as developed when all core categories are saturated. Theoretical saturation is achieved through staying in the field until no new evidence emerges which can inform or underpin the development of a theoretical point. There are no clear-cut rules of thumb for when this will occur, but it is important to saturate the data if the theory is to have substance. This may also involve searching and sampling groups that will stretch the diversity of data in order to ensure that saturation is based on the widest possible range of data (Glaser and Strauss, 1968). When similar incidences occur over again, the researcher may feel confident that the category is saturated.

Another well-documented mistake associated with using grounded theory is coming to 'closure' too early (Glaser, 1978; 1992; Strauss, 1987). All argue the importance of acknowledging variations and issues that do not fit neatly, and the need to make clear that the theory is only one frame of understanding drawn from many possibilities. Theories generated using grounded theory are interpretations made from given perspectives and are therefore fallible. Consequently, if one is to present a credible theory it is crucial to think carefully about:

1 The design of the study
2 The range of sampling
3 The clarity of discourse used to present findings
4 The relationship between the theory and other research
5 The identification of areas for further research. (O'Callaghan, 1996)

A further area of risk is to confuse inductive research with grounded theory. This may not be the case if the inductive research lacks 'creativity' and theoretical sensitivity. Strauss and Corbin (1994) acknowledge the overemphasis on induction in Glaser and Strauss's *Discovery* (1967) which played down the role of theoretical sensitivity thus creating confusion and misinterpretation. However, this is explicated in Glaser's (1978) publication *Theoretical Sensitivity* and in his later (1992) work, where the role of theoretical sensitivity is emphasised as a vital component of the end product. This is also linked to how the researcher contextualises the developed theory in the light of existing theory on the subject.

## Using the Literature to Enhance Theoretical Sensitivity

As mentioned, it is commonly thought that grounded theory methodology requires the researcher to enter the field with a very limited knowledge of the problem under investigation. This, however, is not necessarily the case. Reading is not forsaken during the initial stages – it is vital – but in a substantive field it is different from the research. The grounded theory researcher should read for ideas and conceptually connect these to the developing theory in order to enhance theoretical sensitivity. Nonetheless, only when the theory has substance should the researcher review the literature directly related to the field of study. This is proposed in order to avoid bringing into the field preconceptions and expectations borrowed from the work of others.

It is interesting to note the use of the literature and its role in developing theory in the case of Parry's (1998) work on leadership. The position adopted was that to research leadership, one must observe or interview in depth about social processes and change. In order to do this one must know what one is observing or questioning. On the face of it, this would seem to go against the inductive principles of grounded theory, but rather than starting with specific hypotheses, Parry chose to interview people in depth about concepts which are subordinate to the overarching concepts of leadership. The concepts chosen were derived from the literature and confirmed as being closely associated with it. Parry suggests, for example, that:

> rather than asking people about 'leaders' or 'leadership', they can be asked about people who are going to get them through a particular change process, who they look to for a lead, who have the most impact on their attitudes and motivation at work, or who they see as being exceptional and influential. Further in-depth interviewing about processes by which these outcomes are achieved can shed light on the social influence processes at work. (Parry, 1998)

A social process is a process which is concerned with human beings in their relations to each other. Social processes are ubiquitous throughout an organisation, and are not concerned with any particular rank or level. Another example of using the literature to sensitise the research is Sperber-Richie et al.'s (1997) study of career developments of highly achieving women in which they looked at eighteen prominent women in the USA across eight occupational fields. To begin with they constructed a rudimentary conceptual framework from the existing literature. They also developed a set of research questions which allowed researchers to do multiple site research and consequently generate data that were comparable across cases. This is obviously an important issue if there are a number of researchers working on the same study. There has to be some form of defining boundary and in order to ensure consistency the process they followed consisted of a series of distinct stages' as follows.

To begin with the general literature was consulted in order to construct a possible conceptual framework. Using this as a basis for further research an interview schedule was put together using open-ended questions. The interviews were then piloted in order to provide practical interviewing experience and feedback regarding the interview protocol. After this trial interviews were conducted and taped. They were simultaneously transcribed and notations were also made of pauses, laughter and tone of voice. The final copies of the transcripts were then sent to the informants for feedback on accuracy. The resulting data were subjected to multiple analysis using a twelve-member team approach to overcome individual bias. They were analysed using open coding (of which there were approx 3,000 concepts to begin with, which were subsequently reduced to 123). These were then grouped under fifteen higher order categories. The research team continued to interrogate the data and only deemed the categories saturated when nothing new emerged. The process revealed the need for the reorganisation of categories, which were ultimately reduced to five. These five categories then became the central elements of the theory. In addition to the presentation of these core categories, the properties of each were identified and a narrative was written to describe each property and its dimensions. Using these as the foundation, one construct was chosen by the team to be the core narrative or story that was most generally expressive of the experience of participants as a whole.

The end story focused on the beliefs the women held about themselves. These in turn were related to a number of socio-cultural conditions, such as sexism and the reality of being a women in a patriarchal environment. Other factors were identified as being important, such as personal background conditions, for example fathers who held traditional values, and current contextual conditions such as the amount of support from a spouse and/or co-workers. The interpretation of actions and consequences largely centred on how women conducted their working lives and the degree of passion and commitment to the job which usually resulted in high personal standards. The study and the description of the process provides a useful example of the methodology, its process, the development of core categories and the layering of influences, and how, ultimately, these relate to form a theory.

### Summary

This chapter has largely concentrated on sources of data and the nature of sampling. However, with grounded theory in practice, the researcher does not separate the data collection stages from the interpretive process. Consequently, whilst the next chapter is primarily concerned with the analysis and interpretation of data, it is important to bear in mind this relationship which is one based on the simultaneous collection and interpretation of data throughout the process.

Student exercises

1 Using grounded theory as your methodology, you are to construct a research proposal of no more than 1,500 words. The research may be academic (i.e. for a dissertation) or practical (for a manager).

- Give the research a title.
- Provide a brief rationale for the study.
- List your objectives.
- State the broad questions that are driving the research.
- Justify your use of grounded theory.
- Discuss how you would implement the method in terms of

(a) Theoretical sampling
(b) The collection of data
(c) An indicative time scale for the research.

# 4

## Analysis, Interpretation and the Writing Process

### Introduction

This chapter looks at the process of handling the data and the various stages associated with abstraction and interpretation. It begins with a description of the most elemental stage in the interpretive endeavour, that of open coding, and proceeds to discuss the more abstract and theoretical stages of the research. In this section the focus is on the nature of axial coding and the identification of relationships across concepts which have emerged from the data as having meaning to the phenomenon under study. Dimensionalisation of concepts into properties forms the basis for the subsequent discussion which also provides an overview of the work of Schatzman (1991) who developed the concept of dimensional analysis as an alternative form of grounded theory. This may provide food for thought for researchers considering using grounded theory, but who may be unsure of the version that will have the best fit to their preferred way of working. The section on dimensional analysis is followed by a brief summary of theoretical coding using grounded theory with a particular emphasis on analytical frameworks, the concept of basic social process, and the conditional matrix. At the pinnacle of theoretical coding are core categories which are higher order categories which represent the developed theory. The nature and explanatory power of core categories is presented, before attention is turned to the writing process and the challenges faced by researchers when presenting their theoretical interpretations. The chapter concludes with a brief discussion of computer-assisted interpretation and its potential and possible shortcomings in relation to grounded theory analysis. It is, however, important to note that this chapter deals with strategies specific to grounded theory, and for additional information on the various techniques available for representing qualitative analysis, readers may wish to refer to Miles and Huberman (1994).

### Interpreting the Data using Coding Strategies

The analytical process involves coding strategies: the process of breaking down interviews, observations and other forms of appropriate data into distinct units of meaning which are labelled to generate concepts. These concepts are initially clustered into descriptive categories. They are then re-evaluated for their interrelationships and through a series of analytical steps are gradually subsumed into higher order categories, or one underlying core category, which suggests an emergent theory. Each stage of the coding process presents dilemmas of interpretation. How these dilemmas are dealt with depends on how one conceptualises the method, and over the years this conceptualisation has reflected tensions in philosophical definitions. However, throughout the process it is important to use inference and prepositional thinking, otherwise the researcher becomes lost in a sea of facts. Turner (1994) refers to the coding process as a set of procedures which lead the researcher into a maze. One method of overcoming this problem is to recognise that enquiry is always context bound and facts should be viewed as both theory laden and value laden. Knowledge is seen as actively constructed with meanings of existence only relevant to an experiential world. Therefore the focus centres on how people behave within an individual and social context. In order to proceed, O'Callaghan (1996) argues that the researcher should have: a perspective to build analysis from; an awareness of substantive issues guiding the research questions; a school of thought to help sensitise the emergent concepts; and a degree of personal experience, values and priorities. These help to distinguish between what is known and what can be discovered (see Guba and Lincoln (1994) for a fuller discussion of this issue). However, it is generally advised that during the early stages of the research, the researcher should not steep him/herself too heavily in the literature directly related to the research topic. According to Glaser (1978) it is important not to 'contaminate' perceptions and ideas with preconceived concepts. This, he maintains, will only force the data in the wrong direction and is more applicable to deductive approaches. The grounded theory approach calls for early data collection, analysis, further theoretical sampling and category saturation.

## Open Coding

As already mentioned in Chapter 3, the researcher using grounded theory enters the field early on in the process. Furthermore, analysis is done at the same time as the data are being collected rather than after all the information has been gathered. The analytical process should start with the writing of memos which describe the scene, events and behaviours under study. As noted in Chapter 3, memos are notes written immediately after data collection as a means of documenting the impressions of the researcher and describing the situation. These are vital as they provide a bank of ideas which can be revisited in order to map out the emerging theory. Essentially, memos are ideas which have been noted during the data collection process which help to reorientate the researcher at a later date. At the same time, data, for example in the form of interviews, should be transcribed and analysed for meaning. This usually involves a series of analytical stages associated with employing specific coding techniques for abstracting meaning from the data. However, this is not to be confused with quantitative coding. Strauss (1987: 278) warns that researchers must stop themselves from thinking in quantitative terms; for example, 'what percentage of x will do y, with what probability?' However, the very term itself with its connotations of quantitative analysis has caused confusion, as indicated by Charmaz:

> Qualitative coding is not the same as quantitative coding. The term itself provides a case in point in which the language may obscure meaning and method. Quantitative coding requires preconceived, logically deduced codes into which the data are placed. Qualitative coding, in contrast, means creating categories from interpretation of the data. Rather than relying on preconceived categories and standardized procedures, qualitative coding has its own distinctive structure, logic and purpose. (Charmaz, 1983: 111)

This distinction lies in the way in which data are collected and handled. In the early days, the analysis will be very broad and lack focus. As the data are collected they should be analysed simultaneously by looking for all possible interpretations. This involves utilising particular coding procedures, which normally begins with open coding. Open coding is the process of breaking down the data into distinct units of meaning. As a rule, this starts with a full transcription of an interview, after which the text is analysed line by line in an attempt to identify key words or phrases which connect the informant's account to the experience under investigation. This process is associated with early concept development which consists of 'identifying a chunk or unit of data (a passage of text of any length) as belonging to, representing, or being an example of some more general phenomenon' (Spiggle, 1994: 493).

## Line-by-line Analysis

Glaser (1978) warns that in many cases, the area of original intent may change as ideas and unexpected actions emerge from the data. The researcher should be willing to adapt to these and remain flexible to the evolving conceptual nature of the emerging theory. In terms of analysing the actual data this normally starts with a line-by-line analysis during which every line of the transcribed interview is searched for key words or phrases which give some insight into the behaviour under study. These are then highlighted and abstracted from the interview. According to Miles and Huberman (1994: 58):

> Of these inductive coding techniques, one of the most helpful is that of Strauss (1987) described best in Strauss and Corbin (1990). Initial data are collected, written up and reviewed line by line, typically within a paragraph. Beside or below the paragraph, categories or labels are generated, and a list of them grows. The labels are reviewed and, typically, a slightly more abstract category is attributed to several incidents or observations.

During the early stage of line-by-line analysis it is not unusual to identify hundreds of codes which are 'open' and unrelated. The next stage is to continue transcribing further interviews and repeat the process of line-by-line analysis. This is done until the researcher sees some sort of pattern emerging. Codes are then clustered into groups that seem to indicate a relationship which says something about the behaviour. This starts the process of abstraction and moves the interpretation on from merely describing what is occurring, to linking codes together with the aim of developing explanatory concepts. Open coding carries with it verification, correction and the opportunity for saturation. Glaser (1992) provides a useful set of definitions which help to distinguish the various levels of theoretical coding. These include:

- *Coding* – This is the conceptualisation of data by the constant comparison of incident with incident, and incident with concept, in order to develop categories and their properties.
- *Open coding* – This is the initial stage of constant comparison during which the data are scrutinised for every possible meaning.
- *Concept* – A concept is basically the underlying meaning, uniformity and/or pattern within a set of descriptive incidents.
- *Constant comparative coding* – This is a fundamental part of the constant comparative method where incidents are coded for properties and categories that connect them together.
- *Property* – A property is a type of conceptual characteristic of a concept or category.
- *Category* – Categories are higher order concepts. They have much wider explanatory power, and pull together all the identified concepts into a theoretical framework.

### The Process of Abstraction

Throughout the various stages of data collection and interpretation, the analysis employs more sophisticated techniques for theoretically coding. It is vital, with grounded theory, to lift the analysis to a more abstract level, away from description, to theory development. Strauss (1987) proposes that the researcher must ask theoretically relevant qualitative questions of the data such as: what are the strategies which result in particular behaviours? What are the different conditions involved? And what kind of theoretically derived comparisons would be useful here? Through the process of abstraction the researcher collapses more empirically grounded categories into higher order conceptual constructs. These abstract constructs encompass a number of more concrete instances found in the data that share common features. The process of abstraction further requires the integration of theoretical concepts into a conceptually complex integrated theory (Spiggle, 1994). To do this it is important to move beyond open coding, which

77

basically describes what is happening in the data, to a more sophisticated conceptual form of analysis known as axial coding.

### Axial Coding, Concepts, Properties and Dimensional Range

Axial coding involves moving to a higher level of abstraction and is achieved by specifying relationships and delineating a core category or construct around which the other concepts revolve. Axial coding is the appreciation of concepts in terms of their dynamic interrelationships. These should form the basis for the construction of the theory.

> Abstract concepts encompass a number of more concrete instances found in the data. The theoretical significance of a concept springs from its relationship to other concepts or its connection to a broader gestalt of an individual's experience. (Spiggle, 1994: 494)

Once a concept has been identified, its attributes may be explored in greater depth, and its characteristics dimensionalised in terms of their intensity or weakness. Using axial coding, the researcher develops a category by specifying the conditions that gave rise to it, the context in which it is embedded, and the action/interactional strategies by which it is handled, managed and carried out. These conditions, contexts, strategies and outcomes tend to be clustered together and the connections may be hierarchical or ungraded, linear or recursive (Spiggle, 1994). Moreover, evolution is an important aspect in the generation of theory. Theory development is a gradual process which can be incredibly time consuming. In terms of process, concept analysis is an integral step in the development of the theory and is a way to prepare for theory construction (Jezewski, 1995). Jezewski proposes that:

> The theoretical definition that emerges from concept analysis summarises insights that form while creating conceptual meaning and describes the essential meaning of the concept. (1995: 16)

It is also important to note that all concepts have properties; they are not stand-alone codes. For example, high staff turnover may be related to stress at work (the concept). However, stress may have many properties such as the nature of the role or job itself, unrealistic targets, poor communication, lack of positive feedback and so on. These may be the properties of the concept. These properties, in turn, may be dimensionalised in terms of their intensity. For instance, the nature of the job may carry with it a high boredom level or a low or high degree of challenge. By recognising these properties it becomes possible to compare and contrast cases in terms of intensity. The next section looks in some detail at the technique of dimensional analysis as this has formed the basis for what might arguably be described as an alternative version of grounded theory associated with the work of Schatzman, a contemporary of the two original authors.

## Dimensional Analysis: An Alternative Version of Grounded Theory

At the same time as Glaser and Strauss were following their own divergent paths, an alternative method to grounded theory began to be taught at the University of California, the birthplace of grounded theory. This new method, labelled 'dimensional analysis', sometimes referred to as 'natural analysis', was pioneered by Schatzman, a long-standing colleague and past collaborator of the two original authors (Kools et al., 1996). Schatzman's main critique of grounded theory was its lack of disclosure of the operations involved in the discovery of theory. He proposed that dimensional analysis could be described as an alternative method which would allow for the articulation of the discovery process. Accordingly, analysis in the context of research is linked to the interpretive actions that one naturally and commonly employs every day. Consequently research is considered to be an exaggerated, intentional and sustained form of natural analysis (Kools et al., 1996). Nonetheless, in order to move the interpretation from a descriptive to an explanatory level it is necessary to have a framework for identifying the relationship between and across emerging phenomena. Dimensional analysis uses as its foundation conditions, process, context and consequences which can be shown to effect the outcome of the informant's story:

> In natural analysis, when we listen to a story, we consider attributes as they are described. We consider actions taken in relation to the context, conditions and consequences. If any part of the story presents problems in understanding, we ask questions. What the listener considers the main issues of the story represents a point of view, or perspective. Scientific analysis is an extension of the natural analytical process, it is distinguishable from everyday thinking by the recognition and consideration of greater numbers and kinds of attributes within a situation ... The perspective of analytical thinking focuses on events in the natural setting where interactions occur between human beings. The aim of analysis is to discover the meanings of these interactions as they create the observed situation, rather than discover the basic social process. (Robrecht, 1995: 172–3)

One of the key questions which often surrounds the use of qualitative data is: how do researchers arrive at their interpretations? All too often the problem is that the analytical methods are not made clear. This often leads to perceptions that their insights are the results of their interpretive abilities rather than a standard methodology. The purpose of the method suggested by Schatzman was to provide a structure or methodological perspective for analysis and explanation. The explanation or story informs us of the relationship between actions and consequences under selected conditions in a

**Conditions**
(These facilitate, block or shape action or interaction)

↓

**Process**
(This is impelled by prevailing conditions and results in intended/unintended
actions or interactions)

↓

**Contexts**
(These are the boundaries of situations/environments which give
rise to consequences)

↓

**Consequences**
(These are the outcomes of these specific actions/interactions)

↓

**Dimensions**
(All salient dimensions are given the opportunity to act as
a perspective – that is, each one is
analysed for its degree of explanatory power before
selecting the main perspective or storyline)

↓

**Perspective**
(This is a dimension which has significant explanatory power and
acts as the main storyline)

FIGURE 4.1  *Explanatory matrix (Adapted from Kools et al. 1996: 320)*

specific context (Robrecht, 1995). The act of designation moves a particular observation towards a more abstract representation of a situation. Data are collected and scrutinised until a critical mass of dimensions is assembled which represent emerging pathways that possess explanatory power. These in turn are presented in the form of an explanatory matrix and are summarised in Figure 4.1.

If we consider, for example, any act of consumer behaviour it is not too difficult to accept this as a structure for analysis. One situation may be the act of shopping. This may involve motivations which instigate actions. Conditions may be influenced by a range of factors such as mood, emotion, disposable income or even compulsion. The process may involve planning the shopping trip, selection and purchase, while specific contexts may include the various retail environments. The consequences of these actions may range from satisfaction levels to falling into debt. Within each one of these there may be a range of influencing factors (dimensions) which contribute to the experience. However, there will usually be a small number of dominant motivators driving the behaviour which allows the researcher to take a 'perspective' as to the main theme of the story. This form of analysis, however, must go beyond mere description to incorporate abstract theorising which offers a plausible explanation of the phenomenon under study. This starts with the very simplest of assumptions:

TABLE 4.1   *The dimensions of dress codes*

**Conservatism versus fashion**

Conservatism in dress was often framed in opposition to fashion. Participants generally held one meaning on a continuum higher than the other. Maintaining a balance between conservatism and fashion keeps an individual from being perceived as extreme (passé or exhibitionist)

**Conformity versus creativity**

Conformity was seen as the effort by an individual to fit into the group. Creativity included the expression of personal characteristics and play with dress. Conformity was a professional priority needed for career advancement, while creativity was a personal priority

**Masculinity versus femininity/sexuality**

While women were aware of the wisdom of adopting male symbols of power, they believed it was a mistake to imitate men in their dress. Furthermore, looking too masculine was often considered a gender norm violation in some organisations. The other extreme, however, was also avoided, that is looking too sexy (low-cut blouses, short skirts)

**The importance of attractiveness (no opposite)**

In addition to these components it was also found that women were expected to cultivate physical attractiveness in their business image. Attractiveness and dressing appropriately were associated with positive characteristics. Attention to grooming communicated a measure of self-respect. The opposite indicated a lack of self-respect which extended to perceptions of a lack of consciousness over performing work duties

Through the learning of language and the ability to engage in social interaction, human beings refine their talent to perform natural analysis and develop the cognitive attribute of dimensionality. (Kools et al., 1996: 315)

Dimensionalisation entails the naming of data bits and the expansion of these into their various attributes. A dimension is an abstract concept with associated properties that provide parameters for the purpose of description. For example, gender is a dimension with the properties of female and male. Designation is the labelling of dimensions and properties observed in the data. Through designation the researcher develops a vocabulary with which to continue analysis. By way of illustration, the work of Kimle and Damhorst (1997) into the ideal dress for business women provides an example of dimensionalisation. The background to the study was the increase in women entering executive positions in the workplace. The study focused on women's business dress to explore the social meanings that role players convey through dress in the work context. They took the position that 'talk about dressing for a role' was 'identity talk' which could help illuminate the notion of 'identity work'. They collected data in the form of interviews with twenty-four women and analysed the transcripts for recurring themes. These themes were then presented as important dimensions of meaning and were incorporated into a model which charts the process of how these multiple meanings are handled (Table 4.1).

The authors concluded that women's business dress serves as a rich text from which complex layers of identities can be read. There is no such thing as a uniform for female executives in the same way as males have the 'suit' which encodes their behaviour and is read similarly across situational contexts. Business women must contend with overlapping identity games which add complexity to the assemblage of a work identity.

### Theorising using Dimensional Analysis

One further distinctive feature of dimensional analysis is the recognition of the need for a supporting theoretical framework to help construct the story. Dimensional analysis draws on past experience and knowledge as a cumulative and integral part of the individual's thinking process. There is pragmatic recognition that, although grounded theory generally rejects the use of received theory as a basis for analysis, in reality, rarely do researchers totally abandon prior substantive or methodological knowledge in the pursuit of understanding a complex social phenomenon (Kools et al., 1996).

According to Robrecht (1995), as a story or problem is revealed to the researcher, the dimensions of the problem have no form until the researcher takes a perspective or viewpoint on the information. From an interpretive position, a researcher strives for objectivity in the selection of a perspective. This objectivity is not to be confused with the position adopted by positivist researchers, rather it involves keeping an open mind as to the array of possible theoretical positions that may be adopted to offer the best and most plausible explanation. That is, the researcher strives for the capacity to entertain multiple theoretical perspectives on a given situation. Each perspective gives a different configuration to the data; it tells a different story. The chosen perspective becomes the theme that configurates the story, making the phenomenon understandable.

Ellis (1993) suggests that when the analysis is nearing completion and the categories and their properties are saturated, analysis gives way to exposition. This is linked with the practical issue of selection – that is, selecting examples from the transcripts to illustrate the abstract features of the model. These examples provide a concrete embodiment for the dimensions and properties of the theory. This aids exposition and allows the reader to confirm that the interpretation fits the data and that the theory provides a fair view of the underlying reality. For example, a particular dimension or property may be noted as occurring across several transcripts. Consequently, quotations are chosen that best illustrate the point or convey the essential meaning of this dimension. If a dimension has properties that embody slight variations in meaning or emphasis, then examples may be chosen to illustrate these nuances. If, on the other hand, it is intended to reinforce a very general or frequently occurring theme, a bank of similar statements may be used to indicate the pervasiveness of the concept or theme in the different contexts. The result should be that the reader has some authentic feel for the overall theory, its dimensions and properties, and the specific instances from which it is derived (Ellis, 1993). Ultimately, conviction lies in the researcher's ability to dissect the narratives of the respondents, and using particular junctures in the story, create a credible explanation which is grounded in the words and stories of the informants. It is possible, therefore, to argue that rather than two, there are in fact three versions of grounded theory and for a detailed discussion of dimensional analysis the reader should refer to the work of Schatzman (1991) and Schatzman and Strauss (1973).

### Causal Conditions, Phenomenon, Intervening Conditions, Interactional Strategies, Consequences

While dimensional analysis involves the use of a coding family which encompasses conditions, process, context, consequence, dimensions and perspective, grounded theory employs similar strategies for describing process and developing theoretical frameworks. The most commonly adopted coding family traces the phenomenon under study, through the description and explication of causal conditions, the phenomenon, the intervening conditions, interactional strategies, and the consequences of these. According to Baszanger (1998: 370):

> For each event or occurrence identified, the researcher asks four questions: What are the conditions of the action, the interactions between the actors, their strategies and tactics, and the consequences of the action? What we are dealing with here is a strategy for conscious recording through which the researcher's own experience is transformed.

For example, Crook and Kumar (1998) in a study of electronic data interchange (EDI) used across four organisations, described the relationship between the central phenomenon of interest, the causal conditions that related to that phenomenon, the context in which the phenomenon existed and the strategies and consequences which related to that phenomenon. In the case of their research the context was the organisation which was analysed in terms of size, IT capability and so on. The causal conditions included customer-initiated innovations, improved customer service and reaction to competition. The phenomenon included such things as the integration of EDI with other applications, and strategies comprised of technical support and building long-term relationships. The outcomes or consequences of these actions consisted of competitive advantage and improved customer service.

A non-managerial, but nevertheless useful, illustrative description of the sequence of fragmenting the data to look for specific relationships in relation to process and handling strategies is Morison and Moir's (1998) work on the coping strategies of parents. The purpose of the study was to

| **Causal conditions** |
| Bed wetting is defined by the parent as inappropriate behaviour for the young person's age<br>Parent believes that the bed wetting is within the young person's control<br>Parent believes that he/she has:<br>    the capacity to influence the situation now<br>    the capacity to influence the situation in the future |
| **Phenomenon** |
| Parents' overall attitude to the young person's bed wetting |
| **Intervening conditions** |
| Parents beliefs and feelings about parenting (e.g. attitudes towards punishment)<br>The young person as an individual and family member<br>The quality of their relationship<br>The attitudes of the wider family |
| **Interactional strategies** |
| Parent takes responsibility for helping the young person stay dry at night<br>Parent blames young person |
| **Consequences for young person** |
| Supportive emotional and social environment in which to learn to stay dry at night |
| **Consequences for parent** |
| Anger towards the young person<br>Frustration at the situation |

FIGURE 4.2   *Parental coping strategies and bed wetting (Adapted from Morison and Moir, 1998: 113)*

explore families' experiences of living with a young person who wets the bed (see Figure 4.2). However, the concepts could just as easily be applied to the management of people within a working organisation, in terms of definitions of appropriate management style and behaviour. For example, such concepts as control, influence over the situation, attitudes to employees, company loyalty, the degree of responsibility, the nature of support in the environment, and the ultimate outcomes, might well emerge from a study of mistakes at work (Figure 4.3).

## Theoretical Coding and Basic Social Process

However, Glaser (1978) warns of the dangers of placing too much emphasis on one particular coding family or forcing the data to fit within the parameters of these theoretical codes. He refers to the range of other coding families which could be equally as valid for the interpretation. These include the identity and self family, which consists of self-image,

| Causal conditions |
| --- |
| Appropriate employee behaviour defined by management<br>Mistakes are seen as employee's fault<br>Management believe they (management) have the capacity to influence the situation now<br>Management believe they (management) can develop the capability to influence behaviour in the future |

| Phenomenon |
| --- |
| Management attitude to employee mistakes |

| Intervening conditions |
| --- |
| Management's beliefs and feelings towards employees<br>Management's attitudes to reward and punishment<br>The employee regarded as individual or part of a team<br>The trust and quality of management/employee relationship<br>Attitudes of the wider organisation |

| Interactional strategies |
| --- |
| Manager takes responsibility for helping employee to recognise and avoid mistakes<br>Manager attributes blame |

| Consequences for employee |
| --- |
| Supportive environment which encourages risk and communication<br>Fear of risk taking, closed communication |

| Consequences for management |
| --- |
| Creative trusting environment<br>Anger and frustration towards employee |

FIGURE 4.3    *Hypothetical Case: Mistakes at work*

self-concept, self-worth, self-evaluation, identity, social worth, self-realisation, transformations of self, and conversions of identity. Conversely, the research may be better analysed in terms of the 'cultural family' consisting of social norms, social values, social beliefs and sentiments; or the 'unit family' which is made up of collective group, nation, organisation, aggregate, situation, context, arena, social world, behavioural pattern, territorial units, society and family. However, these are only proposed as possible theoretical codes or analytical frameworks. If the research does not fit into any of these, then the advice is: do not force it, describe it in terms of the theoretical codes that emerge from the data which have fit and explanatory power in the context of the research.

According to Glaser (1978) the goal of grounded theory is to generate theory that accounts for a pattern of behaviour that is both relevant and problematic to those being studied. The developed theory will normally take account of a basic social process. This is something which occurs and changes over time. Basic social processes are summaries of the patterned, systematic uniformity of social life which people experience and which can be conceptually captured. They give the theory density. A number of studies in the field of management have used the notion of social process as a starting point for analysis. For example, Hunt and Ropo (1995) offer an illustration of the grounded theory process as applied to the analysis of multi-level leadership using the case of General Motors. In their study they identify processes of force or dynamism in relationship to leadership theory. Other work in the area is also useful for exploring this concept. For example, Parry (1998) looked at leadership as a social influence process in relation to change. He suggested that mainstream leadership methodologies have been partially unsuccessful in theorising about the nature of these processes. He selected grounded theory as an alternative to the limiting, but still dominant, use of quantitative methodologies associated with psychology arguing that these approaches have not led to an enduring theory of leadership. Furthermore, while change is an enduring theme in the literature, change is inherently longitudinal. Consequently an appropriate methodology was needed to reflect this. Essentially, his position was one which viewed leadership as a social influence process. Accordingly, from this perspective he thought it necessary that leadership research should incorporate the variety of variables that impact upon the social influence process. In other words, leadership research should be about processes rather than what leaders do. Parry traced the process he engaged in and the series of outputs which emerged. These included an analytical chronology of the case (descriptive), a diagnosis of the case (the iterative process of inductive pattern generation and theory generation) and the interpretive/theoretical outputs. He described how he linked theoretical codes and emerging themes into a more complex explanation of the phenomena; and finally he discussed the meta-level analysis across cases and the analysis of a number of replicated studies of similar cases needed to develop a formal theory.

De la Cuesta (1994) conducted a study into the effectiveness of marketing in relation to health visiting. Grounded theory was chosen because it brings *process* into the analysis of data. The idea of process provided a focus for interviews and observations which were guided by theoretical sampling. Collection and analysis of data were conducted simultaneously, beginning with line-by-line analysis of interview transcripts and the assignation of conceptual labels to describe events. Categories were built through the constant comparison of data and concepts. The emergent theory was further guided by the *conditions* under which interactions took place, the *interaction* among informants and health visitors, the *strategies* and tactics that informants used, and the *consequences* of the actions and interactions. Analytical memos were also a crucial part when writing the theory. Informants were also asked to check emerging concepts in order to ensure that they had 'fit' to the actual experience.

De La Cuesta findings centred primarily around client attitudes, and identified tactics which could enhance selling in health visiting, strategies for *gaining clientele* (transforming cases into clients), and methods for influencing behaviour in order to encourage primary prevention. In the discussion the author addresses the issue of 'process' in health visiting, and the need to promote the service through personal presentations and advertising. The research had further practical implications by identifying tactics for raising awareness by getting clients to recognise problems early.

Other concepts which emerged from the data and were subsequently integrated into the written output included an analysis of factors which influenced the behaviour of clients. These included personal selling and the influence of the health visitor's appearance and personality. A further factor was the need to display information in a clear and informative way and a willingness to adjust delivery to make take-up of the service easy. Bargaining and negotiation (mainly to gain access, i.e. to see a baby, and then inform about immunisation) were a further feature of the interactional process, as was timing and opportunism. Important to the interactions was a willingness to alter pace with regard to the amount of service given, as was flexibility in adjusting to clients' needs. With regard to specific marketing strategies, the findings highlighted the importance of tailoring the product, arranging the agenda in order to adapt to clients' perceptions of priorities, and a willingness to negotiate and compromise. In summary De La Cuesta concluded that health visitors use a combination of tactics to make their service acceptable, relevant and accessible to clients. These tactics bear great similarity to those used in commercial marketing. The study provided a better understanding of how health services are provided and offered strategies for improving delivery.

### The Conditional Matrix

A further feature of the methodology which is related to theoretical coding is referred to as the conditional matrix. This, however, has been the source of some conflict between Glaser and Strauss, the two original authors, particularly with regard to parsimony and fidelity to the data. The conditional matrix is essentially a device for tracking the various levels of influences upon the phenomenon under study. It is usually represented in the form of a diagram comprising concentric circles. The outer circle usually represents the macro influences, while the inner circles relate more to the actions and consequences of the behaviour. Corbin and Strauss (1990: 11) state that:

> broader structural conditions must be analysed, however microscopic the research. The analysis of a setting must not be restricted to the conditions that bear immediately on the phenomenon of central interest. Broader conditions affecting the phenomenon may include economic conditions, cultural values, political trends, social movements and so on.

Strauss and Corbin (1994) suggest other conditions may run from international through national, community, organisation and sub-organisational groups, individuals and collectives, to action pertaining to the individual. They further suggest that it is useful when describing such conditions to:

> think in terms of a 'conditional matrix.' With this image we suggest the worth of attending to a set of decreasingly inclusive circles embracing different conditions, beginning with the broad ones just noted and moving inward to conditions progressively narrower in scope. (Corbin and Strauss, 1990: 11)

The researcher is further required to show specific linkages between these conditions and to integrate them into the developed theory. However, the idea of the conditional matrix and particularly the notion that '*the analysis of a setting must not be restricted to the conditions that bear immediately on the phenomenon of central interest*' is a source of conflict between researchers adopting the Strauss and Corbin approach and those using the principles advocated by Glaser. For Glaser (1992) the compulsory use of the conditional matrix smacks of forcing the data into predefined categories for which there may be no evidence. This in turn inhibits the process of emergence and stifles theoretical sensitivity. Nonetheless, Strauss and Corbin (1994) justify the use of the conditional matrix, arguing that the key benefit is that the user can respond to change with the times. Conditions that effect behaviour may change, and these changes can be analysed through the application of new ideas or emergent perspectives.

## Developing Core Categories

The final stage in the process of theory development is the construction of a core category. Through the process of coding and abstraction the data are finally subsumed into a higher order or core category which the researcher has to justify as the basis for the emergent theory. A core category pulls together all the strands in order to offer an explanation of the behaviour under study. It has theoretical significance and its development should be traceable back through the data. This is usually when the theory is written up and integrated with existing theories to show relevance and new perspective. Nonetheless, a theory is usually only considered valid if the researcher has reached the point of saturation. This involves staying in the field until no new evidence emerges from data collected through an ongoing process of theoretical sampling. A core category is also based on the assumption that a full interrogation of the data has been conducted, and negative cases, where found, have been identified and accounted for. According to Glaser (1978), a core category is a main theme which sums up a pattern of behaviour. It is the substance of what is going on in the data. A core category should be saturated as much as possible for its explanatory power and should be based on full theoretical sampling in order to maximise differences in data. Furthermore, it must be explained in relation to its relevance to other categories. Glaser specifies the criteria that a core category must meet. These include:

- It must be central and account for a large proportion of behaviour.
- It must be based on reoccurrence in the data.
- A core category takes longer to saturate than other categories/concepts.
- It must relate meaningfully to other categories.
- It should have clear implications for the development of formal theory.
- The theoretical analysis should be based on the core category.
- It should be highly variable and modifiable.

### Ensuring Credibility through Member Checking

In terms of ensuring the credibility and consistency of the interpretation, it is often recommended in the literature that the researcher invites other, sometimes external reviewers to consider the data and offer their interpretations of it in order to check consistency (Riley, 1996). This process of 'member checking' is well documented in the literature as a prime strategy for the validation of findings. Returning to the original informants and obtaining their opinions of the developing theory is also recommended in all the key texts on grounded theory, although this is only done during the early stages of data collection and interpretation before the researcher begins the process of abstraction. Nuefeldt et al. (1996), for example, discussed this in relation to reflectivity as part of the process. Interviews with clinical psychologists were conducted in order to ascertain how they resolved problems. They were asked about their decision points, locations and solutions. Data collection and analysis was a simultaneous process and in order to check concepts the original informants were reinterviewed to allow for changes in behaviour due to context and mood. They also took the unusual step of asking their informants not only to check the resulting interpretation, but actively to criticise it and expand on earlier comments.

Hirschman and Thompson (1997) offer a good example of using others to ensure consistency of findings. They used grounded theory for the collection and analysis of data when researching the impact of the media and advertising from a consumer-based frame of reference. Their investigation centred largely on the meaning that was sought from advertising rather than stopping at the level of information provided and internalised. The choice of grounded theory was justified on the grounds of its strength in developing consumer-based constructs and theories, rather than researcher hypotheses. The process they followed adhered to the principles of grounded theory in relation to allowing theory to emerge from the data, memoing, constant comparison, and category development and saturation.

In selecting a sample they were aware of the 'types' of viewers who were of particular interest to advertisers, namely middle- and upper middle-class consumers, and this group formed the starting point for investigation. Data consisted of semi-structured interviews with twenty-eight informants. These interviews were transcribed verbatim and the most salient metaphors identified. These resulted in the development of three key categories based around the interpretive strategies of those who participated in the research and can be summarised as: 'motivational interpretations' (inspiring and aspirational role models who influence behaviour); 'critical interpretations' (deconstruction and rejection of the overtly economic motivations of advertisers); and 'personalising interpretations' (the manner in which individuals negotiate self-perceptions and personal goals in relation to the media). Essentially, the research indicated that advertisers need to cultivate their sensitivity towards the cultural consumption codes that are largely inherent in television programmes. Individual celebrities represent culturally shared perceptions (they give the example of 'Roseanne' who is perceived as a 'blue-collar housewife'), and such programmes and 'codes' were viewed with much less scepticism in terms of the information they project than advertisers.

Whilst their paper is a useful discussion of a process of data collection and analysis, it is particularly strong in relation to the use of others to ensure validity and consistency of interpretation. To begin with, a number of trained and experienced qualitative researchers were involved in the interviews, thus overcoming some of the problems associated with researcher subjectivity. Moreover, the original informants were given copies of their interview transcripts and provisional analysis. Their opinion was then sought as to the fidelity of the interpretation. Any inconsistencies were amended in order to provide an accurate reflection. As concepts were abstracted from the data other academics were given copies of transcripts and coding procedures and were invited to assess the paucity of the interpretation. However, one of the biggest problems faced by grounded theory researchers, who normally amass vast amounts of data from which theory is developed, is how to represent the main findings to an external audience without losing the sense of process.

## Writing the Theory

When the theory is fully developed the researcher is faced with the challenge of writing it up. This stage is fraught with dilemmas over the structure the story should take, the degree of methodological detail to include, and the amount of data to present in order to provide evidence and support for the core categories. The author should also write the theory in such a way that it demonstrates to the reader how concepts 'emerged' and developed from the data, how the researcher moved from description through the process of abstraction, and how core categories were generated. This calls for a degree of creativity. According to Glaser (1978: 22) creativity:

> requires an historical approach to the work. One must write as no one else has ever on the subject. Then explore the literature to see what new property of an idea he has offered, or how it is embedded with others.

There appears to be no strict formula for presenting the theory. The form in which theory is presented may be independent of the process by which it was generated. It may take the form of a well-codified set of propositions, or it may consist of a running theoretical discussion using conceptual categories and their properties (Glaser and Strauss, 1968). Glaser and Strauss further maintain that the author needs to ensure that the reader understands the theoretical framework by providing an extensive abstract of the overall framework and its principal associated theoretical statements. These are usually made at the start or end of the publication.

The standard approach is to present data as evidence for conclusions, indicating how the analyst obtained theory from the data. Nevertheless, there is recognition that qualitative research does not lend itself easily to summary, as in the case of quantitative results. Consequently, characteristic illustrations and diagrams may help to convey the message. Glaser (1978) maintains that credibility should be won through the theory's integration, relevance and workability, and not by illustration used as if it were proof. This is not the aim, and the reader should be advised that all concepts are grounded, and as such they are not proven, they are only suggested. The end theory should be an integrated set of hypotheses, not of findings, and it should be made clear that the enormous effort that makes up the process of generating theory cannot be shown in a single publication (Glaser, 1978).

Glaser and Strauss also suggest that if the theory encompasses a multitude of ideas, illustrating each one may be far too cumbersome and disruptive to the flow of the narrative and general idea. In order to avoid being swept away on a tide of data, they propose that the writer presents only enough material to facilitate understanding. Glaser (1978) argues that it is not incumbent upon the analyst to provide the reader with descriptions of how each concept was reached, rather the method should be stated and possibly an example of how a code or hypotheses was grounded should be included. Indicators for concepts should be used only for illustration and imagery, not the story itself (Glaser, 1978). The researcher may also quote directly from interviews or conversations, include dramatic segments of on-the-spot field notes, construct case studies of events or persons, or quote telling phrases dropped by informants (Glaser and Strauss, 1968). They suggest that the theory will gain credibility on the part of the readers if they become caught up in the descriptions so vicariously that they feel they have been in the field. This presents an interesting challenge and may require numerous drafts and redrafts until this sense of reality can be described in such vivid terms. In order for the readers to feel this, they should be told about how the researcher came to the conclusions reached, the range of events the researcher observed, who he/she interviewed, who talked to him/her, and what diverse groups were compared. Strauss (1987) proposes that the presentation may either be very abstract, or utilise a good deal of data which will speak for themselves. However, data should only be used to give credence to the theoretical construct, they should not merely be included to provide low levels of description. Consequently, Strauss warns against presenting data with little analytical comment. He advocates inter-weaving discursive propositions using the results of coding and memos, with carefully selected words or phrases combined with theoretical points. This provides a sense of reality and helps the reader to understand the context and evolution. The writer can also summarise events by constructing readable case studies which describe events and acts. These offer a rich context by describing places and spaces, in detail and can include examples of personal experience.

In terms of recasting the theory in the light of other extant theory, Strauss (1987) maintains that it is likely, when the theory is developed, that the findings will differ from those derived from studies in related areas. The developed theory needs to be recast in terms of fit, extension or the degree of challenge offered to extant explanations. In other words, it should either be integrated with the existing work, or act as a critique of it. Conversely, it may be an approach that is so different from any other that it may lead to results which need to be discussed in relation to a more general disciplinary theory. With regard to ending the writing up, Glaser (1978) advises that summaries are not always necessary, although conclusions are worthwhile. Conclusions should incorporate the key variable and the subordinate variables which worked well within the integrative framework. They should then be discussed in relation to their use and potential contribution to the development of more formal theory and other realms of enquiry. Nonetheless, the theory must also be traceable back through the data to provide evidence, and it is possibly this problem that in recent years has seen a movement away from the complicated and often frustrating process of manual interpretation, to the use of computer software for the analysis of qualitatively derived data.

## A Short Note on Manual and Computer-Aided Analysis

At this point it is worth deviating slightly from the subject of grounded theory method to address the issue of qualitative data analysis, although not necessarily the analysis of diverse methodologically derived data, but the means and tools for analysis which require justification in the light of current technological developments.

> In the last 15 years there has been a proliferation of computer software packages – designed to facilitate qualitative data analysis. The programmes can be classified, according to function, into a number of broad categories such as: text retrieval; text based management; coding and retrieval; code based theory building; and conceptual-network building. The programmes vary enormously in the extent to which they can facilitate the diverse analytical processes involved. The decision to use computer software to aid analysis on a particular project may be influenced by a number of factors, such as the nature of the data and the researcher's preferred approach to data analysis which will have at its basis certain epistemological and ontological assumptions. (Morison and Moir, 1998: 106)

92

Qualitative data analysis programs are software packages developed explicitly for the purpose of handling data that consist of 'qualitative data' – unstructured narrative text or similar material, such as videotapes (Yuen and Richards, 1994). At present there is some debate regarding the use of computers in the analysis of qualitative data, particularly with the growing number of software packages designed to handle such unstructured sources of data. For the purpose of this discussion, however, only one will be discussed, probably the most sophisticated of the range, namely NUDIST. For a fuller discussion of the range and capabilities of these packages, Richards and Richards (1994), the designers of NUDIST, provide a detailed analysis of a number of the key software packages available. They outline the merits and limitations of each and conclude with an explanation and explication of the NUDIST package. Advocates of the NUDIST software package claim that it eases the sometimes laborious and time-consuming process of transcribing, identifying and cross-checking concept development, although there are still many who argue for the use of manual interpretation of data as the true route to theory generation.

In a critical and constructive argument Richards and Richards (1994) suggest that, increasingly, qualitative researchers are experiencing pressure to incorporate the use of computers in the analysis of their data, largely because computers are less concerned with emotional experiences and more concerned with structure, which in the eyes of many still equates to credibility of findings. However, traditionally, most packages have been limited to code and retrieve facilities, which while useful for working with structures are limited in their analysis of content. Richards and Richards (1991) propose that NUDIST has extended the scope of computer analysis in order to address the many challenges and criticisms associated with the limitations of earlier software by aiming at theory construction and development through a range of flexible and varied tools and applications. These tools transcend code and retrieval to incorporate the handling of manuscripts, notebooks, text and unit indexing whilst allowing for searches to create new indexing categories.

They further argue that context can be preserved through the retention of headers and sub-headers with retrieval and index systems which can be structurally reorganised to support the emergence of theory. In addition to this the program also provides freedom to change the content of categories and the creation of new categories in as wide a variety of ways as possible. Coupled with this is the ability to attach memos to indexing categories to record ongoing thoughts. Finally and importantly, the system ensures minimisation of clerical effort and error, thus, it may be argued, legitimising the findings over and above those derived from manual interpretation. Indeed when the labour-saving qualities are explained it is easy to see the appeal of such a program and the many advantages it has to offer in terms of simplifying the process. Nevertheless, the developers of the program are also aware of the pitfalls associated with too heavy a reliance on computers in the process.

Denzin and Lincoln (1994) discuss the limitations of software packages in general terms suggesting that many still remain limited to pure code and retrieval procedures which consequently ignore, or do not have the ability to incorporate, situational and contextual factors. A further danger is the tendency of researchers to reduce field materials to only codable data, which may result in the loss of rich and valuable sources of concepts and theory development. In line with this is the temptation to focus only on those aspects of the research that can be helped by computer methods, or even designing the research itself to fit the available software, which could have undesirable consequences for the range and scope of qualitative research projects.

Whilst Richards and Richards (1994) maintain that NUDIST deals with many of these issues, they acknowledge that they still face a number of challenges in the quest for total analysis of unstructured data. There is still recognition that ideas, concepts and categories discovered in the data are woven by the researcher into a fabric of theory. This process still remains a challenge to software designers. Software packages do not address the crucial tasks of theory construction. Theory construction is a mental activity. It is a process of developing ideas that can allow us to explain and understand the phenomenon (Yuen and Richards, 1994). This cannot easily, if at all, be formalised. Most of the time during qualitative data analysis is spent on reading, rereading, interpreting, comparing and refelecting on texts.

A further potential problem relates to the fact that while the system removes many constraints on size and variety of records, which releases the researcher, the actual result is a form of methodological anomie. This must surely create problems if one is claiming a grounded theory analysis, a phenomenological analysis or any other defined paradigm, as each has its own distinct philosophy, practice and procedure. There are also certain constraints in the area of theory development and the NUDIST package. Richards and Richards (1994) point out that the program does not allow for the visual display of conceptual-level diagrams and models that show emerging theory. This means that the researcher may still have to revert to pencil and paper to do this in order to trace developments and continue. In their earlier article (1991) Richards and Richards called for greater debate with regard to the challenges and meaning associated with the transformation from manual analysis to computer-assisted forms, proposing that computational knowledge means transforming qualitative methods, not merely smartening up old ones. They propose that the considerations that need to be debated include:

- An acknowledgement that researchers can contextualise an interpretation and return to it later. Any technique that relies on segmenting and decontextualising puts this ability at risk as context is not simply achieved by attaching a file name to it. Dembrowski and Hammer-Lloyd (1995) further point to the concern that the machine may take over to the detriment of the thinking process which is so vital to qualitative analysis, although they do point out that the machine can only do what it is directed to do and the main burden still remains with the researcher.

- The fact that context is more than sequence is also an issue. It involves an understanding of the process and the ability to draw knowledge from outside of the text such as literature and personal reflections, which are beyond the scope of any program. This loss of the wider picture and non-textual sources of information is also highlighted by Dembrowski and Hammer-Lloyd (1995) who discuss the fear that data analysis may become mechanistic to the detriment of intuition and creativity. Additionally, there remains for many the misconception that code and retrieval techniques are the path to grounded theory, a misconception that would be strongly disputed by the original authors of the method, who warn against overemphasising coding at the expense of theory emergence (Glaser and Strauss, 1968). And finally:

Users should be aware that many computer techniques are only marginal to, may even be inimical to, the tasks of 'grounded theory'. The process of theory emergence requires a different ability: to see the data as a whole, then to leave data behind, exploring the lines of this segment of that text. To code and retrieve text is to cut it up. The 'grounded theory' method leaves text almost untouched. The researchers' contact with the data is light, hovering above the text and rethinking its meanings, then rising from it to comparative, imaginative reflections. It is the difference between the touch of scissors and that of a butterfly. (Richards and Richards, 1991: 260)

These issues, questions and the obvious potential of computers certainly provide food for thought for any researcher engaged in qualitative research. However, there is a further, and in this case a more important, issue at stake, and that is the nature of the researcher him/herself, his/her relationship with the data and level of involvement in the process, preferred patterns of working and own mental processes of collecting, reading, making sense of, and interpreting his/her findings.

### Summary

This chapter has attempted to describe the process of data interpretation through identifying the stages of coding and interpretation associated with grounded theory research. It has examined some of the issues surrounding theoretical coding and the development of analytical frameworks and has looked at the criteria for identifying a core category which forms the basis for the theory under which concepts and their properties are subsumed. The chapter then considered the challenges faced when writing up the research and concluded by considering the role of computer-assisted analysis. In effect, this chapter represents the culmination of the research process which has been progressively developed through Chapters 1 to 4. Nonetheless, although examples of work have been used to illustrate particular aspects of theory development, there has been no attempt to show the detailed process of theory emergence in any one of these studies. This is largely due to the fact that the work is the intellectual property of the respective authors, and as such the experience belongs to them. Consequently, the next two chapters draw upon the author's own research in an attempt to take the reader through the various stages of the grounded theory process, from identifying a problem and the debates that gave rise to research questions, through to the abstraction of the data and their integration with the literature.

---

**Student exercises**

The following interview was conducted as part of a study into the nature of dance or rave culture. The objective of the research was to gain an understanding of the consumer experience which has seen rave develop into a multi-billion-pound enterprise, impacting on tourism, fashion, breweries and the music industry.

As part of the exercise, you are to

1   Read the transcript very carefully and note down any initial impressions in the form of a memo.
2   Conduct a line-by-line analysis highlighting key words, sentences or phrases that may have explanatory power.
3   Describe what you see as the main themes emerging from the data.
4   State any links or relationship that may emerge.
5   Try to identify as many preliminary concepts as possible.
6   If possible, compare and discuss your findings with those of your colleagues and justify your interpretation.

---

### Interview with Andrew

Andrew is 34 and has been on the rave scene since the 1980s. He has a degree and works in interior design.

*Interviewer*:   Can you tell me a little about your experiences with rave, for example, when did you first start going?

*Andrew*:   I've been on the rave scene now for quite a few years. I started going before it became widespread and legitimate. My first experiences were the early field parties. This was back in the late 1980s. I was about 20 at the time and living in London. I was a student and some of the people I knew suggested that I come along with them to a venue. They had 'gotten the word' that there was a big event being organised somewhere in Kent, so I went and that was the start of it. I'd heard about the scene but this was something else. There were literally thousands of people, thousands of cars heading in one direction to this point in the middle of nowhere. However, it was dynamic. The conditions were terrible, no toilets or anything, well apart from a few very smelly portaloos, but that didn't matter, the sound, the stage, the music, the lighting, the vibe, it was totally electric. To me it was like some sort of awakening and after that I was hooked. I couldn't wait until the next one, but I had to, there was no way of finding out. It was all underground. Someone would receive a flyer and pass the word on, might not seem very sophisticated as a way of communicating to the hordes, but it was effective. It was usually last minute because as you can imagine the police hated it. They couldn't control it so any leakage would have put an end to the whole thing. As it stood at the time, if you were heading in the direction of a suspected venue you stood a good chance of being stopped and searched for drugs. Consequently the whole thing had to be kept secret up until the last minute. But this was also a big part of the attraction, the anticipation, the being ready to go at the last minute, the mystery and the feeling that you shared a secret with a group of like-minded individuals.

*Interviewer*:   This notion of community and shared experiences seems to be a common part of the experience, do you think you could tell me a bit more about it?

*Andrew*:   It's the whole essence of the thing really. I mean it's bound up with the music, the drugs and so on, but it has always been about sharing the feeling, or the 'happy vibe' as it's called. I mean things are a little different now, but community is still central. In the early days rave attracted people who were, what shall we say, not exactly mainstream. New age travellers for example liked the rave scene, it fitted in with their ethos. They would set up tents, get high, mingle with the rest of us, we were like them. We hadn't opted out, but we shared a commonality. It was the same with everyone. You all came for the same thing. Lets face it, you'd defied all odds, you'd got there and the party just went on until the police came to break it up. When field parties became impossible to arrange venues would be set up in disused warehouses and then eventually in clubs, although not in nightclubs as most people define them. DJs and organisers would rent out a club for a night and hold an event in it. The secrecy thing was still the same, phone calls to certain people, underground flyers and then you'd turn up and the queue would be down the street and around the corner. Of course by this time you'd know everyone. They were all familiar faces, we had a common history. Inevitably this changed, around about the early 1990s was the time. Clubs such as Ministry in London and Cream in Liverpool opened around then. Rave became much more accessible, but the stress was still the same, music, uplifting experiences, the happy vibe and community.

*Interviewer*:   You have mentioned drugs when describing your experience. It also seems that when we read about rave it is always linked to drugs such as ecstasy. Can you tell me your views on this?

| | |
|---|---|
| *Andrew*: | Don't let anyone tell you that you can have rave without the drugs, the two are inseparable. |
| *Interviewer*: | What about people who describe getting high on the dancing and music? |
| *Andrew*: | People say you can, but I don't know. I don't think I could. It's like a communion of mind, body, heightened senses and the music. On ecstasy your senses are alert to the sound, to the light, even touch, it heightens your emotions, you love the world. You've heard about being loved up. Well you don't get loved up from the music alone, it's the combination. |
| *Interviewer*: | Is it just ecstasy or are other drugs taken as well? |
| *Andrew*: | Drugs are taken at different times and for different moods. It's not a good idea to drink, in fact the majority of serious ravers don't touch alcohol. The normal thing is to meet up at someone's place and start to get in the mood for the evening by taking maybe one or two e's or maybe a line of Charlie. This gets you going, you lose your inhibitions, you're lifted. It marks the start of the weekend. Your full of confidence and good will. |

That's what makes the difference between mainstream nightclubs and dance venues. You'll get a group of blokes out for the evening with two things on their mind, getting pissed and pulling. Who needs the hassle? They drink, they get drunk and aggressive, you can't relax in an atmosphere like that. That's the one thing about rave, people don't get drunk. I think the fact that it has lasted so long is because it doesn't attract the boozy brigade. Anyway I'm going off the track. Sorry, about the drugs, yeah. Well after the ceremonial popping or snorting, we'll move on to the club. You may well do another line or an e waiting in the queue depending on the effect of the first. If it's coke the effects don't last too long. With me usually about an hour and a half, but I usually revert to e's once I'm inside and the evening has started. You get into the music and that's when you really feel yourself coming up. It is an incredibly sensuous experience. I think what heightens it though is the music and the dancing. You just get on the floor and lose it to the music. You feel euphoric. I suppose that's the best way to describe it. It's like this feeling of happiness and contentment. You look around and everyone is feeling the same. You're on a different plane, you're all feeling it together. You don't have to talk, you just know. You want to dance for hours and hours and make the feeling last. And that's what we try to do. Usually around 2.00 a.m. people will start to drift to the chill out room or maybe even home where they can smoke a little weed and come down gradually, listen to some easy sounds and get the old heart beat back on an even keel. Sometimes we don't bother going home, it might be the case of taking a couple more tabs of e and looking for a party, something to keep us going for the weekend.

| | |
|---|---|
| *Interviewer*: | What about sleep? |
| *Andrew*: | Sleep's for the week, the weekends are too precious to waste sleeping. |
| *Interviewer*: | Doesn't it effect you, not sleeping for days? |

*Andrew*: Yeah, Mondays can be a real downer, but you just have to get on with it.

*Interviewer*: Do you take drugs or go to raves in the week?

*Andrew*: No I don't. I think I would be on the slippery slope if I started that. I don't think there's much worth going to in the week and as for drugs, I take them to heighten an experience. I'm not too keen on just taking drugs and sitting around. I like the effect of the whole thing, the atmosphere, the music, the dancing and so on. It's the whole package that gives you the feeling, but it's not the kind of thing you could do every night, besides I think it would lose its appeal.

*Interviewer*: Can you describe the differences between your week and the weekend?

*Andrew*: Well in the week I work for a design company. We do a lot of the design and arrangement for companies looking to advertise themselves on television like *** [famous furniture store]. Some days I'm in the office, some days I'm on the set, some days I'm travelling around the country. It's a case of early to bed, early to rise. If there are a few of us and we're booked into a hotel we might have a few drinks, but that's about it. I quite like my job, so the last thing I want is for any of the crowd I work with to find out about my other self. But, come Friday night I'm off, up and away.

*Interviewer*: That's quite interesting, so you have a different set of people that you mix with during the week and at the weekend?

*Andrew*: Absolutely. I don't think the two would mix, although maybe people at work are doing the same thing. But you talk to most people about rave and they immediately think it's linked to drug addiction. I mean drugs are involved, but I wouldn't call myself an addict. It's not like taking heroin, or having to take drugs everyday. The drugs associated with rave are recreational drugs. They're part of a scene and they only get taken at the weekend, so what's the real harm in that?

*Interviewer*: I've heard that the latest dance drug is something called ketamine, do you know anything about that?

*Andrew*: Yes I do, I've tried it a couple of times, but I'm a little wary of it as I had a bit of an experience, a bit of a bad trip. It's a form of horse tranquilliser that when mixed with cocaine or taken in various degrees has an hallucinogenic effect. I know quite a few people who love it, say they're up with the stars on it, but I think I'll stick to what I know and like.

*Interviewer*: You talk about being lifted, of experiencing things that you can't experience by taking alcohol for example, do you think you could elaborate on this a little more?

*Andrew*: Well, as I said, it's a gradual process that you go through during the course of the night and it involves an initial lift, while you're getting ready to go out, followed by a full-on surge when you're in the club, surrounded by the music and the people. You dance for hours and the feeling just seems to get better, drugs help to loosen you up, but the music, the lights, the people, the atmosphere all serve to bring you up higher. I mean, take the lighting, the strobe lights darting with the beat of the music, it's almost hypnotic. There's also this feeling of great freedom and exhilaration that you get from dancing. It's like nothing bad can touch you, any cares or worries that you have just disappear, you're a free spirit, your mind can take you wherever you want it to go.

*Interviewer*: This sounds quite an individual experience, although you talk about this notion of community, how do you explain that?

*Andrew*: Well yes it is very individual. You don't go to raves and dance with a partner, it's not like that. And you don't go to chat up people or have in-depth conversations. But you don't need to in order to feel close to the crowd. You can share something without talking about it, you can communicate on different levels. People are there for the music, that's one thing we all have in common, people are also there for the vibe, that's another thing, and there's the feeling of escape and freedom that comes with dancing and the love drugs. Also there's no threat, no aggression, it's just something we're all into together.

# Part Two

## GROUNDED THEORY: AN ILLUSTRATION OF THE PROCESS

# 5

## Researching the Consumer Experience

### An Illustration of the Grounded Theory Method

#### Introduction

While there are many papers which describe and explain what grounded theory is and how to use it, one of the most common requests of the two original authors (Glaser and Strauss, 1967) is for illustrations of the process to show how theories are developed (Strauss and Corbin, 1994). An obvious response to this is to direct enquiries to published reports, papers or theses. However, as with any methodology, within the final body of the work, the actual processes of coding, reduction and concept development become subsumed and invisible in this final interpretation and presentation of the analysis. Therefore, the main aim of this chapter is to demonstrate the application of the method by drawing upon examples from the author's research into consumer behaviour and the meanings derived from visiting heritage sites. This chapter is split into a number of sections which chart the process of collecting and analysing grounded theory data. To begin with, a brief discussion of the issues and debates surrounding heritage consumption which led to an interest in the topic and subsequent research questions is presented in order to locate the research and give a sense of the rationale for conducting the enquiry. This is followed by an overview of the aims of the research and the reasons why grounded theory was chosen as the most appropriate methodology. The location of the study and the process of collecting and analysing the data is next discussed in order to give a picture of the theory-building process.

The rest of the chapter is concerned with the various stages of developing the theory. It begins with an example of an interview transcript and presents a memo that accompanied the early analysis. This is followed by a line-by-line analysis in order to demonstrate how one concept was developed. By way of illustration, the process of abstraction is discussed in relation to the development of the concept of nostalgia, the properties of this concept, and, finally, its dimensions. The other concepts which emerged are then presented to give a sense of the developing theory. After this a brief explanation of the three core categories is offered and in order to show the process a diagram detailing the concepts which were the foundation for the categories is briefly explained. This is followed by an overview of theory which provided the starting point for theoretical abstraction. In essence this chapter is about process, emergence and abstraction in the context of analysing the consumption behaviours of visitors to heritage sites and should be of assistance to those unfamiliar with methods of handling inductively derived data.

## Researching the Consumer Experience

The objectives behind the research were to explore the motivations and the nature of the experiences gained from visiting contemporary museums and heritage sites. This was of interest because at the time that the research was being developed there was a great deal of academic debate about the nature of visitor behaviour, but very little work involving the consumers themselves. Essentially, the question of what influenced heritage consumption had been largely ignored or given only cursory attention. Furthermore, much of the existing work was derived using inadequate methodological frameworks as noted by Moscardo (1996: 379) in the suggestion that:

> whilst there is a growing body of literature relating to visitor behaviour at museums few attempts have been made to integrate the results into a coherent framework or to apply theory to understand or explain the results. This lack of theory in museum visitor research and the atheoretical nature of the research conducted has resulted in poor methodology and limited impact.

This view was reinforced by Masberg and Silverman (1996: 20) whose analysis of the literature on the subject led them to the conclusion that:

> there is a surprising lack of understanding of visitors' perspectives on the experience of visiting a heritage site. Previous studies used quantitative approaches that did not shed light on visitors' perspectives, terms and meanings. Much of the existing research in the quantitative vein utilises predetermined categories defined and supplied by the researcher rather than the respondents themselves.

However, to imply that this was the only approach to visitor studies at heritage sites would be misleading. Over the last two decades we have seen a growing body of ethnographic research conducted at museums (see, for example, Kelly, 1985; McManus, 1989; Delaney, 1992; Squire, 1994; Boisvert and Slez, 1995). Nevertheless, much of this research focused almost exclusively on the experiential aspects of the visit, ignoring in the process the motivating forces that influenced individuals. Given the lack of theory in the area of heritage consumer motivations, the research sought to use the voices and actions of those who took part in the research to construct an integrated account which had both empirical and conceptual relevance. However, before any research questions could be formulated it was necessary to define what was meant by heritage. Myerson (1994) suggests that there are three types of museums:

1) Traditional object based museums.
2) Museums that are not object based but imaginative at creating experiences.
3) Those with no scholarly purpose that fall under the wider umbrella of the leisure industry.

Each of these will attract different individuals with varying and distinct motivations, tastes and expectations (Myerson, 1994). Horne (1984) argues that it is a misconception to talk about the public as if they are a homogeneous mass. We are after all many publics and we will negotiate meanings and approach the museum on our own terms. One thing that became clear, however, was that the entire presentation and interpretation philosophy was in transition. This transition was partly attributable to economic pressures, but also needed to be evaluated in the context of the growing interest, awareness and changes in visitor composition and motivations that saw an increase in the number of museum visitors rise from approximately 28 million in 1970 to 80 million in 1993 (Myerson, 1994).

### The Research Questions

It is important to note that the ideologies underpinning the nature of historical interpretation occupied prime place on the discursive agenda. However, the nature of the consumer and his/her motivations and experiences tended to be discussed in very general, and sometimes patronising, terms. There was very little to hint at any systematic effort at developing insights that lifted the debate beyond broad and unfounded assumptions, despite objectives to become more 'customer-friendly'. Against this backdrop the following research questions were developed.

1   What are the main motivational factors behind visits to museums and heritage attractions?
2   How do these motivations differ between individuals and groups?
3   What is the nature of the experience derived from such visits and how does this differ between individuals and groups?

These questions needed to be evaluated in the light of existing work and in the context of the aims of the research. As indicated, there was a lack of integrated theory particularly in relation to the motivations and experiences of the heritage consumer. Consequently, to begin with, work in the broader field of tourism was evaluated in order to assess existing theories and models that may have had application. However, many research publications based around tourist behaviour claim to be motivational studies and measurements of motivation, but the majority are derived from a quantitative position which pre-empts the range and scope of motivation through the use of survey techniques. Furthermore, as Fodness (1994) observed, such measures of motivation frequently consist of a series of responses that are fixed and inflexible and as such fail to penetrate surface answers for underlying influences. Therefore, rather than models of motivation they are lists of possibilities. Given this lack of attention to consumer-based accounts a decision had to be made regarding the main aims of the research. It is a well-accepted fact that no method allows the researcher access to a fount of indisputable truths. Whichever method is adopted the findings will only be one perspective drawn from a range of possibilities. This did mean, however, that in order to adopt a credible position, the questions, the methodology chosen and the aims of the research had to be closely integrated in as cohesive and logical a manner as possible. Upon reflection of the above, the aims became:

- To *build* theory that is grounded in the voices, actions and experiences of those studied.
- To provide a new perspective on the motivations and experiences of heritage consumers.
- To apply and critically evaluate an interpretivist methodology to the study.
- To develop and incorporate the findings into a theoretical framework that has explanatory as well as descriptive power.

### Choosing the Methodology: A Grounded Theory Approach

With regard to choosing a methodology to research the area of heritage consumption, grounded theory was selected after an evaluative process of the strengths and weaknesses of a range of possible approaches. Table 5.1 summarises the key points which influenced the final decision.

As discussed in Chapter 2, in recent years there has been a divergence in thought between the two original authors of the methodology. It is now common for researchers using the approach to specify which model was adopted, the Glaser or the Strauss and Corbin version. In the case of this research, data were collected in keeping with Glaser's description of the methodology with the emphasis on emergence and theoretical sensitivity. Consequently, some of the techniques associated with Strauss and Corbin's account, such as the continual use of the conditional matrix, do not form a central role in the interpretation. However, the basic principles of open coding, axial coding, theoretical sampling, theoretical emergence and the process of abstraction remain pivotal.

The research was conducted in three stages. The first stage involved in-depth interviews and observations of behaviour at Blist Hill in Ironbridge, Shropshire, a living museum. The second stage took the research into different locations which included repeat observations of behaviour at Blist Hill Living Museum, in addition to observations at an English Heritage property, Buildwas Abbey, and an orthodox museum, Birmingham Museum and Art Gallery. The final stage of the research consisted of a series of focus group discussions which encouraged participants to reflect on their experiences.

### Location

In keeping with the concept of theoretical sampling the researcher should start the process of data collection by going to the places and talking to the

TABLE 5.1   *Choosing the methodology*

Grounded theory was chosen for the following reasons:

- It is a methodology that has as its central aim the objective of theory building, rather than theory testing. Given the lack of an integrated theory in the literature regarding heritage consumption, an inductive approach which allowed theory to emerge from the experiential accounts of the visitors themselves seemed the most appropriate and relevant
- It has a set of established guidelines both for conducting research and for interpreting the data which offered a sense of security when delving into the unknown territory that became the research. Furthermore, whilst there has been some debate regarding the divergence in application of grounded theory between the two originators, there is less disagreement over the nature of theory development than, for example, with phenomenology
- It is an interpretivist mode of enquiry that has its roots in symbolic interactionism and as such discourse, gestures, expressions and actions are all considered primary to the experience. The research described in this chapter, being largely experiential in nature, needed to incorporate observations of behaviour, as it was expected that visitors would not necessarily be able to articulate fully the complete range of their experiences and feelings. Consequently methodologies such as phenomenology, which rely almost entirely on descriptive accounts, were rejected in favour of grounded theory, which allows for a much wider range of data
- It is a methodology that encourages creativity and self-development. This is normally achieved through the process which stimulates eclectic analysis through the application of theoretical sensitivity. Again, given the nature of the research which focused on behaviour, it was clear that theories from across disciplines could have explanatory power
- Contrary to popular misconceptions, grounded theory is not 'atheoretical' but requires an understanding of related theory and empirical work in order to enhance theoretical sensitivity. In an area such as this where there is little formal theory, the incorporation of work in substantive areas proved to be thought-provoking without overshadowing the analysis or predetermining perceptions regarding what to look for
- It is especially renowned for its application to the study of human behaviour, the central theme of this research
- Finally, it is an established and credible methodology, particularly in such disciplines as nursing studies, but it has been largely unused in the field of consumer behaviour. This therefore provided the opportunity to apply a legitimate methodology in a different field

people who are most likely to provide some insight into the problem and offer guidance for further data collection. The initial location for the research was Blist Hill Living Museum in Ironbridge, Shropshire. Ironbridge itself is of significant historical importance as it is recognised as the birthplace of industry. In Britain the area itself remains the only designated world heritage site in the country. It is where iron was first smelted, and the oldest iron bridge was built. Blist Hill is an outdoor, reconstructed, nineteenth-century village which aims to replicate the social and working conditions of the nineteenth century and is typical of the type of museum which generated debate over authenticity and consumer experiences.

The visitor enters this world through a visitor centre and, in effect, is expected to leave the twentieth century behind for the three hours that it takes to explore the site. The museum is completely themed. All workers dress in period costume and will recite tales of their work and home life.

However, there is very little information in text. So, as one enters the museum, there is nothing to locate the buildings in terms of a specific date. This is left largely to the imagination. Although Blist Hill is an industrial living museum the emphasis is predominantly on the High Street and the retail outlets which confront the visitor first. There is a bank where money can be exchanged for old currency, a chemist's, a butcher's, a candle maker's, a baker's, an undertaker's, a working mine, and an array of houses and cottages. In addition to the living interpretation, reproduction products can be purchased in all of these shops. Past the High Street shops and houses lies an old iron smelting furnace, beyond which is the school and the Victorian tea rooms. Towards the end of the museum there is the squatters' cottage, a two-roomed dwelling which once housed a family of eleven, but at the time that the research was being conducted, played host to an elderly woman and her cat.

## Process: Theoretical Sampling and Data Collection

### The In-depth Interviews

According to Glaser and Strauss (1967) and Glaser (1978, 1992), at this stage in the research no preconceived perceptions or opinions should be allowed to colour the investigation. The researcher should remain open in terms of the structure and direction of the interviews in order to let concepts emerge rather than 'forcing' them into predefined categories.

Before approaching the visitors two interviews with demonstrators working at the Blist Hill site were conducted. One was with the policeman, the other with the inhabitant and demonstrator in the squatter's cottage. Both had worked at the museum for several years and were in constant close contact with visitors on a daily basis, this being the main reason they were chosen. These interviews provided an understanding of the institution from ground level, as opposed to management views on why visitors came and what they experienced at the site.

Following on from these interviews sampling was conducted openly with as wide a cross-section of visitors in terms of age, social class and party composition as possible, bearing in mind that these variables should not determine the sample at this stage as they had not at this point 'earned' their place as any real concrete basis for difference. Whilst there were a number of overseas visitors (largely German, Japanese, French and American), for the purpose of the research they were excluded in order to avoid ambiguity and cross-cultural perceptions. The informants ranged in age from 18 to over 80, were all domestic visitors, were diverse in terms of social and educational background, and were drawn from locations as far away as Newcastle in the north east, and Surrey in the south. However, whilst this may seem like a rather diverse spectrum of visitors, it was not entirely untypical of the profile of visitors to Blist Hill (Horne, 1994).

Collecting data in the form of interviews was not, however, an easy task. Visitors had to be approached, stopped and persuaded to discuss their reasons for coming. Individuals are often reluctant to stop and complete questionnaires, so the idea of talking to a stranger armed with a tape recorder proved at times to be even more daunting. That was an obstacle that took time to overcome. Ultimately, however, twenty usable interviews were obtained, two with the demonstrators at the site and eighteen with visitors. In terms of conducting the interviews, it was essential that informants were approached tactfully, and informed about the general nature of the research. Not all the interviews were taped. If an informant felt uncomfortable with the tape recorder it was removed and the interview conducted in the form of a conversation. This involved memoing and coding immediately after the interview in order to keep the findings fresh and alive.

According to Riley (1996) formally structured questions should be minimised, thus allowing the informants to speak about their life and influences before introducing the topic questions. Consequently, most of the interviews commenced with a general discussion about leisure activities, the degree of engagement and the variety of visits. General questions were asked regarding the types of heritage sites informants visited, who they visited with, who and what influenced choice, why they came, and the nature of their experience at different exhibits and settings. Additionally, they were asked about particular objects they could relate to or remember, and what these meant to them. There was also an emphasis on what they considered to be real and faithful representations of the period. However, while there was a general structure to the interview in order to avoid confusion, this was not rigid. Informants were encouraged to elaborate on themes that they felt were integral to their expectations and actual experiences at the museum, which sometimes took the conversation into other areas. With regard to the length of the interviews, these varied substantially. Some lasted well over an hour, others only about forty minutes. However, although some were short, this did not devalue their contribution. A number of informants were very sure and forthcoming in their answers, and in many cases it was the shorter interviews that yielded the most revealing statements and produced *in vivo* codes. Others were happy, once started, to develop the conversation virtually unprompted, and describe in their own words their feelings, motivations and experiences. A sample profile is provided in Table 5.2 in order to show the diversity of the individuals who were interviewed.

As can be seen from this table, the informants ranged quite dramatically in terms of age, social class, where they lived and how many they visited with. Informants had not been selected on the basis of numbers, or division by characteristics to begin with. However, common sense alone dictated that if one is trying to establish reasons for visiting for a broad range of individuals, then in the early stages at least, the sample should be as diverse as possible.

TABLE 5.2   *Sample profile of visitors interviewed at Blist Hill*

| Number | Sex | Age | Class | Party | Distance |
|--------|-----|-----|-------|-------|----------|
| 1 | F | 80+ | Retired | Group | Manchester |
| 2 | M | 70 | Retired | 4 | Shropshire |
| 3 | M | 76 | Retired | 3 | Stafford |
| 4 | F | 65 | Retired | 5 | Swansea |
| 5 | M | 55 | D | Group | Birmingham |
| 6 | M | 60 | B | 2 | London |
| 7 | M | 40 | C1 | 1 | Birmingham |
| 8 | M | 20 | Student | 2 | Wolverhampton |
| 9 | F | 18 | C2 | 2 | Wolverhampton |
| 10 | F | 33 | C1 | 4 | E. Anglia |
| 11 | M | 45 | B | 2 | Bucks |
| 12 | M | 40 | B | 4 | Cheltenham |
| 13 | F | 26 | B | 6 | Leicester |
| 14 | F | 50 | D | Group | Cheshire |
| 15 | F | 28 | B | 2 | Kent |
| 16 | F | 35 | B | 4 | Lancs |
| 17 | F | 40 | C2 | 3 | Chester |
| 18 | M | 40 | B | 4 | Yorks |

Only when particular themes and patterns started to emerge that were indicated by certain characteristics did sampling become more focused.

## Simultaneous Analysis

With regard to the analysis of the data, each interview was accompanied by a memo, clarifying ideas and incorporating codes and their possible meaning. Memos were also useful for describing the intensity of actions or reactions that had some bearing on the experience, and their consequent theoretical implications. These memos were then sorted like with like on the basis of emerging themes rather than individual characteristics. The first few interviews were transcribed verbatim and a line-by-line analysis was conducted to identify the full range of possible codes. This is a process of analysis that Glaser (1992) suggests is time consuming and not always necessary. He suggests that the researcher should transcribe one interview in full, and the rest in part while listening to tapes to identify codes and themes. This, however, did not work in practice and full transcription was not abandoned until a sense of recurring themes was noted consistently in the data. At this point data were extracted rather than develop the entire range of possible codes. These codes were then grouped together to form clusters that might have conceptual value in identifying patterns, similarities and also differences. To begin with there were hundreds of codes, far too many to manage. This called for a return to the data in order to re-sort, prioritise and reduce the number and include only those that had explanatory power.

## Observation of Behaviour

The extraction of early codes provided a provisional framework of concepts. These subsequently directed the enquiry to the next stage of the research. The second method used to collect data was that of 'observation' of naturalistic behaviour in the context of the heritage setting. Again the site of Blist Hill was used, largely to check out the emerging concepts from the in-depth interviews and to look for instances that extended, challenged or substantiated these. The approach was based on the rationale that sometimes actions speak louder than words (Grove and Fiske, 1992; Adler and Adler, 1994). Whilst the interviews provided a rich source of information, it had to be acknowledged that when asked about experiences, informants were not always fully aware of them, or able to articulate their feelings. Consequently observation became a complementary part of the process of data collection.

Visitors at Blist Hill were observed using a video camera in addition to manual observations. These observations were conducted over two separate fortnights during the height of the season. During this time the weather varied from extremely warm, to cold, wet and windy. This in itself provided an opportunity to note differences in behaviour. Visitors were observed alone, in couples, and with family and friends. Observations included the whole age spectrum. At this stage observations were focused on a number of areas felt to be relevant to the analysis. These included interaction with each other, interaction with the objects on display, and exchange between visitor and demonstrator. Other factors included the amount of attention given to particular demonstrations, the level of enquiry, the nature of enquiry (social, academic, exchange of information), the time spent at each display, the degree of familiarity as evinced by a number of the older visitors, the level of knowledge regarding the period, descriptions of authenticity, and nostalgic reactions. In addition to these, body language which indicated boredom, excitement, engagement and frustration was noted. Observations revealed five general modes of behaviour, interaction and experience and can be summarised as:

- Visitors who sought only to interact on a one-to-one basis with the demonstrator.
- Total silent observation of the demonstration.
- Participatory observation with communication occurring as part of a social group in addition to interaction with the demonstrator.
- Removed exploration and interpretation where the experience is divorced from the interpreter and placed on the immediate social group and tangible objects of memorabilia.
- Nostalgic escapism and withdrawal from the present.

Observational methods do, however, have their limitations. In the context of this research the technique yielded interesting and valuable data relating to the heritage experience, which in keeping with many experiences is often hard to articulate, but there are nonetheless restrictions in its suitability to studies of motivation.

## Taking the Research into Different Locations

By combining the findings of the two sets of data it became clear that there were recognisable sets of patterns occurring. However, although Blist Hill attracts a wide range of heritage visitors in terms of composition, it was felt that to conclude at this stage would have been premature. In order to add substance to the emerging concepts it was considered essential to check for similar behavioural signs in more diverse sites. Consequently the next stage of the research involved observations conducted at two different forms of heritage museums. Before changing locations a return visit was made to Blist Hill in order to double-check the concepts that had been identified from the original visit to see if they still had substance. The second site used for observation was Buildwas Abbey, an English Heritage property which could legitimately be labelled 'uninterpreted'. The final setting for analysis was Birmingham Museum and Art Gallery, a more traditional or orthodox museum which incorporated a range of interpretation methods, including static displays, textual and documentary evidence interactive exhibits.

One major difference, however, was that by this stage a framework had developed which provided a greater focus than before. Therefore observations had a more defined structure to them whilst still allowing for differences to be noted. Nonetheless, with observational research there are questions of validity which call for multiple observations, the search for negative cases and the repetition of observations in different settings (Adler and Adler, 1994). These were addressed through an extended period in the field observing behaviour at the Blist Hill site, and then by taking the research into the more diverse locations described.

Locating observations within different contexts not only allowed for a wider range of heritage consumers, but afforded the opportunity to observe individuals with similar characteristics as those observed at Blist Hill. This enabled comparison of behaviour in these quite often contrasting forms of heritage interpretation. For example, while such concepts as the use of imagination were noted during the interview stage, Buildwas Abbey provided a focus for the experience given its lack of information and the solitude of the setting. Birmingham Museum and Art Gallery again provided a different form of interpretation which mixed static and interactive displays and consequently allowed greater scope for the analysis of 'problem' solving and personal involvement in the process as an aspect of the experience. Furthermore, other issues such as the layout of the resource and a sense of physical and mental orientation were explored in greater depth than was possible at a single open-air site.

## The Focus Groups

The final stage in the process was to explore these issues in a totally different context, away from the immediate museum or heritage site itself, through the method of group discussions and debate over motivations and experiences regarding heritage consumption. This method was chosen for a number of reasons, namely:

1  It allowed for greater numbers in a single sitting.
2  It provided a social context which can stimulate discussion and generate new ideas.
3  According to Hedges (1993), groups can help bring out subconscious reasons for behaviour.

Therefore, the role of focus groups in generating understanding and insights was thought to be sound justification for their use. Having developed a framework, this meant that these concepts could provide a catalyst for the ensuing discussions, unlike the earlier interviews which were less structured. Consequently, a briefing sheet listing the broad areas for exploration was used. Nevertheless, this was not rigid. New contributions which took the conversation in different directions were noted and compared against existing data.

The discussions were conducted away from the heritage site in what might be termed neutral locations. This was done for two reasons. The first of these was the matter of convenience for the participants. Two private houses were used in order to provide a comfortable and relaxing environment in which those involved could get to know each other informally before starting the sessions. The second reason concerned the need to get people to talk about their reasons for visiting and their expectations of experiences at heritage sites, away from the actual sites themselves. This provided the opportunity for reflection and evaluation outside of a stimulus context; it also became possible to check if similar themes emerged as from those who were interviewed on site. These groups were also used to develop a fuller picture of opinions regarding historical representations through the exchange of views in a socially interactive situation. In order to avoid any feelings of intimidation, the groups were divided on the basis of age which ranged from 16 to 81. Individuals were mixed in terms of educational history, social class and gender. In all thirty-three people participated in these sessions.

## Analysis

With regard to the analysis of the data, this included full transcription of interviews which were then analysed line by line in order to identify the full range of possible codes. This stage was associated with open coding and was followed until a recurring pattern was noted across the data sets. Once patterns were identified open coding was forsaken for more focused axial coding. This meant that codes were clustered on the basis of their explanatory relationship to each other. These were then labelled to generate concepts. These concepts were initially grouped into descriptive categories. They were then re-evaluated for their interrelationships and through a series of analytical steps were gradually subsumed into higher order categories which suggested an emergent theory. Figure 5.1 provides a summary of the experience. Essentially it reflects the process of grounding the theory in data, from the initial identification of the research problem which emerged from a provisional review of the literature. In this case the lack of theory in the area of heritage consumption resulted in the objective of theory building and the selection of grounded theory, which was designed with this purpose in mind.

In keeping with the methodology the researcher is expected to enter the field during the early stages of the research. This resulted in early data collection (field research 1), at a contemporary living museum, known to attract a cross-section of visitors. Data were initially collected in the form of interviews with demonstrators and visitors, and observations of behaviours at the site. Grounded theory calls for the simultaneous collection and analysis of data. Consequently interviews were transcribed and fragmented through a process of line-by-line analysis. This was done in order to identify the full range of possible codes. At the same time, researcher memos were scrutinised in order to identify any patterns in observed behaviour.

The process of constant comparison of the data resulted in early conceptual categorisation, or a form of preliminary axial coding. Each of the concepts was analysed in terms of their properties and their relationship to each other. At this stage many provisional concepts were rejected owing to their lack of recurrence in the data or explanatory power. However, by this time a preliminary framework had emerged. Conceptual categories were examined in terms of their fit with the literature on behaviour in order to enhance theoretical focus, and were then checked through further theoretical sampling which consisted of observations at a wider range of heritage sites.

Categories were checked against there subsequent data and were refined and prioritised. The last method of data collection was through a series of focus group sessions which allowed visitors to reflect on their motivations and experiences of heritage in a neutral environment. The final stage centred on a full critical review of the data and necessitated a process of abstraction which moved the analysis from the descriptive level to a theoretical interpretation. This involved presenting the core categories that had emerged as having explanatory power through their integration with the literature.

### Example of the Process

This chapter, until now, has been largely concerned with providing context and the bigger picture of the research. The remainder of the chapter aims to

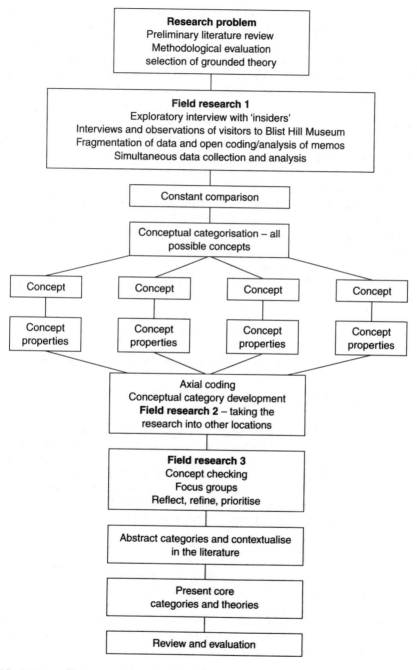

FIGURE 5.1    *Theory building through the research process*

offer more specific, in-depth examples of how the data were analysed and abstracted, beginning with the basic analytical techniques of line-by-line analysis and open coding. What follows is a section taken from a transcript of an interview with a female visitor to a living industrial museum in Shropshire. She was aged approximately 80, was visiting with an organised group and was not a regular visitor to museums. The interview took the form of a semi-structured conversation, allowing her to elaborate on themes and issues that she felt were important to her experience at the museum. She also talked about her life, her family, and the past. One of the important factors that emerged was that of familiarity with a number of artefacts at the museum. These in turn induced nostalgic memories. The concept of nostalgia is described in the literature as being a 'rose-tinted' form of remembrance, or a longing for the past set against an unfavourable perception of the present (Davis, 1979). The concept was identified by taking the whole script and conducting a line-by-line analysis. The interview transcript was then broken up and emerging themes grouped together. In this case the themes relating to perceptions of the past and present have been merged to provide a picture of the nostalgic reaction.

## Interview Transcript

On the issue of who she was visiting with and how the site was chosen:

> I'm here with a group of other elderly people. We belong to a club that organises trips for us about every few months.

> it was suggested to us by the organisers, we don't tend to find out about these places ... in fact I hadn't heard of it before, but we like these sort of places, you know, old houses, gardens, all the people dressed up in the old costumes. The old ways of working ... and you can buy nearly everything they make. You can stop and talk to the workers, have a chat ... they've got time ... like it used to be. That's how it was years ago, people used to leave their doors open and be in and out of each others' houses. Everyone knew everyone else.

On perceptions of the past as the 'good old days':

> Well ... yes, well they were. People knew each other, you helped each other out if you were in trouble. Today people are frightened to open their doors. Back when I was young you might not have the things that are around today, but you made your own fun. You worked hard, you gave your wages to your mother and she'd give you your spending money. Life was a lot simpler then ... it was slower. I wouldn't like to be growing up today.

On perceptions of the present:

> it's rush here, there and everywhere. You turn the telly on and all the news is about murders and robberies. People see things they can't have and just go out

and get them. There's no respect left for anyone, teachers don't or can't control the kids and the old are just easy targets. It isn't a society that values the older generations, but I remember when it did. You respected your elders and betters, you got a clout 'round the head if you didn't, but you learned lessons that saw you through life.

On positive aspects of contemporary life, role changes, support networks and health:

Oh I'm painting a really black picture. Of course there are some things that are better now ... it's only when you come to a place like this it makes you realise the sort of thing you miss. I mean, it takes you back. I've lost most of my family, my husband's dead and so are a lot of my old friends, the ones I've known for years. So when you see things you can remember it brings back happy memories. I'm not able to get around as much as I used to be ... the old bones are getting stiff [laugh].

On perceptions of Blist Hill:

It's not like a normal museum is it ... there's so much going on here ... I spent over an hour in the squatter's cottage down the hill talking to the lady in there. I had a go at the peg rug, and she told me all about the history of the place. I've just been in the chemist, I could spend hours in there looking at all the old potions and bottles ... it's like going back in time.

On the degree of authentic representation:

I mean you really get a feel for the time. All the objects on display are really old, and the clothes are in keeping and the buildings ... I'd say its all very real ... Well they can't show it all, but you get a pretty good picture. I mean there's the shops, the doctor's ... the candle maker's is really stuffy, really let's you see what conditions would have been like, working all those hours.

On the past:

Well you worked hard, but there were other things that compensated for that, family, community, you felt safe.

On the disappearance of these social aspects and feelings of isolation:

To some extent they have. People are always moving from one place to another, you lose touch. At one time if you lived in a street every one would know each other. Half the time you don't know who your neighbour is these days.

On this as an added appeal of living heritage:

You can sense that it would have been a community. I mean you don't get that with the new towns. People are only interested in getting on with their own lives, they don't have the time for anyone else.

On visiting other museums:

> I don't, no ... it's not the same, they don't give you a feel for the past and they tend to be full of really old things, you know, mummies and vases, not like here where you can relate to what's going on.

On similar museums and other heritage:

> No not museums like this ... I've been to a lot of old houses ... but although they're interesting you can't really touch anything. Here you can relax much more and there's so much to see and do, and of course you've got people acting out the part.

On the appeal of the 'live' aspect:

> Oh very much so ... well it makes it so much more interesting, you can feel a part of it ... join in, exchange stories, you can't do that in other museums.

On other forms of socialising:

> I do when I can, but I have to rely on others for transport so I don't get around as much as I'd like. I belong to the club, so I get out a bit ... they pick me up and drop me back every week, but I don't see that many people apart from that.

On her favourite exhibit:

> I think the squatter's cottage. The lady in there was really friendly and chatty and it was snug and cosy. She's got her cat, Tabitha.

On taking over her job:

> Yes I would. I could sit all day talking to people about what it used to be like. You get a lot of people my age in there and they don't want to move ... they stay there swapping stories with each other.

On interest in history in general:

> Not all history, dates and battles, that sort of thing, but later history, history about everyday life, like this is much more interesting ... it brings that past to life.

On the media and history:

> Sometimes I watch historical programmes, but it depends what they're about. If there's something about the war I might watch it ... but remember I lived through that.

On media distortions of the past:

> I think they have to tell a story, everyone likes a bit of romance ... a good love story.

On other activities:

> Well I have a fair bit of time on my hands. I used to have a garden but I've moved into a flat. I watch television, do a bit of baking, but I can't do as much as I used to, I have arthritis in my hands so that stops me from doing a lot of things. I do enjoy these outings though and the afternoon club. It gets you out of the house, you meet other people, have a game of bingo or whatever's on offer.

Immediately after the conversation had taken place a memo was written to capture initial ideas and to provide a sense of reorientation for the future. A memo may consist of a few lines or may be several pages long. The following memo relates to the extract presented previously and offers an example of some of the initial ideas about what was occurring in the data.

## Memo Relating to the Transcript

It is an interesting fact that although the woman is in her early eighties, she seemed to be relating personally to the era depicted at the museum even though the setting is supposed to be mid-nineteenth century. However, there is very little to pinpoint its exact date. There is nothing at the entrance to 'periodise' it. Architecture is mixed, ranging from seventeenth century to Victorian. It is almost as if a lack of any dating allows the visitor to decide what period it is. Personal identification then comes from being able to relate to it through association with *familiar* objects. These objects then constitute the criteria against which authenticity is evaluated and measured. Also noted is the constant use of such words as 'remember', 'old days', 'community', 'safe', 'real'. It is almost as if she is transposing her own past and memories onto the 'themed' setting. The experience is personal and the living museum provides a backdrop for these memories. Contributing to this near idealisation of the past are perceptions of contemporary society and changes in role, security, community and belonging. The past is contrasted with the present and seems to represent a near polar opposite. Memories are selective (nostalgic – wistful longing for a past with the pain removed). Even negative aspects ('clout' around the head) are rationalised or compensated for. Factors that appear to influence this nostalgic reaction include:

Dissempowerment (devaluation of self in eyes of others)
Isolation (from community and security)
Dependency
Alienation and loss of social contact
Loss of significant others
Geographical displacement
Levels of anxiety and mistrust of the present

The experience is largely one of fantasy and escape, evoked through stories, exchange of information and imagination.

## The Process of Abstraction

According to Glaser (1978), after the interview has been transcribed and a memo recorded, the next stage is to analyse the data line by line looking for codes in each sentence. The following is an example of some of the codes that emerged from the interview.

### Line-by-line Analysis

Self-concept = elderly
Dependence on others
'Old' associated with 'good'
Nostalgic reflections on the past
Need to belong
Community lost
Loss of social interaction
Fear and mistrust of the modern
Loss of 'simplicity'
Non-materialistic idealisation of personal past
Present = rush, crime, loss of respect and control
The present devalues the old
Ability to turn a negative into a positive if associated with the past
Disempowerment
Alienation
Loss of significant others
Physical deterioration
More than a museum – a step back in time
Imagination an important factor in experience
Authenticity attached to 'familiar' objects, not processes
Distorted and selective perception of the past
New = isolation/alienation
Need to identify personally with the past
Past = security
Non-questioning attitude to 'invisible' issues
Enjoyment/entertainment through escape
Interaction 'starvation'
Shared 'common' experience with similar others
Gratitude for attention and time
Need for physical and social interaction
Need for involvement and participation
Loss of independence and mobility
Lack of social contact = norm
Unique and personal nature of experience
Selective attention to history
Little need for historical 'truths' – distorted reality

Other modes of presenting the past (TV) also personal
Geographical displacement
Ability loss and role stripping

## Nostalgia: An Example of a Concept

At this stage the coding was largely unfocused and 'open'. Coding is the process of analysing data and at this point the researcher may identify hundreds of codes which could have potential meaning and relevance. However, as a result of constant comparison of subsequent data these are reduced and grouped into meaningful categories. Codes are the building blocks of theory. By coding in every way possible, this allows for direction before becoming selective. It begins by fracturing the data into analytical pieces which can then be raised to a conceptual level (Glaser and Strauss, 1967; O'Callaghan, 1996). Analysis on this level forces the generation of core categories and guides theoretical sampling. Open codes need to be grouped and constantly compared in order to generate a conceptual code. This conceptual code should have properties which can be dimensionalised, but it is also important to note that the focus should not be on quantitative values but on meaning. Consequently, by taking the transcript relating to one emerging concept, in this case that of nostalgia, it is possible to identify properties relating to the nostalgic reaction and in turn their dimensional range. It is important to note that there are varying degrees of nostalgia. Davis (1979) describes the various orders of nostalgia at three levels. Level 1 or first-order nostalgia is extreme nostalgia, which can involve a withdrawal from the present as a result of disaffection with current life circumstances. As a result the individual focuses on the 'rosy' days of the past, filtering out any negative memories. In the case of the heritage experience, this can involve a transposition of life experiences onto the ersatz setting of the heritage site. Level 2 or second-order nostalgia is a much more objective stance whereby the individual questions the source of the emotion, while level 3 or third-order nostalgia is a phenomenological deconstruction of the nostalgic feeling. The concept of nostalgia also has a number of properties (Table 5.3). These were derived from the coding procedure, from words, sentences and phrases that indicated an array of influences and behavioural implications, yet in isolation answered only a fraction of the problem. So, for example, negative perceptions of the present would not have constituted nostalgia if the past was not perceived in the opposite light as better than the present.

These codes and dimensions can be used to compare the presence or absence of nostalgia from the data provided by subsequent informants. Essentially, they may offer an initial basis for further analysis. Concepts explain aspects of behaviour, but not the whole. They unite certain influences under an explanatory conceptual heading. For example, the interview revealed a reduced role repertoire, a lack of social affiliation, disaffection

TABLE 5.3    *Concept: Nostalgia; its properties and dimensional range*

| Level 1/first-order nostalgia | Level 3/third-order nostalgia |
| --- | --- |
| Empty role repertoire | Full role repertoire |
| Low social contact | High social contact |
| Disaffection with the present | Satisfaction with the present |
| Out of control | In control |
| Rose-tinted memory | Realistic memory |
| Fantasy and escape | Leisure and recreation |
| Withdrawal from the present | Contentment in the present |
| Transposition of experience | Collective evaluation |

with the present and the loss of control. In contrast with the present, the past was perceived as a much simpler, better time. It was remembered affectionately, although in a somewhat coloured manner. The painful aspects were selectively filtered out or justified, thus enhancing the nostalgic feeling. For these individuals, nostalgia is a form of escape and is congruent with Davis's account of level 1, first-order nostalgia. However, nostalgia, as noted, is a matter of degree and individuals who were satisfied with their roles, enjoyed a good social support network, were happy in the present, felt in control, and used their memories and related imagery for leisure, were less likely to experience nostalgia. The emotion, when it did occur, had more in common with Davis's description of level 3, third-order nostalgia which involves a critical assessment of the memories associated with the emotion. Nevertheless, nostalgia was only one concept. In total six concepts, their properties and their dimensional ranges were identified as having a relationship that helped explain the behaviour of the informants (Table 5.4).

TABLE 5.4    *The six concepts relating to consumer behaviour at heritage site*

- The presence of and intensity of alienation
- The degree of cultural and personal identification with the interpretation
- Stimulation of nostalgia through the experience
- The desire for authenticity
- Educational motives
- The need for social interaction

The next part of the process was to review the codes and concepts, to note these recurring themes and to abstract them and cluster them in a way that indicated a relationship between them. The development of a core category, however, involved demonstrating the relationship of these concepts to each other in order to provide a theoretically integrated explanation of behaviour in this particular context. The more one finds concepts that work, the more the core category becomes 'saturated' (Glaser, 1978: 60–4). One must then go on to saturate other core categories. Grounded theory is based on multi-indicator concepts, not single-indicator concepts. A core category is a main theme; it sums up a pattern of behaviour pulling together identified concepts which have a relationship to each other. It is the substance of what is happening in the data. The eventual outcome of the research was the identification of three core categories based on differences in terms of the dimensions of the concepts and their properties. These three categories of behaviour have been labelled 'existential', 'aesthetic' and 'social', terms which sum up their behaviour in the context of using and experiencing the past.

### The 'Existential' Visitor

This group of visitors were largely defined by age. They mainly consisted of the 18–21s along with the oldest group, many of whom were aged over 70. They were predominantly drawn from the lower socio-economic groups with little academic interest in the past. Role deprivation or frustration with roles was also a key feature. For example, a number of the older informants had suffered quite severe role loss. In many cases this resulted in a nostalgic longing for a time long gone. The label 'existential' defines the nature of alienation in the present and the search for meaning and temporary control in the past, which typified the behaviour of these informants.

### The 'Aesthetic' Visitor

This group were mainly middle-class professionals or students. Their ages ranged from 20 to 59, although the majority were in their thirties and forties. This group differed from the first in terms of their perceptions of, and criteria for, what constituted authentic representations. They also differed in how they perceived and used the past. The label 'aesthetic' was applied to describe perceptions of the past in relation to the arts, architecture and craftwork, the consequent idealisation of previous eras and vicarious nostalgia, a desire for authenticity, and their quest for imaginative escapism which was characteristic of this behaviour.

### The 'Social' Visitor

This group constituted a middle ground in terms of behaviour. They might be described as 'mainstream' in so far as they used heritage for both leisure and education. Furthermore, there was little to suggest any disaffection with the present, nor any hint at romantic idealisation of previous times. Their ages ranged from 19 to 80, but the key distinguishing factor between this group and those labelled 'existentials' was the degree of social belonging and security which negated any need for escape into the past. Although there were a number of elderly visitors in this category who could identify with the artefacts on display, particularly at Blist Hill, there was an objective and sometimes critical evaluation of the times associated with such objects.

## Using Diagrams to Assist Axial Coding

Whilst it has been stated that the culmination of the research was the identification of three core categories, the concepts that underpin these categories need to be traced and demonstrated. Figure 5.2 is largely a device for amalgamating these concepts into groups, a type of axial coding that demonstrates process and relationships. It constitutes a form of conceptual map which gives order and structure to the subsequent analysis provided in Chapter 6.

## Explanation of Figure 5.2

The figure entitled *Concept identification and grouping* looks at the dominant concepts and their underlying properties. These concepts are identified as alienation, cultural and personal identification, nostalgia, the search for authenticity, the search for enlightenment, the search for social interaction and the psychological and physical factors that influence the individual's state or orientation.

These concepts have properties or underlying causes which vary in their intensity (their dimensions). To begin with, the concept of alienation appeared to be a contributing factor behind both the motivation and experience of the heritage visitor. Alienation was perceived largely as a product of role repertoire, the degree of control the individual felt to have over his/her life and the extent to which he/she is part of a social group. Those who had a full and satisfying set of roles, were socially secure and felt in control tended to be the least alienated; these, for the purpose of identification, have been identified as 'social' visitors. The reverse was found for those at the opposite end of the spectrum, who have been labelled 'existential', while those holding the middle ground appeared to be experiencing a sense of anxiety or lack of fulfilment with their roles, an awareness of the problems in society but a lack of control over change, and less need for social activities as those identified as 'social'. This group has been labelled 'aesthetic'.

These factors had an influence on how the past was perceived and used, but throughout the data the issue of cultural and personal identification also featured as a significant aspect in the relationship the individual develops with the past. The past, for some, offers a sense of continuity. History defines the present and gives context and meaning to the individuals' lives. However, the association with the past depended on the degree of alienation encountered in the present. Those that are most alienated (the 'existentials') will look for alternative answers away from the present, but these 'alternatives' must have personal and culturally bound meaning. In other

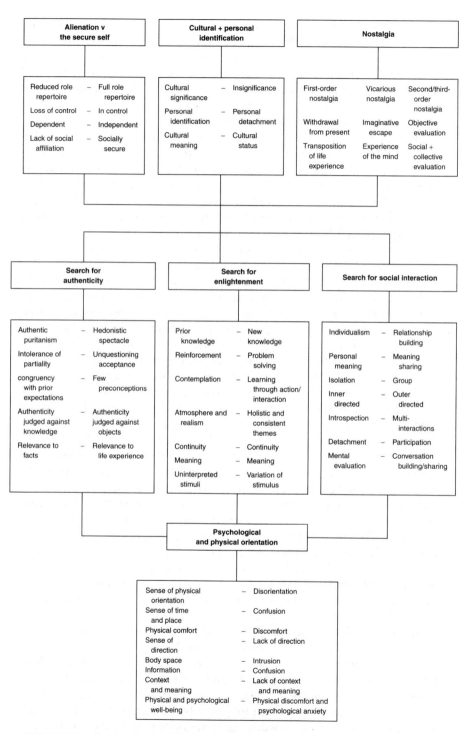

FIGURE 5.2    *Concept indentification and grouping*

words, there needs to be a sense of identification. Those who are emotionally or aesthetically alienated (the aesthetics) will identify with earlier periods (craftswork, poets, artists and so on), which again tended to be culturally defined. The least alienated (the social self) on the other hand did not appear to possess the same need to look for identification in other times and places. On the contrary, they define themselves in the present, and heritage or other cultural activities are merely one aspect of this.

The idea of alienation and cultural identification has a further relationship with the degree of nostalgia experienced by the individual. Again the more alienated the individual is, the more prone he/she is to look back on happier times. For example, those labelled 'existential' showed fairly consistent tendencies that indicated first-order or level 1 nostalgia (Davis, 1979), the uncritical acceptance that life was better then. This took the form of a need for escape, to withdraw temporarily from the present (in this case into the past) and to try to make sense of their lives by transposing their own values and experiences onto this often make-believe time. The 'aesthetics' also experienced nostalgia, but this was not necessarily personal nostalgia. In such cases the nostalgia was vicarious, based on prior knowledge and gained from academic interest which resulted in a nostalgia for an 'idealised' past, not associated with own life experiences, but instigated by a loss of idealism, values and aesthetics in contemporary society. The driving force behind visits to heritage in such cases was the ability to use the imagination as a form of escape, to gain an experience of the mind rather than any interactive or particularly social motivations. Social visitors, on the other hand, evaluated the past in a much more objective and dispassionate manner and, in keeping with Davis's level 3 or third-order nostalgia, tended to use the imagery and interpretation as the basis for critical evaluation of the period depicted.

In turn these three strands of behaviour – 'existential', 'aesthetic' and 'social' – dictated the degree of authenticity that was expected from the resource. This ranged from, at the very extreme, academic purism, intolerance of partial interpretation and expectations of interpretation that is congruent with prior knowledge. This sets the standard for how the resource is evaluated. There is very little search for hedonistic spectacle and a primary desire for factual information and in many cases uninterpreted representations. This desire for authenticity was most manifest in those labelled 'aesthetic'. The opposite of the range, once again at the extreme, was found in the behaviour of those labelled 'existential', while the middle ground was held by those identified as 'social'.

Again in relation to the search for enlightenment, extreme cases could be noted, with the 'aesthetic' highly concerned with building on existing knowledge when possible, but more concerned with contemplation, atmosphere, realism, a sense of continuity and meaning. Others were also concerned with the educational benefits, but tended to engage in more interactive behaviours aimed at problem solving, such as learning through action and participation. However, there was still a need for consistency of theme, a sense of pattern, and a variety of stimuli in order to sustain attention and provide meaning. There was possibly less of a divide between the behaviour of the 'existential' and the 'social' visitor in this case, although in the case of the 'existential' visitor there was more of a need for reinforcement through association with familiar objects, and a higher degree of nostalgia as part of the experience than the 'social'.

Social interaction was a further motivating and experiential influence, although, again, this depended largely on the preceding factors. For example, those labelled 'aesthetic' tended to have less developed social needs in this situation. There was a much stronger emphasis on individual exploration or introspection and the search for personal meaning, through in some cases isolated experiences. The experience was therefore much more inner and mentally directed as averse to outer (group) focused. Those labelled 'social' and 'existential' demonstrated much stronger social behaviour. Meaning was shared with the immediate group, or with similar-minded individuals encountered at the resource. This behaviour could largely be classified as 'outer' directed and multi-interactive with the aim of relationship building.

The final part of the figure concentrates more on the environmental conditions of the heritage resource and how, for example, such factors as a sense of physical and mental orientation are important to the experience. This is largely determined by the inclusion of such things as scene setters which locate the resource in time. Additionally, mapping, routing and crowding density levels may all serve to impact on the experience in either a positive or negative manner.

With regard to abstracting the interpretation, this involves identifying the most salient literature which gives theoretical credence to the interpretation. The remainder of this chapter looks at the initial starting point for analysis which involved an examination of the concept of 'selfhood' and the issue of contemporary feelings of alienation.

### The Concept of the 'Self': A Starting Point for Analysis

Possibly the most appropriate starting point for analysis is to examine the concept of the 'self' in relation to the past. This research was in part concerned with the motivations of heritage visitors, and whilst acknowledging that no general theory of motivation exists, Weiner (1992) suggests that any theory of motivation should include the self. He argues that while the self lies at the very core of human existence it has only been given vague or superficial treatment in the field of human motivation studies.

It is no great revelation to say that we all have a sense of 'pastness' whether this is gained in the home from family stories, the education system or the museum. As this research progressed, the different configurations of the self became a focus for attention in the context of consuming the past. The literature on the self also served to enhance theoretical understanding of the nature of interactions. But instead of providing neat little categories against which behaviour could be checked in the light of the data, it generated a list of questions that took the analysis in a number of directions. Questions such as: how many selves are there? Are we alienated? If so, are we only alienated if we know about it? Is alienation a conscious condition? What determines it? Is it constant? And is it a prime motivator in looking to the past for answers?

According to psychodynamic theories, a consistent and unitary self cannot be assumed; our selfhood changes as we develop and age. We employ defensive manoeuvres to establish, and at times re-establish, a sense of wholeness, and we utilise defences such as identity as a mechanism whose function is to provide a sense of continuity (Stevens, 1996). It is therefore impossible to categorise individuals into constant, unchanging 'types', nor was it the intention of this research to do so. Therefore the ultimate aim was to move away from the analysis of individuals to focus primarily on the identification of common behaviours based around distinguishing themes. These are, however, context and time specific and while the analysis emphasised the self and meaning in relation to the consumption of the past, it is recognised that this is only one aspect of the self and it does not necessarily explain the multiplicity of selves that make up the individual (see, for example, Higgins [1987] on the domains of the self and Markus and Nurius [1986] on possible selves). This research looked predominantly at the aspect of the self that relates to the past in a purposeful manner. The museum or heritage site was used as a means of gaining access to individuals in the process of interacting with tangible representations of the past in an attempt to penetrate the meaning gained from such experiences.

In terms of conceptualisation, the term 'motivation' was interpreted as a broad social and psychological concept. Similarly experiences were defined in the light of personal constructions of interactions and the meaning derived from these. However, as the analysis developed and the theoretical interpretations unfolded or 'emerged', further, more subtle existential questions were raised in relation to the way in which individuals create meaning and how this construction differs across individuals, or groups of individuals. Stevens (1996) analyses the dimensions of being a person, which, he proposes, consist of a number of separate but interrelated components. These include:

1 'Embodiment' (related to the inhabitancy of a particular body). This research included a number of informants ranging in age, and consequently stages of physical development and deterioration. For example, some informants were very elderly and less physically mobile. This tended to have an impact on how they related to the past, to the days when they were active and in their prime. It proved a useful construct to keep in mind while looking for clues regarding behaviour.

2 Subjective experience (consciousness and a sense of self and agency). This idea was incorporated into the analysis in terms of how people made use of the past in the context of the heritage resource, how they engaged in activities and where, in certain cases, the heritage background constituted a stimulus for active behaviour aimed at regaining control, albeit for a temporary period.

3  Cognitions for processing and making sense of experience. These were considered in the interview and discussion stages in order to ascertain how expectations and motivations were consciously evaluated in the light of experiences and the criteria used for judging the adequacy of the visit (authenticity, orientation, crowding and so on).

4  It is generally accepted that we exist in a social medium of meanings and customs. Whilst the issue of culture is a feature that cannot be dismissed in terms of behavioural influences, the nature of this research was set against the backdrop of cultural resources which utilise history, tradition and customs to create a picture of the past. In turn, the behaviour of the visitor was observed to ascertain the nature of interactions (social, isolation or self-directed) as a consequence of his/her reading of displays.

5  It is also acknowledged that we experience unconscious feelings. There is no intention to claim that the research penetrated the subconscious of those individuals whose behaviour formed the basis of the findings. However, subtle clues were given off, particularly during the non-intrusive observation stages which provided insights. Subconscious motivations were also indicated at times during conversations with individuals, particularly when the discussion moved into other, less direct areas, such as the nature of society and their place within it.

6  Finally, we need the ability to draw together these strands and make sense of their complex interactions. It was certainly beyond the scope of this research to claim that all aspects of meaning have been identified. We do not tend to think holistically about each diverse strand of our being, nor do we necessarily consider each and every experience in relation to the general pattern of life, at least not on a conscious level. However, wherever possible, themes were identified and related to each other in as meaningful a manner as possible.

### The Quest for Meaning and the Concept of Alienation

While such constructs as role repertoire, social affiliation and control have been used to explore perceptions of the past, in a similar vein Yalom (1980), on the subject of choice and experience, argues that individuals will strive to give their lives purpose by engaging in specific behaviours which will provide meaning and a sense of autonomy. He proposes that:

Engagement is the answer to meaningless. Wholehearted engagement in any of the infinite array of life's activities … enhances the possibility of one's completing the patterning of the events of one's life in some coherent fashion. To find a home, to care about other individuals, about ideas or projects, to search, to create, to build – these and all other form of engagement are twice rewarding, they are intrinsically enriching, and they alleviate the dysphoria that stems from being bombarded with the unassembled brute data of existence. (Yalom, 1980: 482)

Csikszentmihalyi (1992) on the other hand looks primarily at the pursuit of happiness through the channelling and control over what he terms 'flow'. This concerns conscious effort and the direction of psychic energy to produce a feeling of well-being. A flow experience is autotelic (an end in itself) and is congruent with goals which involve absorption in an activity. This demands real engagement (not passive spectating) and real involvement. This proved a useful concept in terms of evaluating the nature of the experience during the observation stage, given that there was a heavy emphasis on interaction and involvement in the process. However, much of the literature on the nature of contemporary society seems to suggest fragmentation, loss of control, interference and the disruption of 'flow'.

Cushman (1990), for example, describes the modern self as 'empty'; it is starved of community experiences and emotional, intellectual and social bonds (Cushman, 1990; Laenen, 1989). Conversely Gergen (1991) proposes that rather than being empty, the contemporary self is 'saturated'; it is too full, overflowing with complex technological and impersonal communications and indirect interactions which often intrude into personal lives. This death of the social has resulted in a quasi-religious searching for answers through consumption (Belk et al., 1989; O'Guinn and Belk, 1989) and retrospective reflection.

From the data, there was some evidence of this, of a searching for meaning or substance unique to the past which has been lost or buried in contemporary life. The museum is one way of accessing the past, and through the course of this research this is how museums and heritage sites came to be perceived, not just as institutions full of treasures, artefacts and images, but as gateways to the past and behaviour settings (Falk et al., 1985). In other words, they were perceived as a stage where motivations and experiences were determined more by social and environmental factors than the quality of display. What did become apparent is that modern individuals are searching for something and the past offers some answers. The following conversation between two males from the focus groups, one aged 59, the other 54, provides some evidence for this:

| | |
|---|---|
| *First informant:* | But I wonder if it really is just a trendy fad, all these people flocking to museums … or is it something deeper? I think we're all looking for something, if you look back over the last thirty years or so you can see that … I mean in the 1960s it wasn't museums but there was a reaction against all sorts of things and a need to fill their place … it was much more political then… |
| *Second informant:* | That's true, but we were all very idealistic, reacting against our parents, thinking we had all the answers. |
| *First informant:* | But we didn't and that's the thing … I don't think people are ever satisfied … so what happened was, in the '60s people questioned established religions, but they still needed something so we had a sort of spiritual searching, you know the |

|                    | whole hippy movement was about finding something deep and meaningful, a rejection of war... |
| :--- | :--- |
| *Second informant:* | Yeah and look what Charles Manson did for them. |
| *First informant:* | But that's just the point ... it didn't last ... people move on ... the whole social, commune thing didn't work so you look elsewhere. Whatever people are doing today it's no different, better or worse ... people are looking for answers ... I think they're searching for meaning ... I don't know maybe they're trying to find them in museums ... the institutions that let us know what we are and why we're like it ... maybe that's reading too much into it, but look around at the people you know ... how many can you say are really satisfied, don't feel pressure or anxiety? Aren't worried that they'll be the next to be made redundant? We seem to be constantly living under a threat where if we don't conform we just get tossed aside ... people think it wasn't always like this ... I don't know you go to these new museums and they show you a different way of life ... you don't see the old miner worrying about how he's going to pay off his Access bill at the end of the month ... the emphasis is on simplicity ... maybe if you can't have it yourself you get it second hand ... that I think is why we can talk about a nostalgic society ... We're all under pressure and we're all under somebody's eye ... if they can't phone you they can fax you, or get you on the computer ... it's hard to get away from it ... and yet we get shown images of an unobtainable ideal ... so what do we do ... we live it for a while. I don't think there's anything really wrong with that ... people know it wasn't really like that, but if you can pretend and if it helps you relax and switch off for a while then so what ... today it's museums tomorrow it'll be something else. |

Here there is an indication of the alienating nature of modern society. Phrases and words like *'searching for something'*, *'threat'*, *'worry'*, *'lost simplicity'* give an insight not only into quite common conditions endemic to the present, but also into perceptions that these are consequences of modern life which exacerbate the search for meaning and alternatives. It would be a wild exaggeration to suggest that these individuals considered museums to be some form of haven from the realities and pressures of everyday life, but they do serve a purpose. They are part of a continuing quest for meaning although paradoxically it is recognised that what is on offer is only an impression. Such descriptions of life do, however, seem to support Yalom's suggestion that:

The more we search for pleasure, the more it eludes us. The search for meaning is similarly paradoxical: the more we rationally seek it, the less we find it, the questions that one can pose about meaning will always outlast the answers. (Yalom, 1980: 482)

In the context of this research, the past and history provide one form of meaning. The term 'the history kaleidoscope' has been used to describe the museum, a lens for accessing and making sense of the past. However, perceptions and the construction of meaning alter depending on the individual, his/her state of need and location within society. The past may often look greener because we are offered endless aesthetic images of it (McRobbie, 1994; Stern, 1992; Babich, 1994) and this in some cases may only serve to accentuate a sense of alienation. However, this is not to imply that this is a condition ascribed to everyone who visits museums. From the data it appeared that a conscious awareness of being alienated only served to deepen the feeling, particularly when accompanied by a sense of powerlessness.

After multiple reflections on the data, three strands of alienation were identified which related closely to the core categories of 'existential' (alienated), 'aesthetic' (semi-alienated) and 'social' (non-alienated). In short these categories were largely influenced by such factors as role, social support and the degree of control that the individuals felt they had over their life. These in turn tended to determine the significance of the past (cultural and personal) and a longing to return to an ideal state, experience it vicariously (nostalgia) or objectify it and see it as a distant and alien time. These states had a strong impact on the nature of the experience that was both sought and gained (authentic, enlightening or social) and are discussed in more detail in Chapter 6.

## Summary

The aim of this chapter was to demonstrate the process of using grounded theory, from the identification of an area of interest, through the various stages of data collection and analysis, to concept development and a form of axial coding represented in diagrammatic form. The chapter concluded by providing an overview of the conceptual literature that provided a starting point for analysis, or the abstraction of the analysis onto a theoretical level. The next chapter aims to explore the theoretical significance of those concepts outlined in Figure 5.2, and relate these to the three distinct types of behaviour identified as 'existential', 'aesthetic' and 'social'.

# 6

## The Identification and Explanation of Concepts and Categories

### Introduction

The preceding chapter highlighted the concepts which formed the basis for the theory and charted the relationships between them. This chapter continues this process by reorganising the data into categories which are the result of reduction and re-sorting. Furthermore, these categories or visitor types, with illustrative examples from the data, are located, contextualised and evaluated in the literature which informed the theoretical development.

The three types of visitor introduced in the last chapter, namely the 'existential', the 'aesthetic' and the 'social', are considered in relation to those concepts identified as significant in Figure 5.2. The chapter concludes with a discussion of environmental factors such as scene setting, mapping and routing and crowd density levels, all of which have implications for the operational management of heritage sites. It must be acknowledged, however, that it is quite rare for the researcher to present the full findings of a grounded theory study in a single paper, or in this case a chapter. Each concept should be fully integrated with the literature and should represent the basis for a paper in itself (Glaser, 1992). Indeed this was the case with the research described here. For example, see Goulding (2000b) for a discussion of authenticity in the heritage context, Goulding (1999b) for an analysis of nostalgia and age-related heritage experiences, and Goulding (2000a) for an overview of the environmental aspects of heritage interpretation and the consumer experience.

### Locating the Interpretation in Theory

#### Summary of the Research Findings

With regard to the emergence of theory, this centred largely around the relationship the individual has with his/her own personal pasts, or pasts outside of his/her living memories. This relationship was derived from the data and offered an alternative means of conceptualising the problem. This does not mean that more standard methods of differentiating the market, such as age, gender, social class and educational levels, were ignored, only that they were considered in the light of other influential factors which provided insights into underlying conditions for motivation. It is nonetheless impossible, whatever the criteria used, to present a uniform and standard picture of the contemporary heritage/museum consumer. It is acknowledged that individuals change as their life circumstances alter and therefore there was no intention to present profiles of individual behaviour in the final analysis, rather sets of behavioural patterns that are dependent on both internal and external influences.

To begin with, early analysis appeared to suggest that age played a significant part in the propensity to visit heritage sites and particularly the kind of resource chosen. However, as the analysis progressed this was questioned and there were indications that age was less potent than social factors, life stages and perceptions of self. These tended to transcend age alone and necessitated a re-evaluation of early findings. With regard to gender, there were very few differences identified, both in terms of motivation and the nature of the experience. Social class and educational levels were possibly more important in terms of evaluating the nature of the experience, but this to a large degree was also dependent on levels of personal interest in history and background knowledge gained prior to the event.

The aim of this research was to theory-build, to explore areas that have previously been ignored in studies of heritage visiting. This evolved into the incorporation of ideas and theories relating particularly to issues of the self, whilst acknowledging that these findings represent an insight into only one of those 'selves': that which relates to and uses the past for specific means.

The following represents a summary of the theory that has evolved from the data and the integration of theoretical ideas from relevant literatures. It offers an explanation that addresses the research questions which revolve around both motivations and experiences. However, in keeping with the interpretivist position, it does not strive to separate cause (motivation) from effect (experience).

## The Existential Visitor, Motivations and Experiences at Heritage Sites

Whilst the label 'existential' has been used to explain the nature of behaviour indicated by this core category it is not the first time it has been applied as a conceptual umbrella. Cohen (1988) applied the term when describing the 'existential' tourist, who, alienated from the immediate environment, seeks alternative arrangements in other settings. Elliott et al. (1996) used the label in relation to addictive consumption. Here the 'existential' consumer searches for meaning, control and creativity in his/her life through the act of shopping which helps to construct identity and is an expression of self. Whilst these may be different behavioural contexts, there remain consistencies which centre predominantly around meaning, choice and control. S. Brown (1995) highlights this by reference to existential phenomenology which purports that humans are self-creating, they are aware of their existence, they make decisions and have the potential to control their lives through a series of intentional actions.

In this instance the label has been applied to demonstrate the nature of meaning derived from the consumption of images and representations of the past. This group are 'existential' by virtue of their ability to construct their own values and ideologies (family, community or respect) which provide a degree of escapist self-determination, and then to transpose these values to another time belonging to their own experiences or 'significant' and relevant pasts. This rests on needs that exist in the present which are influenced by the extent of alienation experienced by the individual, the search for identity, nostalgic reactions to the past, a need for association through familiarity and a desire to share experiences.

Whilst there was no intention to categorise behaviour on the basis of age, social class or education, the data suggested that those most likely to fall into this group tend to be elderly, are from the lower socio-economic groups and have little experience of higher education. They conform to the profile of those classified by Merriman (1991) as non-visitors. However, Merriman's study was largely confined to traditional museums, while this research incorporated the living museum as part of the overall context. This provided a different picture, particularly of the retired, who constitute approximately 20 per cent of Blist Hill's visitor base (Horne, 1994).

Those who fall into the category 'existential' appeared to be experiencing periods of transition, through role uncertainty or lack of autonomy, boredom, anxieties over the future and feelings of identity confusion and isolation. For example, the 80 year old informant described in Chapter 5 illustrates such feelings:

> I have a fair bit of time on my hands, I used to have a garden, but I've moved to a flat ... I watch television, I do a bit of baking, but I can't do as much as I used to do ... I have arthritis in my hands.
>
> I've lost my family ... my husband's dead and so are most of my friends.
>
> When you come to a place like this it makes you realise the things you miss ... it takes you back.
>
> People are always moving from one place to another, you lose touch ... half the time you don't know who your neighbour is.

This isolation from the social seems to accentuate feelings of loss of control and fear (Kamptner, 1989; Connor, 1995; Baumeister and O'Leary, 1995):

> There's no respect left for anyone, teachers don't or can't control the kids and the old are just easy targets.

Coupled with this, the ability to engage in any form of social activity rests in the power of others:

> I have to rely on others for transport ... they pick me up and drop me back every week.

These feelings are factors associated with the condition referred to as the 'empty self' by Cushman (1990). This behaviour can be further contextualised in the light of Yalom's (1980) description of existential isolation which results in individuals struggling to give their lives purpose through engagement. In this case it is engagement through fantasy and escape, through representations of meaningful pasts as offered by the museum, or other more personally relevant simulations. For example, the same informant described more orthodox museums as follows:

> They don't give you a feel for the past ... they tend to be full of really old things, you know mummies and vases ... not like here where you can relate to what's going on.

whilst her experience of Blist Hill tended to be of a more personal nature:

> I could sit all day talking to people about what it used to be like ... you get a lot of people my age in here and they don't want to move ... they stay here swapping stories with each other.

Such engagement with personal or 'significant' pasts allows for the confirmation and reaffirmation of identity and offers a mode of self-expression. The past becomes recontextualised and selective, drawing upon either lived experiences or media interpretations. Through the use of imagination, a sense of escape and consequent control is temporarily gained. This group find themselves locked into something of a dichotomy, alienated from their immediate centre (the present) in which they have very little power, but alienated also from their alternative centres (the past) through distance in time. This results in the consumption of fairly specific forms of representations (living museums, special themed events) which allow for engagement and interaction with similar others. These representations in turn heighten the nostalgic reaction.

In keeping with Davis's (1979) analysis, the roots of nostalgia tended to be located within the context of the present, but it was also found that the reaction can be triggered by fears and uncertainties over the future. For example, the elderly informant described previously illustrates the contrast between the experiences of the past with those of the present:

| | |
|---|---|
| *On the past:* | People knew each other, helped each other out if you were in trouble. |
| *On the present:* | People are frightened to open their doors. |
| *On the past:* | Back when I was young you might not have had the things you have today, but you made your own fun. |
| *On the present:* | I wouldn't like to be growing up today. |
| *On the past and Blist Hill:* | You can see it would have been a community. |
| *On the present:* | I mean you don't get that with the new towns, people are only interested in getting on with their own lives ... It's rush here there and everywhere ... it isn't a society that values its older generations but I remember when it did. |

Nevertheless, whilst Davis's (1979) levels of nostalgia could be applied, and in this case the most appropriate is that of level 1 nostalgia (an extreme longing for the past), within this level itself reactions varied in intensity. In its mildest form there was a simple belief that the past was better. More extreme manifestations resulted in the need to immerse the self fully in a construction of the past and consequently withdraw from reality. However, whilst complete withdrawal has been associated with pathological disorder (Kaplan, 1987), the nostalgic experience at heritage sites is temporary, and as such acts as a means of coping with the alienation and isolation that was expressed, although in more subtle terms, as characterising much of everyday life.

Consequently, in order to escape, representations of the past need to have meaning for the individual. As such the quest for personal authenticity is high. The invisibility of the negatives that would have existed and the aggregation and fusing of various periods, as in the case of the Blist Hill museum, is often overlooked. Authenticity is largely attributed to familiar objects and attention to surface detail:

> I mean you get a feel for the time. All the objects on display are really old, and the clothes are in keeping and the buildings.

The criteria for evaluating authenticity are often personal and in turn will differ according to age (Csikszentmihalyi and Rochberg-Halton, 1981) and key socialising influences, such as the family and community in the case of the elderly, and the media for those belonging to the younger age groups.

As the experience tends to be of a highly personal nature, the search for educational enlightenment is not a major priority, rather the social aspects (Blud, 1990) take precedence. This manifests itself in enjoyment through meeting and exchanging common experiences with similar-minded individuals whereby the nostalgic reaction can be shared and reinforced through collective consensus, as illustrated in the following statements given by the elderly informant and the demonstrator at the squatters cottage:

| | |
|---|---|
| *On living museums and the live aspect:* | It makes it so much more interesting, you can feel a part of it, join in, exchange stories, you can't do that in other museums. |
| *On her favourite exhibit, the squatter's cottage:* | The lady in there was really friendly and chatty and it was snug and cosy. She's got her cat Tabitha [realism]. |
| *On taking over the Demonstrator's job:* | I could sit all day talking to people about what it used to be like. You get a lot of people my age in there and they don't want to move ... they stay there swapping stories with each other. |
| *The Demonstrator on the attraction:* | This part of the museum attracts all sorts, especially the senior citizens. I mean there's one old man, just been in, he's 98 and he's a great gay boy. |
| *On nostalgia and familiarity:* | They wanted to stop because they remembered so much. Everything they could see from the range and |

*On interactive*       cooking instruments, it brought back all their memories from when they were young.

*On interactive*
*participation, nostalgia*    One old lady still has a pegged rug, she can still do it
*and familiarity:*      all, she was all 'oh let me have a go love'. That started her talking about years and years ago. They loved it, they got quite carried away.

*On 'it's good to talk':*    We find time to stand and talk and discuss things, people don't talk enough these days ... it makes the day out for people [and] people come in here and what is it? It's a home.

## The Aesthetic Visitor, Motivations and Experiences at Heritage Sites

This group have been labelled 'aesthetic' as a consequence of their desire to recapture the essence of times that are considered more intellectually and artistically superior to today. These individuals tend to be interested in works of art, literature, paintings and architecture, which may possibly be conceptualised as a reaction to postmodern uniformity. This group were largely, although not exclusively, middle aged, middle class and well educated. Most seemed to have a full role repertoire that allowed for challenge in their lives; however, there was still a degree of frustration and disaffection with contemporary society and their place within it. For example:

We're governed by the clock ... it's nice to get away from that for a while, switch off and forget the rat race. (40 year old man)

It isn't something you can think about in isolation ... you can talk about the destruction of the past by visitors and politicians, but it's only part of an overall picture and it needs to be addressed at the most fundamental level ... if you think about the amount of cars that are on the road today, there are no real attempts to solve the problem except to build more roads, so you cut through the natural countryside, destroy it, just to service the needs of people who never consider alternative forms of transport ... then there's the pollution ... the fumes ... the vibrations from the traffic ... what is that doing to historic cities and to the quality of life of those who live there ... what people really need is education ... education about the past, what it can offer, and that without care and attention all we are going to have left is a heap of rubble. (34 year old woman on the problems of pollution and the destruction of natural heritage)

It's important that we don't lose sight of that [history], that we don't get too tied up with the modern ... we need a sense of history, without it we're rootless. (30 year old woman)

I feel quite strongly about preserving the old buildings and crafts, if they are let die out future generations will lose so much. (45 year old man)

I think we're losing sight of the really important things, satisfaction and achievement at work. (20 year old student)

This sense of alienation tended to hinge on an awareness of contemporary social and environmental issues, coupled with feelings of an inability to control or fully influence these issues, even though many were active and constructive in their efforts to support conservation and change behaviour. There were indications of frustration and of searching for meaning. This resulted in the construction of an ideal past, the essence of which was sought largely in resources that placed the emphasis on the individual to construct meaning. Part of this romanticism of the past was based around a sense of loss of aestheticism and intrusion (technology and media) into the personal spheres of private life, as proposed by Gergen (1991) in his theory of the 'saturated self'. In many cases these informants appeared to be intellectually stimulated but aesthetically deprived. With regard to meaning derived from representations of the past, rather than personal association, as in the case of the 'existential' visitor, personal and cultural identification revolved more around intellectual and aesthetic movements.

> Look at the craftsmanship that went into making things ... it's just not there today, houses look like boxes and computers are taking over from skilled people ... people just don't learn those types of skills anymore, it really is a shame that the only place you can see them is in a museum. (45 year old man)

> There's very little to get excited about. ... I'm not keen on modern architecture ... it looks as if it's been thrown up ... to intimidate and make you feel small ... there's no warmth to it. (20 year old man on the present)

> There was so much happening ... paintings ... books ... poetry ... much more than today, you look at what's going on around you and there's very little of any aesthetic value, but there's more to it than that. The contrast, the way people lived ... they may have been awful ... but they were exciting times ... today everything is so mechanical and functional. (40 year old man, on the past)

There was a strong appreciation of former cultural configurations before craftsmanship became stifled by technology. This in turn appears to lead to fairly strong conservationist needs and a form of nostalgia as illustrated in the following statements:

> I'm not a great visitor to museums ... they are fine and I've nothing against them, but I can't stand spending hours peering at things in glass cases, I don't think that gives you any real sense of the past ... but you get away from all that ... out into the open ... you might think I'm weird but some of the ancient stones out in the wild countryside ... lie down at night and you can really feel the atmosphere ... that has more to do with taking you back in time than any reconstruction can. ... but we're losing them. ... look what's happened to Stonehenge ... you can't get near it ... it's been turned into a circus ... traffic, car parking, hordes of spectators. ... we're in danger of losing one of the most mysterious legacies of the past that we've got ... but never mind, you can experience it all through virtual reality ... that about sums it up. ... does it actually mean anything in this type of society, is there a place for it? (33 year old woman)

> Can you imagine what it was like ... it must have been a magnificent spectacle ... I know it's impossible to go back ... but I would love to have been there, just to experience what it was like. (20 year old man on Blist Hill)

The result of such perceptions is a nostalgia, induced by historical stimuli. However, whilst the nostalgic reaction is located within conditions of the present it is not necessarily 'personal' as defined by Davis (1979). This vicarious nostalgia does not manifest itself in a longing for any prior period belonging to the individual's own life experience; rather it is for an idealised and romanticised past. This in itself leads to a search for the unobtainable, for 'real' representations of lost ages.

In such cases imagination and atmosphere become the means of experiencing the past. Imagination replaces the need for tangible objects and artefacts and as such excessive interpretation can be perceived as intrusive.

> I shouldn't really complain about this place, I mean there are enough people enjoying themselves ... it's just not me ... People tell you to come here, that it's exactly like it would have been ... but this is more like a scene from The Railway Children, there's no sense of realism ... I mean it's the birthplace of industry but you wouldn't know it [and] one thing they have done here is recreated the shops well ... but I want the impossible ... I'd like to see it at night with just the gas lights on ... it's all to do with imagination, I don't think you can beat that. (40 year old man on Blist Hill)

However, there was generally an appreciation of detail and authenticity:

> I mean, look at the attention to detail, the research that must have gone into collecting all this stuff, it's not just thrown together ... you talk to any of the demonstrators there's nothing they don't know about their particular role ... I know it would have been a much smellier place had it really existed and working conditions would have been hard, but would anyone really want to see that? (33 year old woman)

In many of these cases there was a highly developed sense of the past based on prior knowledge and interest. Such informants may be described as possessing the keys which unlock and decipher the cultural codes associated with the more cryptic and traditional forms of representations (Bourdieu, 1984). The difference between the two groups identified can also be located within Bourdieu's (1984) distinction between working-class expectations that every image should fulfil a function and the culturally educated who can accept, understand and appreciate more abstract forms of culture. Consequently, heritage visiting tends to transcend social needs, and the experience becomes inner directed and quite often sought through solitude and social and physical space as illustrated in the following statement:

> There's no sense of realism, I get more of that from the Victorian rooms in Birmingham Museum and Art Gallery. At least there you don't have the crowds of people constantly showing you how it was done. It's quiet and you can use your imagination, take your time ... (40 year old man describing Blist Hill)

## The Social Visitor, Motivations and Experiences at Heritage Sites

The third group has been labelled 'social' in terms of both motivations and experiences. This, however, is not to say that such motives cannot be integrated with other educational or entertainment incentives, only that the nature of interactions was largely 'outer' or 'other' directed. This group could possibly be described as more mainstream in their expectations and evaluation of the heritage experience. There was little to suggest either extreme interest or particularly high levels of identification with the resource. Furthermore, nostalgia, when and if it occurred, was transitory and subordinate to other experiences.

While there were variations in terms of age, life-cycle stages, education and occupation, there were similarities in themes or patterns of behaviour that transcended individual differences. These suggested that certain types of museum interpretations could be used to serve needs other than those associated with academic enlightenment, escape or contemplation. With the other two groups, there were indications of psychological alienation and in some instances social isolation which contributed to the construction of experience at heritage and museums. With this group there was little to suggest this in any recognisable form; the curtain covering the stark realities of existence described by Yalom (1980) remained, for the large part, closed. This was primarily related to a strong sense of social integration and acceptance whether by peers or family units. In addition to this there was little to suggest frustrations with role sets or worrying visions of the future. For example, a 77 year old male, known in Ironbridge as the 'Lord Mayor', typified this type of behaviour. It would be fair to describe him as active, incredibly energetic and full of life. His past roles included fighting as a soldier in the Second World War, running the local funeral parlour and owning a building firm. His wife had died some years ago and his new partner had recently moved in with him. During the day he was constantly engaged in a variety of activities from painting and decorating his house to overseeing and participating in his latest project which was building a new house on a plot of land he owns. He described how in the evening he went out for a drink and enjoyed socialising. His son, who also lives in Ironbridge, had taken over the building business and visited him on a regular basis. With regard to the past, he remembered it very much for what it was and there was little evidence of nostalgia or any form of discontent with the present. On the contrary, his self-perception was incredibly positive, he enjoyed life and had little time to dwell on past events. His evaluation of Blist Hill was that:

> It's okay for a day out but I got a bit fed up after a short time, I mean those old days were dreary times, although what they've done there is to clean it all up. I can't say I'd go back again in a hurry, I went out of curiosity but to be honest I'm not one for all that sort of thing, I'd much rather go out for a few drinks in the evening rather than spend my time wandering around a museum ... I suppose the whole of Ironbridge is pretty much like a museum these days ... It wasn't

always like that though. This area was pretty run down years ago, there used to be a lot of mining work so it wasn't the picturesque place it is today ... funny it takes an old bridge and a museum to get people moving into the area and cleaning the place up ... but it's all for the tourists isn't it ... they want to see what it was like a hundred years ago so they go to Blist Hill and talk to the miners and the shop girls in their nice clean aprons ... they don't show you the slag heaps and what the buildings would really have looked like covered in grime from the coal ... but people don't really want to know the reality and I don't blame them you've got to enjoy life ... it's a bit of entertainment that's all.

With regard to history and its place in contributing to a sense of identity, this was not dismissed, but did not appear to be any more influential than other factors such as cultural activities, leisure pursuits or work. There was little personal identification with the past and for those who could associate with the objects and surroundings through familiarity (the elderly in a number of cases particularly at Blist Hill), there was none of the uncompromising acceptance that times were better then.

The main reason I'm here is to see the old butcher's shop. I used to work there as a boy when it was on its original site [but] I remember those days well, cold water, early rising, thank God they're gone. (74 year old man on Blist Hill)

They were hard times for the working classes, it wasn't only the workers in Britain, Wales had its fair share of poverty and hardship. (65 year old Welsh woman reminiscing about the sweet shop and the pub)

I think it's great, it certainly takes me back, I remember a lot of the techniques used around here, even though I was a bit later than this ... mind you they could perhaps have a couple of workers' houses, they've got one extreme to the other with the doctor's surgery and the squatter's cottage [however] It's been entertaining and a bit of fun, one or two things on display brought back a few memories, but you don't go twice to a place like this, once is enough. (70 year old man on Blist Hill)

Overall the general feeling was that such places had an educational value, but in the final analysis a 70 year old man described the visit as:

It's just something to do, visits to these places have become part of general recreation, just like having a game of golf or a drink.

By contrasting the first group, the 'existential' visitors, with this third group, those labelled 'social', it is possible to note, at the extremes, a series of oppositions. These predominantly involve feelings of insecurity versus security, isolation versus integration, low self-esteem versus perceptions of self-worth, a lack of meaningful roles versus reward and satisfaction gained from roles, and pessimism versus optimism over the future. These appeared to impact on the need for retrospective escape and confirmation of self. In the case of this latter group the museum was used largely as a stage on which social identities could be reinforced and explored.

For the social visitor, the idea of the group experience was a consistent theme noted across both interviews and observations. This indicated that for this category the degree of 'engagement' with the past was of a social nature. One further observation was that frequently, for example at Blist Hill, on-site museum behaviour mirrored modern-day consumerism. This was manifest in an emphasis on shopping, the selection and purchase of 'old' products, the play with currency, and the evaluation of retail settings against such criteria as ambience, colour and display. For example:

> I could spend hours just browsing in these shops, especially the chemist, all the different bottles, I think that's what they've got right here ... the ambience ... They invite curiosity [and] it's been great changing the money, it adds to it, although you spend it thinking it's worth nothing. (28 year old woman)

These findings, however, are not an attempt to present the 'social' heritage consumer as either passive or disinterested in the educational value of such institutions. In most cases knowledge was enhanced not only by the tangible interpretations, whether static or interactive, but through discussions, questions and problem solving as noted in the following memo relating to the observation of behaviour of a couple in their middle thirties and a young boy.

> This small group interacted as a social unit, observing the demonstration, commenting among themselves, asking each other questions and discussing themes and methods. The demonstrator in this instance acted as a backdrop, a supplier of information. None of this group displayed any inclination to partici-pate in conversation ... They were concerned with detail and authenticity but gave no indication of identification with their surrounding ... Interaction was con-fined to their personal social group supporting McManus's (1989) theory that visitors react and interact to interpretation as part of a social unit, analysing, questioning and drawing conclusions from the available information and appli-cation of knowledge in a shared situation.

In summary, the behaviour of this group can largely be explained in terms of social expectations. These are largely dictated by the establishment and enhancement of existing group identity and acceptance, as averse to the often transitory nature of group associations common to the 'existential'. The emphasis in many cases was on relationship building and maintenance through interactive forms of communication that allowed for the sharing of information. This supports both Blud's (1990) assertions that heritage and museum visiting is largely a social activity, and McManus's (1989) findings that learning in museums tends to stem from developing questions from group communication as opposed to individual explorations.

## Comments on the Categories

It is important to note that although these three categories have been iden-tified as the basis for differentiation, they are neither mutually inclusive nor mutually exclusive. They are not meant to be constant labels applied to individuals, but should be considered in the context of pertinent life circumstances. Furthermore, they relate to only one aspect of the self, and are bound by the context of the analysis, the historical resource. Within the categories, there are also degrees of motivational and experiential intensity. For example, within the 'existential' category, the extreme end of the spectrum would include individuals experiencing very strong feelings of existential isolation, alienation, boredom, dependency on others, low engagement in a range of fulfilling activities, and powerlessness. In such cases the need to retreat into the past is at its strongest. Others belonging to this category may experience a number of these emotions, but these may be less permanent and enduring and as such the past may be perceived as a temporary refuge.

At the extreme end of the category labelled 'aesthetic' is the need for solitude, individual contemplation and inner directed experiences which are focused on the self. On the other hand, those at the opposite end of the 'aesthetic' category demonstrate conservationist tendencies, seek authentic experiences and have a strong appreciation of, and even nostalgia for, the past, but are willing to engage more fully with others in their actions.

Conversely, those at the furthest end of the 'social' spectrum will emphasise complete social integration and will interact only as a unit to the exclusion of their own personal interests, while the more moderate 'social' visitors will experiment for themselves, talk to others outside of their immediate group and pass on experiences.

One further way of conceptualising these findings is to locate them within Csikszentmihalyi's (1992) analysis of engagement. He distinguishes between 'autotelic' experiences, whereby the action itself is its own reward with the focus primarily upon individual growth, and 'exotelic' experiences, whereby actions are performed for external reasons only. Such actions can also be related to constructions and perceptions of the self which can be either 'differentiated' or 'integrated'.

A self that is only 'differentiated' (not integrated) may attain great individual accomplishments, but risks being mirrored in self centred egotism ... A person whose self is based exclusively on integration will be connected and secure, but lack autonomous individuality. (Csikszentmihalyi, 1992: 42)

Whilst he stresses that most experiences are middle ground, there are similarities between the two extremes he describes and those at the far end of both the 'aesthetic' and 'social' categories. Those labelled 'existential', however, are probably the most likely to experience disruption in flow (happiness) and full engagement through such barriers as described in this research which correspond to his analysis and include attention disorders, lack of clear rules, alienation and boredom.

## The Heritage Environment and Implications
## for Operations Management

So far this chapter has been concerned with highlighting the main differences among individuals and groups in relation to the experience. The data, the analysis and the incorporation of theories derived from the literature have identified three fairly distinct forms of visitor type depending on variations across these themes. Nevertheless, there remain a number of environmental factors which largely transcend motivations and consumer types, but have, nonetheless, the power to enhance or destroy the nature of the experience. The following analysis is largely derived from the observational data described in Chapter 5.

Regardless of the make-up of the individuals, their motivations and hoped-for experiences, it is crucial to acknowledge that all behaviour takes place within a particular setting. According to Shields (1992), contemporary sites are characterised by their new spatial forms. These extend beyond the museum or heritage site into every realm of contemporary life. The separation of home, shopping, work and leisure into carefully designed and distinct 'zones' contributes further to the fragmentation of postmodern living. Zukin (1991) proposes that all identifiable activities are controlled and legitimated into liminal zones. As such the leisure zone, or in this case the heritage zone, provides a refuge that should satisfy the quest for alternative social arrangements.

However, the psychological well-being of the individual and ultimate desired experience will depend on a number of controlled or uncontrolled factors encountered at the heritage site. According to Rapaport (1982), environments communicate meanings that trigger appropriate behaviours. These behaviours and experiences, in this instance, were analysed against the following three factors:

1   Scene setting
2   Routing and mapping
3   Crowding and density levels

### Scene Setters

The argument proposed by Pearce and Stringer (1991) is that the visitor needs to feel well oriented to enjoy the visit. In the case of the heritage site or museum, this starts at the entrance in the form of a scene setter which serves the purpose of locating the individual in terms of either time (particularly relevant to the reconstructed, living forms of interpretation) or space (applicable to all forms of interpretation). This is where the experience begins, and lack of information at this stage results in disorientation and confusion.

None of the heritage sites/museums that were the object of analysis could be described as having adequate 'scene setters', and this did tend to impact upon the visit. For example, at Blist Hill there was confusion as to the exact period the reconstruction was supposed to be located in. Differences in period estimates on the part of the visitor varied by as much as a hundred years. This indicated a degree of confusion which in turn had implications for the educational quality. Buildwas Abbey provided no information at all, but attracted visitors who appeared to have prior knowledge of the histories of such places and therefore were not disappointed or confused by this absence. At Birmingham Museum and Art Gallery there was a confusing array of information which did little to orientate or direct the visitor, which resulted in blind exploration and anxiety over the unexpected or the possibility of missing an interesting exhibit. The following factors therefore emerge as important:

- That a clear, cohesive and periodising 'scene setter' enhances understanding, orientation and satisfaction.
- Lack of such will be perceived as negative unless the individual is already familiar with the environment or knowledgeable about the subject.
- 'Scene setters' need to be complemented with a coherent and precise map of the site/museum.

### Routing and Mapping

Spatial knowledge acquisition involves internalising a large number of spatial relationships some of which will be more precise than others. Learning an area requires the analysis of a series of perceptual and sensory impressions which have to be organised so as to identify common features which then have to be synthesised into a coherent component. However, one's cognitive system has certain limitations, such as memory capacity and information processing speed, which the structure of the physical environment can either help or hinder (Ryozo, 1991).

These concepts are a progression of the need for a scene setter as a means of orientation, but have greater implications for the need to include both some form of map and clear signs or pointers for the visitor to follow. Again the lack of clarity in the maps provided at both Blist Hill and the Birmingham Museum proved to be a source of frustration.

If the individual is to concentrate on processing information regarding artefact, display or demonstration, he/she does not have the additional capacity to carry around a developed cognitive map of the environment, especially if it is spread over a large geographical area, or on a series of levels. The extra effort required to find displays that are not immediately apparent further adds to the frustration which in turn impinges on the emotional well-being of the individual. Therefore the following conclusions can be derived:

- More is required than a complicated map situated at the entrance. Clear and concise images of the site should be included which refer the visitor to key features and exhibits. Alternatively leaflets incorporating maps should be available to avoid the individual having to carry around the information mentally.
- Maps should be reinforced with signs and pointers which direct attention and enhance memory and information retention, the result of which would free the individual to concentrate on the nature of the display.
- Maps and signing can act as a form of spatial control providing a clearly directed route which may help to overcome congestion at certain popular features.

### Crowding and Density Levels

The third aspect of the environment that impacts upon the experience is that of crowding and density levels at certain sites and areas within the museum. The fundamental axiom underlying many social psychologists' conception of crowding is that crowding perceptions represent a negative psychological evaluation of physical density (Schmidt and Keating, 1979). According to James and Burdges (1984), such perceived crowding correlates with the visitor's exposure to threatening behaviour resulting in physical movement constraint. This is in keeping with a major conceptual tradition known as 'social interference' theory which attributes this negative evaluation to incompatibilities between a given level of physical density and the valued psychological goals or expectations a person holds for an experience (Stokols, 1976).

There was evidence of varying reactions to crowding levels, especially at Blist Hill which was particularly busy during the time the research was being conducted. This revealed reactions similar to those proposed by Stokols (1976) with regard to the following:

- Crowding increased awareness of other people.
- Spatial needs varied between individuals.
- Crowding modified the behaviour of certain 'types'.

However, these factors did not apply universally, but varied in intensity depending on the level of involvement on the part of the visitor.

### Crowding Types and Determinants of Outdoor Recreation

1 Goal related – The degree of density compatibility of valued psychological goals motivating a behaviour.

Here the level of involvement and personal identification with the resource influenced the tolerance level of the individual in relation to crowding density. Most groups found crowding a negative factor which impinged on behaviour and impacted upon the experience. For example, there was a reluctance to ask questions, physical discomfort and irritability. However, those that were deeply involved had the ability to filter out the presence of others to such a degree that the level of immersion in the experience increased tolerance (as with weather conditions) to the extent that they were simply not noticed.

2   Behavioural crowding – The amount of exposure to threatening or objectionable behaviour (noise, rowdiness, litter).

In this case it was primarily the older groups who exhibited objectionable behaviour, particularly in the form of noise, and in doing so restricted the behaviour of others. This was particularly marked in popular exhibits such as the printer's where the level of information imparted depended on the demonstrator's instructions and stories. However, objects and artefacts were on display for all to see, which resulted in certain groups, who could identify with them, relating stories among themselves at the same time as the demonstration was taking place. In such cases it was the level of noise, coupled with high-density crowding, that produced frustration and eventual anger in others.

3   Physical crowding – The amount of space required to pursue an activity in an unconstrained manner.

Again it was Blist Hill that proved to be the most densely populated in terms of visitor numbers at key spots (candle maker's, printer's, chemist's). Birmingham Museum and Buildwas Abbey were not particularly congested, but this was due to two factors:

(a)   In the case of Buildwas Abbey, the attraction appeals to a small minority of visitors and therefore crowding is very seldom an issue. However, the type of visitor to such attractions would tend to resent the presence of crowds possibly more so than visitors to attractions such as Blist Hill, who, it is reasonable to presume, have an expectation of sizeable numbers. Expectations are therefore important in relation to tolerance levels. The element of surprise is more likely to impinge on the experience in a negative manner if motivation and expectations are those of solitude.

(b)   Layout and design can encourage length of stay and density. At Birmingham Museum, the exhibition halls were spacious and airy and could accommodate greater numbers without creating anxiety. Those exhibitions that were not too heavily attended also incorporated seating areas, which again encouraged the individual to pause and contemplate what was on offer. As such the combination of expectations, layout and design can serve either to enhance or detract from the visit.

Having looked at Stokol's types and determinants of crowding experience, there is another aspect of crowding that must be considered in relation to this analysis, and that is the effect that crowds have upon communication. Crowding experience is mediated by stress, and arousal attributed to violation of distance norms, which according to Rustemli (1992) is the necessary condition of crowding and ultimate behaviour restriction. Evans and Lepore (1992) suggest that high density is problematic because it restricts access to valued resources – in this case, the heritage resource. The anthropological characterisation of interpersonal distances has come broadly to describe the active use people make of the spatial context in which the interaction occurs; that this context can be actively manipulated implies that such manipulation is in itself an effective determinant of behaviour (Hall, 1966).

Hall emphasises the communicatory aspects of personal spacing, arguing that spatial context is a communication medium and as such regulates the amount, intensity, type and quality of communications. Communication involves multiple sensory systems which are differently affected by distance. He distinguishes four interactional zones:

1 Intimate
2 Personal
3 Social
4 Public

These four are dictated by distance and desire. In the case of crowding at Blist Hill, there was evidence of a mismatch between the social and publicly accepted distances, through close physical contact, which resulted in distance, usually reserved for the personal or even intimate situation, occurring in the public. The effect of this was distraction, irritation and loss of concentration and communication. Many with lower tolerance thresholds left the more congested exhibits missing out on demonstrations that they had planned to visit. However, it must also be noted that a number of factors such as gender, personality and culture affect personal spacing, and in this context age was noticed as a determinant of crowding tolerance, and must be evaluated in this light.

With regard to culture, an important determinant, the research concentrated on the British population only. Therefore, any analysis of environmental effects on the consumer must be set against a framework that acknowledges that meanings are not just constructed, they are given by the culture and social structure within which the person operates. The extent to which the environment works as a source of cues for appropriate behaviour is culturally specific and hence not necessarily cross-culturally transferable (Saegert and Winkel, 1990).

By way of a summary to this section on environmental conditions and their impact on the experience, it must be noted that although the interpretation, artefacts, authenticity and entertainment may provide the expectations of the experience and will be perceived as either positive or negative, the amount of information provided at the start of the visit, directions and clear mapping and crowding density will also either contribute towards an enjoyable, informative experience or conversely result in feelings of disorientation, frustration and psychological anxiety.

## Implications of the Research

There is growing recognition among marketing and management scholars working in the area of cultural consumption that there is a greater need for visitor orientation (Prentice, 1996) and experiential segmentation. Essentially what museums offer is a service, and the effectiveness of communicating historical information, the core product, relies on the ability to construct images, convey information and engage the visitor. Consequently, what we term the delivery of a service, in this case, might just as easily be described as selling an experience. In the present climate the need to understand the nature of the experience has never been greater. Since the late 1980s there has been increasing competition and pressure on museums to widen their appeal in order to attract larger and more diverse audiences. The findings of this research contribute towards a broader understanding of museum publics, particularly in relation to issues of heritage interpretation, product development and the service encounter. It is not enough to assume that visitors want to be entertained or engage in nostalgia. Some do, but a significant number want more from the visit than that: they want thought-provoking stimulus which results in mindful experiences. This in turn has implications for the segmentation and targeting of markets.

The findings also highlight some weaknesses in the literature on 'popular' heritage management, particularly Hewison's (1987) theory. While he presents a seductive argument, in the final analysis it is primarily one that perceives heritage visitors as manipulated, passive and incapable of creating meaning. This was not in evidence from the data. Most consumers seemed capable of enjoying a range of 'historical' experiences. Furthermore, they constructed meaning, and interacted with the resource according to their own expectations, not necessarily that of the museum professional or academic critic. Additionally, themed, or living, heritage was not perceived as the ultimate heritage experience. There were a number of informants who came away frustrated with the 'intrusive' nature of such reconstruction, preferring interpretation that allowed for solitude and imagination. Therefore it is a question of striking a balance and knowing where and when to stop with regard to interpretation. The danger for museum managers, it would seem, lies in pursuing interpretation policies which deny the use of the imagination for the sake of theming (Goulding, 1999a).

## Final Points Relating to the Data

Before the findings are left behind, there are a number of important issues that need to be addressed in relation to their interpretation and credibility, particularly those associated with validity and transferability. According to Riley (1996: 36–7), legitimate methods of ensuring consistency and reliability involve the use of 'others' in the analysis process.

### Ensuring Credibility

When establishing the credibility of analysis, the tradition of investigator-as-expert is reversed. This process is called 'member checking' and is an invited assessment of the investigator's meaning. Informants can be invited to assess whether the early analyses are an accurate reflection of their conversations.

This is done before the interpretation is abstracted onto a conceptual level and therefore becomes less meaningful to the individual. And on the issue of transferability:

Transferability is not considered the responsibility of the investigator because the knowledge elicited is most influenced by each individual's life context and situation. Indeed the varied social constructions of knowledge are what the investigator is searching for. In its stead the investigator is to accurately describe the contexts and techniques of the study so that subsequent follow-up studies can match them as closely as possible.

Unfortunately, involvement with those who participated in the process was of a very transient nature. However, in order to avoid accusations of reading more into the data then was actually realistic, and to confirm ideas, transcripts were given to other academics during methodology workshops on qualitative research. These academics were given a brief description of what the research was about and asked to code, line by line, raw data. After they had completed this process they were asked to discuss the key factors they felt were occurring in the data and were encouraged to look for the most salient concepts. Finally they were asked to group these concepts into clusters that indicated a relationship between them.

Discussions were then held to establish where, how and why particular concepts had been identified as having significant explanatory power. The academics were then shown the extended analysis of the data, from line-by-line coding and open coding, concept development and memos, and finally they were told why these were integrated into certain categories. Feedback was then sought as to their relevance, plausibility and fit.

### Whose Theory is it Anyway?

A second point that needs clarification rests on the issue of 'ownership', and fits easily under the heading 'whose theory is it anyway?' This requires an evaluation of how and why we make use of informants and how this in turn relates to the key philosophical underpinnings of the methodology employed. For example, had a phenomenological position been adopted, then the emphasis would have been on the voices and actions of those under study, to the exclusion of personal experiences and, to some extent, interpretation. However, when using the grounded theory method, the researcher has an obligation to 'abstract' the data and to think 'theoretically' rather than descriptively.

Therefore, whilst the informants provide the basis for the theory (the data) it is ultimately the researcher's interpretation of the informants' construction of both motivation and experience. Moreover, it is important to stress that these findings are an interpretation; they offer a perspective from which the researcher, actively involved in the experience, cannot be divorced. Others with different academic backgrounds may study the problem from a different vantage point, seek to observe and select different aspects of the phenomena and reach different conclusions. However, that does not mean to say that because we may conflict, one has to be wrong; it merely expands the theory and increases understanding from a broader disciplinary base, and as such is congruent with grounded theory's methodological principles.

### Labelling People or Labelling Behaviour?

Finally, to conclude this chapter, consideration needs to be given to the labelling of identified 'types'. Glaser (1978, 1992) suggests that categories should indicate 'behavioural type', not 'people type'. This allows the people to walk in and out of many behavioural patterns. The emphasis is therefore on behavioural, not personal, patterns. So for example, the 'existential' may be nostalgic when faced with themed stimuli but it does not necessarily follow that they will remain so once removed from the situation. It is important to recognise that most actors engage in a type of behaviour without being 'typed' by it; they engage in other behaviours as well.

### Summary

The aim of this chapter was to describe in some detail the process of abstraction in relation to the key concepts that emerged from the data. This was done in order to demonstrate the similarities and differences which formed the basis of the three identified core categories. Whilst Chapter 5 was concerned with process and early concept identification, this chapter attempted to demonstrate the relationship of the findings to extant theory through their integration with the literature. Nevertheless, what has been presented here is the end product of a long and complicated process which involved extensive coding, recoding, prioritisation and reduction. The next chapter looks in some detail at the frustrations, problems and misconceptions with using grounded theory in order to provide a clearer picture of what the researcher might reasonably expect when choosing the methodology and putting it into practice.

# Part Three

## SOME CONCLUDING REMARKS

# 7

## A Critical Review of the Methodology

### Introduction

Whilst Chapters 5 and 6 set out the details of theory building within a specific context, this chapter briefly discusses some of the decisions and problems associated with the process of data collection, analysis and interpretation. Grounded theory now has an established place in management research (Schroeder and Congden, 1995; Browning et al., 1995; Crook and Kumar, 1998; Kimle and Damhorst, 1993; Hunt and Ropo, 1995; Parry, 1998; Sperber-Richie et al., 1997; A. Brown, 1994, 1995; Manning et al., 1998; King, 1996; Seeley and Targett, 1997; Lang, 1996), and more recently in marketing (Hirschman and Thompson, 1997; Burchill and Fine, 1997; de la Cuesta, 1994; Houston and Venkatesh, 1996; Goulding, 1998, 1999b, 1999c). Nonetheless, it has not escaped criticism. It is suggested that this is largely due to a number of misconceptions regarding the methodology, the split between the two originators which in effect has resulted in two distinct versions, and possibly, most important, the misuse and abuse of its principles and procedures. According to Charmaz (1983), both the assumptions and analytical methods of grounded theory have been criticised by some qualitative researchers on a number of accounts. For example, the suggestion that grounded theorists fail to give proper attention to both data collection techniques and the quality of the gathered material. Such criticisms, she maintains, misinterpret the aims and methods of grounded theory. However, she does acknowledge that many misconceptions arise as a result of certain features of grounded theory such as the language of the method. To a large extent grounded theory relies heavily on terms commonly associated with quantitative research inherent in the use of such terms as open coding, axial coding and verification procedures which elicit images of logico-deductive quantitative procedures. Such attempts to structure, order and interpret data are commonly seen to defile the canons of pure qualitative research where the primacy of the subjective experience of the participant takes precedence over the interpretation of the researcher (Goulding, 1998). However, Coyle (1997), in defence, argues that grounded theory was so revolutionary for its time that a language that was accessible to quantitative methodologists, followers of the dominant paradigm, was needed if the methodology was to be accepted.

However, it is not only the language associated with grounded theory that has created controversy. The following addresses some crucial issues which should be seriously considered when thinking about using grounded theory. They are points which are often overlooked in the texts on the subject, but failure to anticipate them has in some cases resulted in frustration, failure to complete the research, and on occasion, when used for research degrees, failure of the thesis. This chapter attempts to spell out and pull together some of the main dangers or potential problems most commonly associated with grounded theory. It begins by stating that grounded theory is risky. Essentially this lies in the fact that the researchers may expect too much, or a magical formula for developing theory just because they follow the rules and principles of the method. This is followed by a discussion of the divergence in thought of the two original authors, and a requirement that any researchers considering using the method should base their choice on an understanding of the key issues which define and divide the two quite distinct approaches. Some of the main criticisms of the empirical literature published as grounded theory studies in the field of management are next outlined by drawing a distinction between what is termed 'full' and 'partial' grounded theory. Problems with contemporary interpretation are further explored by considering the implications of rewriting the method and the importation of 'non'-grounded theory rules for judging the credibility of grounded theory research. The discussion then focuses on two specific issues which have been the subject of some controversy and misunderstanding: namely, the overemphasis on induction, which is one of the main reasons many reject using the method, and the problem of premature closure. The chapter draws to a close by considering the possibility of writing the theory as a reflection of process and individual working styles.

## Grounded Theory is Risky!

One of the appeals of grounded theory lies in the way that the method is presented in the texts on the subject, particularly Strauss and Corbin's (1990) version. In this book they set out a highly formulistic set of procedures which if followed accordingly would, one presumes, automatically lead to the development of a theory. However, this is not always the case. According to Rennie (1998), grounded theory is attractive to those people who prefer to immerse themselves in data before jumping into theory, and to those who enjoy working with natural language rather than numbers. Nonetheless, the grounded theorist has to acknowledge the risk factors associated with such an approach. These risks are of lesser concern for researchers who define their boundaries to begin with, explore the literature fully, identify key research questions, and collect data to answer them. For example, the nature of theoretical sampling means that sampling is controlled by the data, it is not defined prior to the field research. Consequently the researcher must remain flexible and open, and be prepared to sample across several groups and possible locations before the data start to make sense and the research finds direction. It is not uncommon for researchers to give up at this point, or force interpretations from inadequate data. Even for those who do use the method correctly, it is wrong to assume that a theory will automatically emerge. There may not be a theory to be found, or the researcher may not apply theoretical sensitivity, presenting instead an account based on thick description. Wai-Chung Yeung (1997) discusses the fact that theoretical categories must be grounded in empirical evidence so that abstraction does not occur in a vacuum – they must be abstracted from concrete phenomena. However, he suggests that there are a number of operational problems. For example, researchers may get lost in the field because they lack theoretical sensitivity. The end effect of this may be an eclectic empiricism in which too many categories are combined in an a-theoretical framework whereby causal relations and tendencies between the categories and concepts are lost. In some cases this may be a result of rushing the research, or expecting too much too soon.

These are some of the problems associated with applying grounded theory that students need to be aware of. There are, however, other implications that may have consequences for academics designing proposals for research funding. Given the nature of grounded theory with its emphases on theoretical sampling, emergent theory and staying in the field until saturation is reached, the issues of planning, targeting of journals and timing become problematic. Linked to this is the problem of estimating the cost of the research which in turn has implications for the budget, whether that of a research council or a manager. For many reviewers, the fact that samples, in terms of size, characteristics and location, cannot be strictly defined in the proposal prior to the research, may well result in a lack of confidence that the research will ever get done.

## Time, Space, Insights and the 'Drugless Trip'

Whilst the practicalities and realities of designing grounded theory research need to be considered carefully, other aspects that need to be evaluated include those of time, gaining insights, and what Glaser (1978) calls the 'drugless trip'. The hours and places chosen to conduct the analysis have a further bearing on the preferred method of analysis. It is important to be aware that meaning is not always instantly obvious. Speaking from experience, it is very common to look at the data for days, weeks and even months, and still fail to realise what is occurring within it. The only thing to do at such times is to leave the data alone, let ideas germinate, and wait. Quite often this may mean revisiting the data, sometimes in the middle of the night when a sudden insight occurs. Qualitative data are sometimes very hard to shut out. Expect bouts of insomnia when a particular set of relationships suddenly start to take shape out of the blue. Usually, the only way to capture these and get some sleep is to keep a notepad by the side of the bed in which to write theoretical memos or sketch emerging thoughts. Glaser (1978) talks about the transition that occurs at the various stages of the research. This basically consists of ideas and input, through to periods of depression and an inability to see any conceptual relevance, through to the emergence of ideas and concepts as a result of memoing ideas, getting them down on paper and tracking thoughts. Only when this is accomplished can the researcher feel free to move on to other ideas and memos. Consequently, it is fair to say that the process of simultaneous data collection and interpretation is easier said than done. Transcription is certainly possible, but moving beyond open coding to seeing meaningful patterns in the data can take months. Glaser (1978) refers to this as the 'drugless trip', a period when researchers experience a sense of disorientation, panic and a desire to give up. The 'drugless trip' is not some abstract concept, it is a reality. No matter how hard one might look at the data, nothing of meaning emerges. However, after a period of intense reflection and abstinence, insights will start to occur. This is usually the start of the interpretive process. Furthermore, the idea of 'several journeys' is a constant feature throughout the process. It is par for the course to transcribe interviews and observations and then read and reread them and listen to tapes over and over again in order to grasp fully what is occurring. This becomes very much a part of the routine, as does extended memo writing, the elimination of early codes and the drawing of diagrams to keep identified relationships firmly in mind. Glaser (1978) discusses these journeys as a process composed of a set of double back steps. These steps include the collection of data, open coding, theoretical sampling and the generation of many memos until saturation is established and the core category identified. However, each stage of the research is not necessarily linear. It is common to have to return to any of the coding stages to check the existence of developed concepts. Memos will need to be sorted into theoretical frameworks, and possibly re-sorted at the editing stage of the writing process. Nonetheless, by re-sorting and reworking the final version through creative conceptual integration, the theoretical perspective should be sharpened.

### Which Method do you Choose?

It was mentioned in Chapter 2 that grounded theory has undergone a number of changes over the past few years which have resulted in the development of two rather distinct versions, one associated with Glaser (1978, 1992), which stresses the emergence of theory from the data, the other with Strauss and Corbin (1990). While Strauss and Corbin introduced a new coding process with a strong emphasis on conditions, context, action/interaction strategies and consequences, Glaser's response was to deny that this constituted true grounded theory. This was largely due to its stress on preconceived and forced discovery centring primarily on preordained categories at the expense of allowing the theory to emerge (Skodal-Wilson and Ambler-Hutchinson, 1996). In the management literature, the most common approach adopted is the Strauss and Corbin version, although this perspective has attracted the most criticism for overemphasising the mechanics of the research at the expense of theoretical sensitivity (Glaser, 1992). Coyle (1997) provides the example of sampling. Rather than just discussing the nature of theoretical sampling Strauss and Corbin further fragment the process into open sampling (sampling persons, places and situations to provide the most relevant data about the phenomenon), relational and variational sampling (purposely choosing persons and sites to elicit data regarding variations along dimensions of categories) and indiscriminate sampling (stories, persons and documents which maximise the opportunity for verifying the storyline and relationship between categories). Coyle (1997) proposes that this can only confuse the issue. Glaser's response was that Strauss and Corbin have diluted the principles of theoretical sampling and offered no methodological help. He suggests that there are 'so many rules, strictures, dictums and models to follow one can only get lost in trying to figure it out' (Glaser, 1992: 104). For example, Glaser takes great umbrage with Strauss and Corbin's coding paradigm and the conditional matrix arguing that the conditional matrix is only one of many possible theoretical schema. The danger, apparently, with the conditional matrix lies in the fact that it may rely on conditions not evident in the data, which lead to forcing rather than emergence:

> If you torture the data enough it will give up! This is the underlying approach in the forcing preconceptions of full conceptual description. The data is not allowed to speak for itself, as in grounded theory, and to be heard from infrequently it has to scream. Forcing by preconception constantly derails it from relevance. (Glaser, 1992: 123)

Other scholars have echoed the criticisms of excessive emphasis on the coding process. For example, Melia (1996) talks about Strauss and Corbin's work as problematic and over-formulistic. She argues that their model is verification in nature and oriented to description but not discovery. Furthermore, she maintains that use of Strauss and Corbin's approach leads to overconcepualisation of single incidents and lacks attention to category saturation and theoretical sensitivity. Ultimately, she suggests that it is not helpful to have such a plethora of categories, subcategories, as well as properties and dimensions, and the appearance of so many rules. This results in preconceptions blocking the way and the technical tail wagging the dog. The saving grace is the simplicity of the constant comparison method (Melia, 1996). According to Glaser (1992: 43):

> Strauss's method of labelling and then grouping is totally unnecessary, laborious and is a waste of time. Using constant comparison method gets the analyst to the desired conceptual power, quickly, with ease and joy. Categories emerge upon comparison and properties emerge upon more comparison. And that is all there is to it.

Rennie (1998: 105) goes on to suggest that:

> Strauss and Corbin's modification is fourfold: the investigator's experiences pertaining to the phenomenon under study are accepted as legitimate empirical data; hypothesis testing is made integral to constant comparison; consideration of the conditions influencing the phenomenon should not be limited to those indicated by the data themselves; and the application of an axiomatic scheme that converts all social phenomenon into process is made mandatory.

However, it is worth noting that for many, the model proposed by Glaser appears daunting in that it involves the researcher immersing him/herself in data, and trusting that a theory will eventually emerge. For some, the strict principles and procedures offered by Strauss and Corbin provide a form of guidance and security. Ellis (1993: 477), in defence of the charges made against Strauss and Corbin, argues that:

> Strauss has tried to provide some guidance for researchers attempting to generate theory in the form of a coding paradigm in which data are analysed in terms of conditions, interactions among the actors, strategies and tactics, and consequences ... However, there are disadvantages as well as advantages with its employment. While it does provide the researcher with a high level model of organising structure for data analysis, it might be thought to be inhibiting to the open approach to theory generation that is at the heart of the original grounded theory approach. For those who feel uneasy developing grounded theory without any such guidelines, the use of the coding paradigm does provide some kind of broad structure for data analysis. But, for others, use of the coding paradigm may be restrictive and may stultify the process of full inductive theory generation.

It is worth reading the original text on grounded theory in some depth, followed by the subsequent publications by the two authors, before making a decision about which method to adopt. To attempt to use both only results in confusion as there are differences in terminology and procedures, and any attempts at a pick-and-mix approach tend not to be received with favour by reviewers and examiners.

### Full or Partial Grounded Theory?

Nonetheless, it is not only the overemphasis on the coding procedures that has attracted criticism. Parry (1998) discusses differences in the application of the method, identifying two basic types. The first he terms 'full grounded theory', as described by Glaser and Strauss (1967). This form of research incorporates the whole iterative process which is played out in full. The second, and most commonly used, he calls 'partial grounded theory'. Here data are collected and then theorised upon, but the approach contains many problems. To begin with the analytical process by which concepts are built up to categories is seldom described. Secondly, the relationship between concepts is not undertaken or explained sufficiently when the research is written up. Thirdly, historical events are often ignored. These events which occur before or during data collection can affect the validity of that data collection if not accounted for in some way. According to Robrecht (1995) there are often gaps in publications regarding research procedure which make it difficult to identify the development and strength of the investigator's core category. This is largely attributed to the development of an over-complex set of operations and procedures and the fact that students of the method learn how to analyse the data by adhering to a set of methodologi-cal principles that rely increasingly upon rigid and restrictive operations. However, possibly the accusation that researchers use grounded theory as a pick-and-mix approach has done most harm to its reputation. May (1996) raises questions regarding the state of grounded theory research in contemporary practice. These include: is the method changing, and if so how can these changes be evaluated? Moreover, can evolutionary changes be reliably distinguished from investigator-specific variations? What is the current state of development of grounded theory method? How can we know? How is the method distinct from accepted emergent qualitative methods? What difference does it make? What is methodological legitimacy in regard to the method? Who decides? And are any of these questions even worthwhile? However, they are worth reflecting on before a particular position is adopted. Chapter 1 attempted to highlight some of the common principles that cut across most qualitative methods of data collection and analysis. Nonetheless, it also aimed to identify variations in terms of philosophy, sources of data and techniques for interpreting the data. Chapters 2 and 3 sought to illustrate the subtle differences with regard to the levels of abstraction and theory development between such methods and grounded theory, particularly with regard to sampling, emergence and conceptual categorisation. Indeed by ignoring these differences, the researcher runs the risk of being accused of methodological transgression.

## Methodological Transgression

Locke (1996) points out that while the 1967 publication of *Discovery of Grounded Theory* remains a touchstone for scholars adopting the approach, the method has been rewritten and has evolved. Accordingly:

> The recent publications by each of the authors constitute rewriting of the grounded theory approach. Moreover, when organisational studies researchers make use of the approach and methods as originally specified by Glaser and Strauss, writing them into their research publications, they are also rewriting the discovery of grounded theory. (Locke, 1996)

Locke reviewed the reference made to Glaser and Strauss (1967) in papers published in the *Academy of Management Journal*. Out of nineteen qualitative studies, sixteen cited the original. All sixteen appeared at least two years after Glaser's (1978) publication *Theoretical Sensitivity*, and eleven were published after Strauss and Corbins's basics of qualitative research (1990). However, only one article cited any of these subsequent works. Observations on how the methodology was cited revealed that nine out of sixteen used it to underscore an iterative analytical process during which researchers tested their emerging theoretical frameworks against their data. Seven used the notion of theoretical saturation and three out of the sixteen used *Discovery* to distinguish the study as inductive and theory building. In many articles, theoretical sampling was not discussed, which in effect means that one of the central tenets of the methodology is being written out of the process. Furthermore, authors talked about studies based on, for example, random selection, which is a frank violation of the method and smacks of an 'anything goes' approach to the research. According to Locke (1996: 244):

> Readers need to be able to evaluate the research based on a full report of the procedures. Broad unspecified claims – for example, the statement that "*this research followed Glaser and Strauss (1967)*" with no operational indicators, or indeed with procedures that run counter to the method's specification – cannot stand.

Grounded theory, it would appear, is being selectively rewritten in and drawn from qualitative managerial research and this has little to do with the fact that Glaser and Strauss were following, and advocating, two distinct versions of the methodology. Skodal-Wilson and Ambler-Hutchinson (1996) refer to the number of academics with no first-hand contact of either Glaser or Strauss who have independently invented rigid rules for judging the credibility of grounded theory research. What they refer to as 'cooked up' translations are often guilty of breaching the essence of the method and the inherent creativity of the original. Such later additions include the requirement of a visual diagram with all grounded theories, and a statement that a sample size of twelve be the minimum for any grounded theory study, although it is unclear how this rather arbitrary figure was reached. This in itself appears to go against the whole philosophy of theoretical sampling as it dictates and directs the research design right from the start. This inflexibility has given rise to accusations of distortion of method as demonstrated in the following:

> The importation of rigid rules is counterproductive to the spirit of creativity and the generation of grounded theory. Although certain flexible methodological guidelines, such as simultaneous data collection and analysis and purposive and theoretical sampling principles are undisputed, credible grounded theory ultimately stands on its own as diverse, parsimonious, conceptual and relevant to the data. (Skodal-Wilson and Ambler-Hutchinson, 1996: 123)

They further point to methodological transgressions when using grounded theory. Such transgressions refer to 'the frank violation of the grounded theory philosophy and methodology' (1996: 224), or methodological muddling (Baker et al., 1992; Wells, 1995). Most commonly, this is when the researcher claims to have used grounded theory, but has, for example, conducted the research using a phenomenological framework. It also pertains to cases where the canons of quantitative method are modified and applied to interview or textual data, and where the outcome is a study described in positivist terms such as random sampling, reliability, validity statistics, and independent and dependent variables. For example, Mullins and Roessier (1998) conducted a study of improving employment outcomes. They adopted a planned action model already heavily quoted in the literature to structure the enquiry. Instrumentation included a self-completion mail survey and a structured intention interview. The mail survey consisted of thirty-one empirically derived items and used a rating scale for measurement. Furthermore, theoretical sampling and constant comparison were ignored. The data collection and analysis were expressed in quantitative terms and presented as descriptive statistics, means and standard deviation, and given priority rankings. The findings were then analysed against the model that formed the basis of the enquiry and no theoretical emergence was discussed in relation to the data. This study may well have been rigorously undertaken, and its findings useful and valid. However, given the nature of the research design, it is hard to call it, as claimed, a grounded theory investigation.

While there is nothing that prohibits the combination of quantitative and qualitative forms of data collection when using grounded theory, their purpose should be made clear, as should their methods of analysis. Grounded theorists do not follow the traditional quantitative canons of verification. They do, however, check the development of ideas with further specific observations. They make systematic comparisons and often take the research beyond the initial confines of one topic or setting. It is proposed that it is because they make systematic efforts to check and refine categories that their efforts are sometimes confused with quantitative techniques. However, there are clear and crucial distinctions between quantitative methods and grounded theory which must be understood in order to utilise the method to its full capacity.

### Using the Literature and an Overemphasis on Induction

A further part of the process is the role of literature and the degree of interplay between data collection, memo writing, coding, interpretation and further literature searches as codes and categories evolve that direct the analysis to new literature sources. Grounded theory research does not normally proceed in the usual iterative manner of literature search, hypotheses development followed by field research. As a rule grounded theory evolves from a tentative literature base to begin with. The field data and the consequent development of codes and categories focus attention on the relevant disciplines and extant theory which offer the most sensible fit. In the case of the heritage experience discussed in Chapters 5 and 6, such disciplines proved to be sociology, psychology and cultural studies. This was a feature of the interpretive endeavour, right until the end. Nonetheless, whilst the findings largely directed attention towards specific literatures, there was a degree of familiarity with such behavioural theories before the research commenced.

The overemphasis on induction has been a source of much criticism. However, it is suggested that this is largely due to misunderstandings about Glaser and Strauss's definition of 'induction'. In the original *Discovery* text both authors emphasised avoiding the literature directly related to the field of study in order to avoid contamination. Nonetheless, the notion of induction and entering the field without first consulting the literature is probably responsible for many scholars' rejection of the methodology. Indeed feedback from seminars on the subject has revealed perceptions that Glaser and Strauss have 'conned' those they have influenced by preaching the notion of theoretical avoidance, whilst marching into the field themselves armed with a lifetime of concepts and experiences. However, this is not necessarily true. Grounded theory method stresses discovery and theory development rather than logico-deductive reasoning which relies on prior theoretical frameworks. Grounded theorists shape their data collection from their analytical discoveries and interpretations, and therefore sharpen their observations. Additionally they check and fill out emerging ideas by collecting further data. Such strategies serve to strengthen both the quality of the data and the ideas extracted from them. Moreover, whilst Glaser and Strauss advocate taking a fresh approach to the research problem in order to ground the theory in data, they also acknowledge that it is impossible to erase all previous influences. For example, when discussing the development of formal theory directly, rather than building upon substantive theory they suggest that:

> it is possible to formulate formal theory directly. The core categories can emerge in the sociologist's mind from his reading, life experiences, research and scholarship; [furthermore] no sociologist can possibly erase from his mind all the theory he knows before he begins his research. Indeed the trick is to line up what one takes as theoretically possible or probable with what one is finding in the field. Such existing sources of insight are to be cultivated though not at the expense of insights generated by qualitative research, which are still closer to the data. (Glaser and Strauss, 1968: 253)

Importing concepts is a further area of concern with regard to the development of theory. This is attributed to the researcher adopting established frameworks or concepts for enquiry, and succumbing to the temptation to limit the analysis to conform to such preconceived theories rather than extend, challenge or change them to fit the situation. The importance of grounded theory is that it generates theoretical sensitivity, a quality which requires the combination of 'interpersonal perceptiveness with conceptual thinking' (Skodal-Wilson and Ambler-Hutchinson, 1996: 124). Charmaz (1983) further points to the fact that unlike deductive research, grounded theorists do not rely directly on the literature to shape their ideas, since it is expected that the theory will emerge independently from the analysis. This, however, should not be misinterpreted as commencing from a position of total ignorance, rather the researcher should read in related areas from the start and allow the data to direct the literature to inform the emerging theory and vice versa.

## Premature Closure – not Enough Data or not Enough Interrogation?

Another common problem associated with theoretical sampling is knowing when to withdraw from the field. Skodal-Wilson and Ambler-Hutchinson (1996) on the subject of saturation and bringing the research to a close argue that premature closure is often simply taken to mean leaving the field too early. They extend this to include the under-analysis of textual or narrative data. The method requires that the researcher move through a succession of stages starting with *in vivo* codes (codes derived directly from the data), to more abstract or second-level categorical codes and finally to the last stage of conceptual and theoretical codes which are the building blocks of theory. At each of these levels the theory becomes more refined, integrating abstract concepts that cover behavioural variation. Therefore, while premature closure is usually associated with leaving the field too early, it can also occur in situations where the researcher has collected a wealth of data but fails to move beyond describing what is in that data. As such the grounded theory is based solely on participants' descriptions, and not on developed concepts. It is important therefore that the researcher lifts ideas from the data and explains them theoretically in order to provide meaning and explanation of the behaviour.

Strauss (1987) summarises some of the main problems or stumbling blocks to analysis. These basically centre around learning to persist with line-by-line analysis, which can be very time consuming and tedious. From this, the researcher needs to be able to move from description to analysis by dimensionalising the data. However, the researcher also needs to be able to identify the most salient factors which may prove difficult if there is a mass of data. On the other hand, under-analysis of data may lead to category development which claims to explain a particular phenomenon but is not firmly grounded in evidence to support such claims. So something to beware of is making overly generic claims. Such claims refer to findings that are not situation-specific, but may be applied to any similar situation. For example, Skodal-Wilson and Ambler-Hutchinson (1996) mention a number of cases such as one which included the concepts of disintegrating identity, dealing with broken identity and reconstructing identity. These were derived from a study of heart attack patients, but, they argue, may be applicable to any chronic illness. This, however, should not be confused with the development of formal theory which is theory derived from many empirical studies in different situations which provide evidence for transcending concepts. In essence, the theory should deal with and explain the situation in hand. Finally, grounded theorists aim to develop fresh theoretical interpretations of the data rather than explicitly aim for any final or complete interpretation of it. This in itself is possibly the most crucial part of the process. It is also one which must ultimately be referred back to the method of analysis and interpretation.

## Some Concluding Remarks

With regard to the process of developing grounded theory, it may be argued that there are three basic stages that need to be addressed. The first one deals with the collection and interpretation of the data and is primarily concerned with demonstrating how, why and from where early concepts and categories were derived. In accordance with the principles common to the method, any theory should be traceable back to the data. Consequently, evidence needs to be provided as does the relationship between concepts, categories and this evidence. The second stage is to abstract the concepts and look for theoretical meaning. At this stage the concepts should be sufficiently developed as to warrant an extensive re-evaluation of compatible literature in order to demonstrate the 'fit', relationship and, where applicable, the extension of that literature through the research findings. The final stage should present the theory, uniting the concepts and integrating them into categories which have explanatory power within the specific context of the research. Throughout the course of the research it is common to collect an extensive amount of data in the form of interview transcripts, field notes on observations, memos, diagrams and conceptual maps. These may ultimately amount to hundreds of pages and as such involve making decisions regarding what to present and what to leave out. Unlike quantitative methods where, for example, a copy of the questionnaire and statistical analysis can be inserted in the appendix for justification and evidence of findings, with qualitative research it is impossible to provide the full evidence in a manner that is as immediately accessible to the reader. Consequently, what is included in the work has to be selective, but still presented in such a way as to create a meaningful picture. It is important, therefore, to chart the process as it evolves, to use diagrams to illustrate the emergence of the theory, and to point to critical junctures and breakthroughs in terms of theoretical insights.

It is very hard to convey a real sense of process which accurately reflects the cyclical and episodic nature of data collection and analysis. For example, it may not be possible to include the early development of multiple codes, concepts and their relationships, which appear at first to be like an enormous and complicated jigsaw, without creating disorder, repetition and fragmentation within the text. Therefore, the paper or thesis should be written in a way that allows the reader to identify key stages in the research and highlight conceptual development. It is usually suggested that, when writing up, the researcher obtains examples of work that have adopted or developed similar methods. To gain an indication of style and presentation of process, two contemporary American PhD theses which are often cited in the literature on grounded theory, Lempert (1992) and C. Hall (1992), are recommended, particularly for researchers engaged in doctoral work. Both were awarded by the University of California, the birthplace of grounded theory, and both were in the field of sociology. While there are differences in terms of length and the presentation of evidence – one used a 'typical' case as the basis for analysis (Lempert, 1992) and the other (C. Hall, 1992) wove sections of interviews into the analysis – they demonstrate the process of telling the story of building theory using this method. A more recent example, and one which has more direct implications for management theory, is Haslam's (1999) PhD thesis. This involves a very detailed step-by-step discussion of the methodological process. It presents the stages of induction and deduction, and the abstraction of theoretical codes and their integration into a densely thick theory.

Nonetheless, whilst these practical steps may be taken to provide an indication of process and what grounded theory looks like, questions regarding individual make-up and preferred working styles should also be addressed before making the decision. For example, there is the issue of control in relation to the collection and interpretation of data. Whilst enthusiasts of computer-assisted analysis suggest that the result is greater control over the data on the part of the analyst, this is open to question. For some, the act of interpreting the data is a very personal one which occurs over time and through a process of constant review and re-evaluation of the information at hand. The nature of the data is usually such that it cannot be instantly dissected and understood. On the contrary the data require reflection, a sense of orientation and a personal understanding of context. It is not enough to count for themes, which are important, but may be subordinate at times to the more subtle nuances of behaviour that signal and convey greater meaning than the spoken word. For example, during observation of behaviour at the site of Blist Hill in Shropshire, one group of elderly visitors spoke volumes about their experience without uttering a word. Their expressions, mannerisms, total detachment from others, and their resilience and tolerance of the wind and rain that day provided an insight into their experience that would be hard to transfer onto a computer. In many cases it was the non-verbal signals that revealed clues to the behaviour of visitors – a tone of voice, a facial expression, a heightened enthusiasm or a look of boredom all acted as sources of rich data. This type of data is difficult to code and categorise, but to ignore it would be to detract from the richness of the final picture.

On the issue of interpretation, there is growing support for the idea that there may be a danger in pressurising researchers using qualitative data into using computer packages as their main source of analysis. Qualitative researchers have been using the guidelines and principles laid down by their originators for many years, and the results have been a wealth of insightful works which are the product of involvement in the context studied and painstaking analysis. However, the end product is not always the sole objective. By going through the process, mistakes are made, frustrations are inevitable, doubts and insecurity take over at times and make the researcher question his/her ability and chances of ever producing a coherent and meaningful account, but there is also a positive side to all this. By living and working with the data, by following the guidelines, experiencing the anxieties and eventually emerging from this to develop insights into the data and meaningful pictures, a sense of personal growth and development is achieved which has as much to do with the low periods as it has with the moments of insight and breakthroughs. However, at the end of the day, it is really up to the individual.

---

**Student exercises**

1   Given the information provided on the two approaches to grounded theory, write a 1,000-word justification for the version (i.e. Glaser or Strauss and Corbin) that you feel would best suit your way of working.
2   Discuss the potential problems you might encounter in using grounded theory for:

   (a)  Academic research (i.e. dissertation, PhD)
   (b)  Managerial research

# Glossary

**Abstraction**: Abstraction is the process of lifting the analysis of the data from the descriptive level to a conceptual or theoretical interpretation which offers an explanation of the phenomenon under study.

**Axial coding**: This is a more sophisticated method of coding data which seeks to identify incidents which have a relationship to each other. It is incumbent on the researcher to specify these relationships which are normally the product of constant comparison of data.

**Categories**: The final stage in the process of theory development is the construction of a core category. Through the process of coding and abstraction the data are finally subsumed into a higher order category. Core or higher order categories unite the theoretical concepts to offer an explanation or theory of the phenomenon. A core category is a main theme which sums up a pattern of behaviour and it must be explained in terms of its relevance to other core categories. It has theoretical significance and its development should be traceable back through the data.

**Coding Families**: Coding families provide a theoretical framework for analysing and tracing the causes, conditions and consequences of actions and/or behaviours within a specific context (see Glaser [1978] for a full description of the range of possible coding families).

**Concepts**: A concept is a higher level code which identifies influencing factors on behaviour and describes the relationship between them. The conceptual code should have properties and dimensions and should be interpreted at a theoretical level.

**Conditional matrix**: The conditional matrix is a device for tracking the various levels of influence on the phenomenon studied. The conditional matrix is usually presented in the form of a diagram comprising a series of decreasing circles. The outer circle usually represents the macro conditions affecting the phenomenon while the inner circles relate more to the immediate micro conditions.

**Constant Comparison**: Constant comparison is the exploration of similarities and differences across incidents in the data. By comparing where the facts are similar or different the researcher can generate concepts and concept properties based on recurring patterns of behaviour.

**Dimensional analysis**: An alternative version of grounded theory proposed by Schatzman. Using dimensional analysis data are collected and analysed until a critical mass of dimensions is assembled which represents emerging pathways that possess explanatory power. These are usually presented in an explanatory matrix.

**Dimensional range**: A dimension is an abstract concept with associated properties that provide parameters for the purpose of description and comparison.

**Grounded theory**: An inductive methodology developed by Glaser and Strauss used to generate theory through the systematic and simultaneous process of data collection and analysis.

**Induction**: The process of building theory from the data rather than commencing the research from the position of hypotheses testing.

**Open coding**: Open coding is the process of breaking down the data into distinct units of meaning. It is the product of early analysis and describes what is happening in the data. Open codes may comprise key words, phrases or sentences.

**Theoretical memos**: Memos are a central part of data collection using grounded theory. They may be descriptions of location, behaviour, researcher experience or theoretical insights which occur throughout the process. They help to reorientate the researcher at a later data and may act as a source of direction for further research.

**Theoretical sampling**: Theoretical sampling is sampling directed by the emerging theory. In the initial stages sampling should be open and relatively unfocused. The researcher should go to those people who are likely to provide relevant information. As the data are analysed, the researcher should use the findings to direct the research to further groups and diverse locations which may broaden the interpretation. Theoretical sampling means that the researcher must be flexible and remain open to the full range of possibilities.

**Theoretical saturation**: The researcher should stay in the field until no new information emerges from the collected data, or until the data are saturated. Theoretical saturation also refers to the thorough interrogation of the data before conclusions are arrived at.

**Theory**: The developed theory should consist of a set of relationships which offer the best and most plausible explanation of the research problem. A theory should be conceptually dense and should account for patterns of action and/or interaction between and among various types of social actors.

# Bibliography

Adler, P.A. and Adler, P. (1994) 'Observational techniques', in N.K. Denzin and Y.S. Lincoln (eds), *Handbook of Qualitative Research*. Thousand Oaks, CA: Sage.

Agar, M. (1983) 'Ethnographic evidence', *Urban Life*, 12 (10): 32–48.

Alexander, M., Burt, M. and Colinson, A. (1995) 'Big talk, small talk: BT's use of semiotics in planning its current advertising', *Journal of The Market Research Society*, 37 (2): 91–102.

Anderson, P.F. (1986) 'On method in consumer research: a critical relativist perspective', *Journal of Consumer Research*, 13 (September): 155–73.

Annells, M. (1996) 'Grounded theory method: philosophical perspectives, paradigm of enquiry, and postmodernism', *Qualitative Health Research*, 6 (3): 379–93.

Atkinson, P. and Hammersley, M. (1994) 'Ethnography and participant observation', in G. Guba and Y. Lincoln (eds), *Handbook of Qualitative Research*. Thousand Oaks, CA: Sage.

Atkinson, P. and Hammersley, M. (1995) *Ethnography* 2nd edn. London: Routledge.

Babich, B. (1994) 'On malls, museums and the art world: postmodernism and the vicissitudes of consumer culture', *Art Criticism*, 19 (1): 93–109.

Baker, C., Wuest, J. and Stern, P. (1992) 'Method slurring: the grounded theory/ phenomenology example', *Journal of Advanced Nursing*, 17 (11): 1355–60.

Barnes, D.M. (1996) 'An analysis of the grounded theory method and the concept of culture', *Qualitative Health Research*, 6 (3): 429–441.

Baszanger, I. (1998) 'The work sites of an American interactionist: Anselm L. Strauss, 1917–1996', *Symbolic Interaction*, 21 (4): 353–78.

Baumeister, R. and O'Leary, M. (1995) 'The need to belong: desire for interpersonal attachments as a fundamental human emotion', *Psychological Bulletin*, 117 (3): 497–529.

Beard, C. (1989) 'The market launch for new technology intensive products and processes'. PhD thesis, University of Manchester.

Belk, R.W. (1988) 'Possessions and the extended self', *Journal of Consumer Research*, 15 (September): 139–53.

Belk, R.W., Wallendorf, M. and Sherry, J.F. (1989) 'The sacred and the profane in consumer behaviour: theodicy on the Odyssey', *Journal of Consumer Research*, 16 (June): 1–37.

Bloch, C. (1996) 'Emotions and discourse', *Human Studies*, 16 (3): 323–341.

Blud, L.M. (1990) 'Social interaction and learning among family groups visiting a museum', *Museum Management and Curatorship*, 9: 43–51.

Blumer, H. (1969) *Symbolic Interactionism: Perspective and Method*. Englewood Cliffs, NJ: Prentice Hall.

Blumer, H. (1980) 'Mead and Blumer: the convergent methodological perspectives of social behaviorism and symbolic interactionism', *American Sociological Review*, 45: 409–19.

Boisvert, D. and Slez, D. (1995) 'The relationship between exhibit characteristics and learning associated behaviours in a science museum', *Science Education*, 79 (5): 503–18.

Boje, D.M. (2000) 'Phenomenal complexity theory and change at Disney: response to Letiche', *Journal of Organisational Change*, 13 (6): 558–66.

Borman, K. and Preissle-Goez, J. (1986) 'Ethnographic and qualitative research design and why it doesn't work', *American Behavioral Scientist*, 30 (1): 42–57.

Bourdieu, P. (1984) *Distinction: A Social Critique of the Judgement of Taste*. London: Routledge & Kegan Paul.

Boyle, J.S. (1994) 'Styles of ethnography', in J.M. Morse (ed.), *Critical Issues in Qualitative Research Methods*. Thousand Oaks, CA: Sage.

Brown, A. (1994) 'Politics, symbolic action and myth making in pursuit of legiti- macy', *Organization Studies*, 15 (6): 861–78.

Brown, A. (1995) 'Managing understandings: politics, symbolism, niche marketing and the quest for legitimacy in IT implementation', *Organization Studies*, 16 (6): 951–69.

Brown, A. (1998) 'Narrative, politics and legitimacy in an IT organisation', *Journal for Organisational Studies*, 35 (1): 35–8.

Brown, S. (1995) *Postmodern Marketing*. London: Routledge.

Brown, S. (1998) *Postmodern Marketing 2: Telling Tales*. London: Thompson Business Press.

Brown, S. and Reid, R. (1997) 'Shoppers on the verge of a nervous breakdown: chronicle, composition and confabulation in consumer research', in S. Brown and D. Turley (eds), *Consumer Research: Postcards from the Edge*. London: Routledge.

Browning, L., Beyer, J. and Shetler, J. (1995) 'Building co-operation in a competitive industry: Sematech and the semiconductor industry', *Academy of Management Journal*, 38 (1): 113–51.

Bryman, A. (1984) 'The debate about quantitative and qualitative research: a question of method or epistemology?', *The British Journal of Sociology*, XXXV (1): 75–92.

Bryman, A. and Burgess, R. (1994) 'An introduction', in A. Bryman and R. Burgess (eds), *Developments in Qualitative Data Analysis*. London: Routledge.

Burchill, G. and Fine, C. (1997) 'Time versus market orientation in product concept development: empirically-based theory generation', *Management Science*, 43 (4): 465–78.

Calder, B. and Tybout, A. (1987) 'What consumer research is', *Journal of Consumer Research*, 14 (June): 136–40.

Calloway, L.J. and Ariav, G. (1995) 'Designing with dialogue charts: a qualitative content analysis of end user designers' experiences with a software engineering design tool', *Information Systems*, 5 (2): 75–103.

Charmaz, K. (1983) 'The grounded theory method: an explication and interpretation,' in R. Emerson (ed.), *Contemporary Field Research: A Collection of Readings*. Boston: Little Brown.

Chock, P. (1986) 'Irony and ethnography', *Anthropology Quarterly*, 52 (2): 87–96.

Clegg, J.A., Stander, P. and Jones, G. (1996) 'Striking the Balance: A Grounded Theory Analysis of Staff Perspectives', *British Journal of Clinical Psychology*, 35 (2): 249–64.

Clondinin, D.J. and Connelly, F.M. (1994) 'Personal experience methods', in N. Denzin and Y. Lincoln (eds), *Handbook of Qualitative Research*. London: Sage.

Cohen, E. (1979) 'A phenomenology of tourist experiences', *Sociology*, 13: 179–201.

Cohen, E. (1988) 'Authenticity and commoditization', *Annals of Tourism Research*, 15 (3): 371–86.

Cole, C. (1997) 'Information as process: the difference between corroborating evidence and "information" in humanistic research domains', *Information Processing and Management*, 33 (1): 55–67.

Connor, S. (1995) *Postmodern Culture: An Introduction to Theories of the Contemporary*. London: Routledge.

Corbin, J. (1998) 'Alternative interpretations: valid or not?', *Theory and Psychology*, 8 (1): 121–8.

Corbin, J. and Strauss, A. (1990) 'Grounded theory research: procedures, canons, and evaluative criteria', *Qualitative Sociology*, 13 (1): 3–21.

Costelloe, T. (1996) 'Between the subject and sociology: Alfred Schutz's phenomenology of the life world', *Human Studies*, 19: 247–66.

Coyle, I.T. (1997) 'Sampling in qualitative research: purposeful and theoretical sampling; merging or clear boundaries?', *Journal of Advanced Nursing*, 26 (3): 623–30.

Crook, C. and Kumar, R. (1998) 'Electronic data interchange: a multi-industry investigation using grounded theory', *Information Management*, 34 (2): 75–89.

Csikszentmihalyi, M. (1992) *Flow: The Psychology of Happiness*. London: Rider Press.

Csikszentmihalyi, M. and Rochberg-Halton, E. (1981) *The Meaning of Things*. Cambridge: Cambridge University Press.

Cushman, P. (1990) 'Why the self is empty: toward a historically situated psychology', *American Psychologist*, 45 (5): 599–611.

Cutler, I. (2000) 'The cynical manager', *Management Learning*, 31 (3): 295–312.

Davis, F. (1979) *A Yearning For Yesterday: A Sociology of Nostalgia*. London: Collier Macmillan.

De La Cuesta, C. (1994) 'Marketing: a process in health visiting', *Journal of Advanced Nursing*, 19 (2): 347–53.

Delaney, J. (1992) 'Ritual space in the Canadian Museum of Civilisation', in R. Shields (ed.), *Lifestyle Shopping*. London: Routledge.

Dembrowski, S. and Hammer-Lloyd, S. (1995) 'Computer applications – a new road to qualitative data analysis?', *European Journal of Marketing*, 29 (11): 50–63.

Denzin, N. (1993) 'Where has postmodernism gone?', *Cultural Studies*, 7 (3): 507–14.

Denzin, N. and Lincoln, Y. (1994) 'Methods of collecting and analysing empirical materials', in N. Denzin and Y. Lincoln (eds), *Handbook of Qualitative Research*. Thousand Oaks, CA: Sage.

Dittmar, H. (1992) *The Social Psychology of Material Possessions*. Hemel Hempstead: Harvester Wheatsheaf.

Dreher, M. (1994) 'Qualitative research methods from the reviewer's perspective', in J.M. Morse (ed.), *Critical Issues in Qualitative Research Methods*. Thousand Oaks, CA: Sage.

Egan, M. (1997) 'Getting down to business and off welfare: rural women entrepreneurs', *Affilia*, 12 (Summer): 215–28.

Elliott, R., Eccles, S. and Gournay, K. (1996) 'Revenge, existential choice and addictive consumption', *Psychology and Marketing*, 13 (8): 753–68.

Ellis, D. (1993) 'Modelling the information-seeking patterns of academic researchers: a grounded theory approach', *Library Quarterly*, 63 (4): 469–86.

Ellis, D., Cox, D. and Hall, K. (1993) 'A comparison of the information seeking patterns of researchers in the physical and social sciences', *Journal of Documentation*, 49 (4): 356–69.

Evans, G. and Lepore, S. (1992) 'Conceptual and analytical issues in crowding research', *Journal of Environmental Psychology*, 12 (2): 163–73.

Falk, J.H., Koran, J.J., Dierking, L.D. and Dreblow, L. (1985) 'Predicting visitor behaviour', *Curator*, 28: 249–57.

Feldman, S. (1998) 'Playing with the pieces: deconstruction and the loss of moral culture', *Journal of Management Studies*, 35 (January): 59–78.

Fine, G. and Martin, D. (1990) 'A partisan view: sarcasm, satire, and irony as voices in Erving Goffman's asylums', *Journal of Contemporary Ethnography*, 19 (1): 89–115.

Firat, A. and Venkatesh, A. (1995) 'Liberatory postmodernism and the re-enchantment of consumption', *Journal of Consumer Research*, 22 (3): 239–67.

Fodness, D. (1994) 'Measuring tourist motivation', *Annals of Tourism Research*, 21 (3): 555–68.

Fontana, A. and Frey, J. (1994) 'Interviewing: the art of science', in N. Denzin and Y. Lincoln (eds), *The Handbook of Qualitative Research*. Thousand Oaks, CA: Sage.

Foster, H. (ed.) (1990) *Postmodern Culture*, fourth edition. London: Pluto Press.

Gergen, K.J. (1991) *The Saturated Self: Dilemmas of Identity in Contemporary Life*. New York: Basic Books.

Gherardi, S. and Turner, B.A. (1987) 'Real men don't collect soft data', Quadermo 13, Dippartimento di politica Sociale, University di Trento.

Glaser, B. (1978) *Theoretical Sensitivity*. Mill Valley, CA: Sociology Press.

Glaser, B. (1992) *Basics of Grounded Theory Analysis: Emergence v Forcing*. Mill Valley, CA: Sociology Press.

Glaser, B. (1998) *Doing Grounded Theory: Issues and Discussions*. Mill Valley, CA: Sociology Press.

Glaser, B. and Strauss, A. (1967) *The Discovery of Grounded Theory: Strategies for Qualitative Research*. Chicago: Aldine.

Glaser, B. and Strauss, A. (1968) *The Discovery of Grounded Theory: Strategies for Qualitative Research*. London: Weidenfeld and Nicolson.

Glen, R. (1999) 'Analysis and interpretation in qualitative research: a researcher's perspective', in L. Butterfield (ed.), *Excellence in Advertising*, 2nd edn. Oxford: Butterworth–Heinemann.

Goffman, E. (1959) *The Presentation of Self in Everyday Life*. New York: Doubleday.

Goffman, E. (1961) *Asylums*, ed. D. Cressey, New York: Holt, Reinhart & Winson.

Goffman, E. (1970) *Strategic Interaction*. Oxford: Basil Blackwell.

Gould, S.J. (1991) 'The manipulation of MY pervasive, perceived vital energy through product use: an introspective-praxis perspective', *Journal of Consumer Research*, 18 (September): 194–207.

Gould, S.J. (1995) 'Researcher introspection as a method in consumer research: applications, issues and implications', *Journal of Consumer Research*, 21 (4): 719–22.

Goulding, C. (1998) 'Grounded theory: the missing methodology on the interpretivist agenda', *Qualitative Marketing Research: An International Journal*, 1 (1): 50–7.

Goulding, C. (1999a) 'Consumer research, qualitative paradigms, and methodological ambiguities', *European Journal of Marketing*, 33 (9/10): 859–73.

Goulding, C. (1999b) 'Heritage, nostalgia, and the "grey" consumer', *The Journal of Marketing Practice: Applied Marketing Science*, 5 (6/7/8): 177–99.

Goulding, C. (1999c) 'Museum culture and consumer behaviour', *Journal of Marketing Management*, 15 (November): 647–72.

Goulding, C. (2000a) 'Grounded theory and consumer behaviour: principles, practice, and pitfalls', *Advances in Consumer Research*, 27 (September): 261–6.

Goulding, C. (2000b) 'The museum environment and the visitor experience', *European Journal of Marketing*, 34 (3/4): 433–52.

Goulding, C. (2000c) 'The commodification of the past, postmodern pastiche, and the search for authentic experiences at contemporary heritage attractions', Special Edition of Consumer Behaviour, *European Journal of Marketing*, 34 (7): 835–53.

Goulding, C. and Domic, D. (1999) 'History, identity & social conflict: consuming heritage in the former Yugoslavia', *1st International Conference on 'Consumption & Representation: Consuming Markets Consuming Meaning'*, University of Plymouth, 1–3 September.

Goulding, C., Shankar, A. and Elliott, R. (2002) 'Dance clubs, rave and the consumer experience: an exploration of a sub-culture and its implications for marketing', *European Advances in Consumer Research*, 5 (forthcoming).

Grekova, M. (1996) 'Restructuring of the Life World of Socialism', *International Sociology*, 11 (1): 63–78.

Grove, S.J. and Fiske, R.P. (1992) 'Observational data collection for services marketing: an overview', *Journal of the Academy of Marketing Science*, 20 (3): 217–24.

Grove, W. R. (1994) 'Why we do what we do: a biopsychosocial theory of human motivation', *Social Forces*, 73 (2): 363–94.

Guba, G. and Lincoln, Y. (1994) 'Competing paradigms in qualitative research', in N. Denzin and Y. Lincoln (eds), *Handbook of Qualitative Research*. Thousand Oaks, CA: Sage.

Hall, C. (1992) 'The homecoming: the self at home', PhD thesis, University of California, San Francisco.

Hall, E. (1966) *The Silent Language*. New York: Doubleday.

Hall, S. (1992) 'Our mongrel selves', *New Statesman and Society*, June: 6–9.

Haraven, T. and Langenbach, R. (1981) 'Living places, work places and historical identity', in M. Binney and D. Laventhal (eds), *Our Past Before Us: Why do we Save It?*. London: Temple Smith.

Harvey, D. (1992) *The Condition of Postmodernism*. Oxford: Blackwell.

Haskell, F. (1993) *History and its Images*. New Haven, CT: Yale University Press.

Haslam, S. (1999) 'Personal legitimising: a substantive grounded theory in the context of small consultancy firms', PhD thesis, University of Strathclyde.

Hassard, J. (1993) *Sociology and Organisation Theory: Positivism, Paradigms and Postmodernity*. Cambridge: Cambridge University Press.

Hassard, J. (1994) 'Postmodern organisational analysis: towards a conceptual framework', *Journal of Management Studies*, 31 (3): 303–24.

Hedges, A. (1993) 'Group interviewing', in R. Walker (ed.), *Applied Qualitative Research*. Aldershot: Dartmouth.

Heidegger, M. (1962) *Being and Time*. New York: Harper and Row.

Hewison, R. (1987) *The Heritage Industry: Britain in a Climate of Decline*. London: Methuen.

Higgins, T.E. (1987) 'Self discrepancy: a theory relating self and affect', *Psychological Review*, 94 (3): 319–40.

Hirschman, E. (1985) 'Scientific style and the conduct of consumer research', *Journal of Consumer Research*, 12 (2): 225–39.

Hirschman, E. (1993) 'Ideology in consumer research, 1980 and 1990: a Marxist and feminist critique', *Journal of Consumer Research*, 19 (March): 537–55.

Hirschman, E.C. and Thompson, C. (1997) 'Why media matter: toward a richer understanding of consumers' relationships with advertising and mass media', *The Journal of Advertising*, 26 (1): 43–60.

Holbrook, M.B. and Hirschman, E. (1993) *The Semiotics of Consumption: Interpreting Symbolic Behaviour in Popular Culture and Works of Art*. Berlin: Mouton de Gruyter.

Holstein, J. and Gubrium, J. (1994) 'Phenomenology, ethnography and interpretative practice', in N. Denzin and Y. Lincoln (eds), *Handbook of Qualitative Research*. Thousand Oaks, CA: Sage.

Holt, D. (1997) 'Poststructuralist lifestyle analysis: conceptualizing the social patterning of consumption in postmodernity', *Journal of Consumer Research*, 23 (March): 326–50.

Horne, D. (1984) *The Great Museum*. London: Pluto Press.

Horne, M . (1994) 'Ironbridge Gorge Museum Trust Tourist Survey 1994'.

Houston, H.R. and Venkatesh, A. (1996) 'The health care consumption patterns of Asian immigrants: grounded theory implications for consumer acculturation theory', *Advances in Consumer Research*, 23: 418–23.

Hunt, J.G. and Ropo, A. (1995) 'Multi-level leadership: grounded theory and mainstream theory applied to the case of General Motors.' *Leadership Quarterly*, 6 (3): 379–412.

Hunt, S.D. (1991) 'Positivism and paradigm dominance in consumer research: toward critical pluralism and rapprochement', *Journal of Consumer Research*, 18 (June): 32–44.

Husserl, E. (1962) *The Crisis of European Sciences and Transcendental Phenomenology*, trans. D. Carr. Evanston, IL: Northwestern University Press.

James, M. and Burdges, S. (1984) 'Crowding perception determinants at intensely developed outdoor recreation sites', *Leisure Sciences*, 6: 167–86.

Jameson, F. (1990) 'Postmodernism and consumer society,' in H. Foster (ed.), *Post Modern Culture*. London: Pluto

Jezewski, M.A. (1995) 'Evolution of a grounded theory: conflict resolution through culture brokering', *Advances in Nursing Science*, 17 (3): 14–30.

Jopling, D. (1996) 'Sub-phenomenology', *Human Studies*, 19 (2): 153–73.

Kamptner, L. (1989) 'Personal possessions and their meaning in old age', in S. Spacapan and S. Oskamp (eds), *The Social Psychology of Ageing*, Claremont Symposium on Applied Social Psychology. London: Sage.

Kaplan, H. (1987) 'The psychopathology of nostalgia', *Psychoanalytical Review*, 74 (4): 465–86.

Katz, J. (1983) 'A theory of qualitative methodology: the social system of analytical fieldwork', in R. Emerson (ed.), *Contemporary Field Research: A Collection of Readings*. Boston: Little Brown.

Kellner, D. (1995) *Media Culture*. London: Routledge.

Kelly, R. (1985) 'Museums as status symbols 2: obtaining a state of having been there', in R. Belk (ed.), *Advances in Non Profit Marketing*. Greenwhich, CT: JAI Press.

Kimle, P.A. and Damhorst, M. (1997) 'A grounded theory model of the ideal business image for women', *Symbolic Interaction*, 20 (1): 45–68.

King, S. (1996) 'Case tools and organizational action', *Information Systems*, 6 (3): 173–94.

Knafl, K.A. (1994) 'Promoting academic integrity in qualitative research, in J.M. Morse (ed.), *Critical Issues in Qualitative Research Methods*. Thousand Oaks, CA: Sage.

Kools, S., McCarthy, M., Durham, R. and Robrecht, L. (1996) 'Dimensional analysis: broadening the conception of grounded theory', *Qualitative Health Research*, 6 (3): 312–30.

Kvale, S. (1995) 'The social construction of validity', *Qualitative Inquiry*, 1 (1): 19–40.

Laenan, M. (1989) 'Looking for the future through the past', in D. Uzzell (ed.), *Heritage Interpretation*. London: Belhaven Press.

Lang, J.W. (1996) 'Strategic alliances between large and small high-tech firms', *International Journal of Technology Management*, 12 (7/8): 796–807.

Langenbach, M. (1995) 'Phenomenology, intentionality, and mental experiences', *History of Psychiatry*, 5: 209–24.

Langman, L. (1992) 'Neon cages: shopping for subjectivity', in R. Shields (ed.), *Lifestyle Shopping*. London: Routledge.

Lash, A. (1990) *Sociology of Post Modernism*. London: Routledge.

Lee, M. (1993) *Consumer Culture Reborn: The Cultural Politics of Consumption*. London: Routledge.

Lempert, L. (1992) 'The crucible: violence, help seeking and abused women's transformation of self', PhD thesis, University of California, San Francisco.

Letiche, H. (2000) 'Phenomenal complexity theory as informed by Bergson', *Journal of Organisational Change*, 13 (6): 545–57.

Lincoln, Y. and Guba, E. (1985) *Naturalistic Enquiry*. Beverly Hills, CA: Sage.

Locke, K. (1996) 'Rewriting the discovery of grounded theory after 25 years?', *Journal of Management Inquiry*, 5 (3): 239–45.

Locke, K. and Golden-Biddle, K.A. (1997) 'Constructing opportunities for contribution: structuring intertextual coherence and problemizing in organisational studies', *Academy of Management Journal*, 40 (5): 1023–62.

Lowe, J., Morris, J. and Wilkinson, B. (2000) 'British factory, Japanese factory and Mexican factory: an international comparison of front line management and supervision', *Journal of Management Studies*, 37 (June): 541–62.

Lowenberg, J.S. (1993) 'Interpretive research methodology: broadening the dialogue', *Advances in Nursing Science*, 16 (2): 57–69.

Lyotard, J.F. (1984) *The Postmodern Condition*. Minneapolis: University of Minnesota Press.

Manning, K., Beardon, W. and Rose, R. (1998) 'Development of a theory of retailer response to manufacturers' everyday low cost programs', *Journal of Retailing*, 74 (1): 107–37.

Marcuse, H. (1964) *One Dimensional Man*. Boston: Beacon.

Markus, H. and Nurius, P. (1986) 'Possible selves', *American Psychologist*, 41 (9): 954–69.

Masberg, B. and Silverman, L. (1996) 'Visitor experiences at heritage sites: a phenomenological approach', *Journal of Travel Research*, 34 (4): 20–5.

Maslow, A. (1943) *Motivation and Personality*. New York: Harper Collins.

May, K.A. (1994) 'Abstract knowing: the case for magic in method', in J.M. Morse (ed.), *Critical Issues in Qualitative Research Methods*. Thousand Oaks, CA: Sage.

May, K.A. (1996) 'Diffusion, dilution, or distillation? The case of grounded theory method', *Qualitative Health Research*, 6 (3): 309–11.

McCracken, G. (1988) *The Long Interview*. London: Sage.

McKinley-Wright, M. (1995) 'I never did any fieldwork, but I milked an awful lot of cows! Using rural women's experience to reconceptualise models of work', *Gender and Society*, 9 (2): 216–35.

McManus, P. (1989) 'What people say and how they think in a science museum', in D. Uzzell (ed.) *Heritage Interpretation Volume 1*. London: Belhaven Press.

McQuarrie, E. and McIntyre, S. (1990) 'What the group interview can contribute to research on consumer phenomenology', in E. Hirschman (ed.), *Research in Consumer Behaviour*, Greenwich, CT: JAI Press.

McRobbie, A. (1994) *Postmodernism and Popular Culture*. London: Routledge.

Melia, K.M. (1996) 'Rediscovering Glaser', *Qualitative Health Research*, 6 (3): 368–78.

Merleau-Ponty, M. (1962) *Phenomenology of Perception*, trans. C. Smith London: Routledge & Kegan Paul.

Merriman, N. (1991) *Beyond The Glass Case: The Past, the Heritage and the Public in Britain*. London: Leicester University Press.

Mick, D. (1986) 'Consumer research and semiotics: exploring the morphology of signs, symbols, and significance', *Journal of Consumer Research*, 13 (September): 196–213.

Miles, M.B. and Huberman, A.M. (1994) *Qualitative Data Analysis*, 2nd edn. Thousand Oaks, CA: Sage.

Mills, C.W. (1959) *The Sociological Imagination*. New York: Oxford University Press.

Morison, M. and Moir, J. (1998) 'The role of computer software in the analysis of qualitative data: efficient clerk, research assistant or Trojan horse?', *Journal of Advanced Nursing*, 28 (1): 106–16.

Morse, J.M. (1991) *Strategies for Sampling in Qualitative Research: A Contemporary Dialogue*. Newbury Park, CA: Sage.

Morse, J.M. (1994) 'Emerging from the data: the cognitive process of analysis in qualitative enquiry', in J.M. Morse (ed.), *Critical Issues in Qualitative Research Methods*. Thousand Oaks, CA: Sage.

Morse, J.M., Hutchinson, S.A. and Penrod, J. (1998) 'From theory to practice: the development of assessment guidelines from qualitatively derived theory', *Qualitative Health Research*, 8 (3): 329–40.

Moscardo, G. (1996) 'Mindful visitors: heritage and tourism', *Annals of Tourism Research*, 23 (2): 376–97.

Muecke, M.A. (1994) 'On the evaluation of ethnographies', in J.M. Morse (ed.), *Critical Issues in Qualitative Research Methods*. Thousand Oaks, CA: Sage.

Mullins, J. and Roessier, R. (1998) 'Improving employment outcomes: perspectives of experienced counsellors regarding the importance of counselling tasks', *Journal of Rehabilitation*, 64 (2): 12–18.

Murray, J.B. and Ozanne, J.L. (1991) 'The critical imagination: emancipatory interests in consumer research', *Journal of Consumer Research*, 19 (September): 129–44.

Myerson, J. (1994) 'Talking shop', *Times Higher Education Supplement*, 3 June.

Norse, C. (1991) *What's Wrong with Postmodernism?* Baltimore, MD: Johns Hopkins University Press.

Nuefeldt, S., Mitchell, P. and Nelson, M. (1996) 'A qualitative study of experts' conceptualisation of supervisee reflectivity', *Journal of Counselling Psychology*, 43 (1): 3–9.

O'Callaghan, J. (1996) 'Grounded theory: a potential methodology', *Counselling Psychology Review*, 11 (1): 23–8.

O'Guinn, T. and Belk, R.W. (1989) 'Consumption at Heritage Village USA', *Journal of Consumer Research*, 16: 227–37.

Parker, M. (1995) 'Critique in the name of what? Postmodernism and critical approaches to organisations', *Organisational Studies*, 16 (4): 553–64.

Parry, K.W. (1998) 'Grounded theory and social process: a new direction for leadership research', *Leadership Quarterly*, 9 (1): 85–105.

Patton, M.Q. (1990) *Qualitative Evaluation and Research Methods*, 2nd edn. Newbury Park, CA: Sage.

Pearce, P. and Stringer, P. (1991) 'Psychology of tourism', *Annals of Tourism Research*, 18 (1): 136–54.

Plait, S. (1993) 'Baudrillard's women', in C. Rojek and B. Turner (eds), *Forget Baudrillard*. London: Routledge.

Poster, M. (ed.) (1988) 'Introduction' to *Baudrillard: Selected Writings*. Stanford, CA: Stanford University Press.

Prentice, R. (1996) 'Tourism as experience, tourists as consumers: insight and enlightenment', Queen Margaret College, Edinburgh.

Rabinow, P. and Sullivan, M. (1979) *Interpretive Social Science: A Reader*. Berkeley, CA: University of California Press.

Rappaport, A. (1982) *The Meaning of the Built Environment*. Beverly Hills, CA: Sage.

Ray, M.A. (1994) 'The richness of phenomenology: philosophic, theoretical and methodological concerns', in J.M. Morse (ed.), *Critical Issues in Qualitative Research Methods*. Thousand Oaks, CA: Sage.

Rennie, D.L. (1998) 'Grounded theory methodology: the pressing need for a coherent logic of justification', *Theory and Psychology*, 8 (1): 101–19.

Rheorick, D. and Taylor, G. (1995) 'Thoughtful incoherence: first encounters with the phenomenological-hermeneutic domain', *Human Studies*, 18: 389–414.

Richards, L. and Richards, T.J. (1991) 'Computing in qualitative analysis: a healthy development?', *Qualitative Health Research*, 1 (2): 234–62.

Richards, T.J. and Richards, L. (1994) 'Using computers in qualitative research', in N. Denzin and Y. Lincoln (eds), *Handbook of Qualitative Research*. Thousand Oaks, CA: Sage.

Riley, R. (1995) 'Prestige-worthy tourism behaviour', *Annals of Tourism Research*, 22 (3): 630–49.

Riley, R. (1996) 'Revealing socially constructed knowledge through quasi-structured interviews and grounded theory analysis', *Journal of Travel and Tourism Marketing*, 15 (2): 21–40.

Ritson, M. and Elliott, R. (1999) 'The social uses of advertising: an ethnographic study of adolescent advertising audiences', *Journal of Consumer Research*, 26 (June): 260–77.

Robrecht, L. (1995) 'Grounded theory: evolving methods', *Qualitative Health Research*, 5 (2): 169–77.

Robson, S. and Hedges, A. (1993) 'Analysis and interpretation of qualitative findings – report of the MRS qualitative interest group', *Journal of the Market Research Society*, 35 (1): 23–35.

Rogers, J.K. and Henson, K. (1997) 'Hey why don't you wear a shorter skirt? Structural vulnerability and the organization of sexual harassment in temporary clerical employment', *Gender and Society*, 11 (2): 215–37.

Rosenau, P. (1992) *Postmodernism and the Social Sciences*. Princeton, NJ: Princeton University Press.

Rule, B. (1995) 'Themes for social science', *Journal of the History of Behavioural Sciences*, 13 (3): 220–7.

Rustemli, A. (1992) 'Crowding effects of density and interpersonal distance', *Journal of Social Psychology*, 132 (1): 51–8.

Ryozo, Y. (1991) 'A note on cognitive maps: an optimal spatial knowledge representation', *Journal of Mathematical Psychology*, 35 (3): 371–93.

Saegert, S. and Winkel, G. (1990) 'Environmental psychology', *Annual Review of Psychology*, 41: 441–77.

Sandelowski, M. (1994) 'The proof is in the pottery: toward a poetic for qualitative enquiry', in J.M. Morse (ed.), *Critical Issues in Qualitative Research Methods*. Thousand Oaks, CA: Sage.

Sandelowski, M. (1995) 'Focus on qualitative methods: sample size in qualitative research', *Research in Nursing and Health*, 18: 179–83.

Sandelowski, M., Holditch-Davis, D. and Harris, B.G. (1992) 'Using qualitative and quantitative methods: the transition to parenthood of infertile couples', *in* J.F. Gilgun, K. Daly and G. Handel (eds), *Qualitative Methods in Family Research*. Newbury Park, CA: Sage.

Schatzman, L. (1991) 'Dimensional analysis: notes on an alternative approach to the grounding of theory in qualitative research', in D.R. Maines (ed.), *Social Organisation and Social Process*. New York: Aldine De Gruyter.

Schatzman, L. and Strauss, A. (1973) *Field Research Strategies for a Natural Sociology*. Englewood Cliffs, NJ: Prentice Hall.

Schmidt, D. and Keating, J. (1979) 'Human crowding and personal control: an integration of the research', *Psychological Bulletin*, 86 (4): 680–700.

Schouten, J.W. and McAlexander, J.H. (1995) 'Subcultures of consumption: an ethnography of the new bikers', *Journal of Consumer Research*, 22 (June): 43–62.

Schroeder, D.M. and Congden, C. (1995) 'Linking competitive strategy and manufacturing process technology', *Journal of Management Studies*, 32 (2): 163–89.

Schutz, A. (1966) 'Some structures of the lifeworld', in *Collected Papers Vol. 3*. The Hague: Martinus Nijhoff.

Schutz, A. (1967) *The Phenomenology of the Social World*. Evanston, IL: Northwestern University Press.

Schwandt, T.A. (1994) 'Constructivist, interpretivist approaches to human enquiry', in N.K. Denzin and Y.S. Lincoln (eds), *Handbook of Qualitative Research*. Thousand Oaks, CA: Sage.

Seeley, M. and Targett, D. (1997) 'A senior executive end-user framework', *Information Systems*, 7 (4): 289–308.

Shankar, A., Elliott, R. and Goulding, C. (2001) 'Understanding consumption: contributions from a narrative perspective', *Journal of Marketing Management*, 7 (3/4): 429–54.

Shankar, A. and Goulding, C. (2000) 'Interpretive consumer research: two "new" additions to the canon of interpretive enquiry', Academy of Marketing Conference, Derby, 5–7 July.

Shankar, A. and Goulding, C. (2001) 'Interpretive consumer research: two more contributions to theory and practice', *Qualitative Marketing Research: An International Journal*, 4 (1): 7–16.

Shields, R. (ed.) (1992) *Lifestyle Shopping: The Subject of Consumption*. London: Routledge.

Skodal-Wilson, H. and Ambler-Hutchinson, S. (1996) 'Methodological mistakes in grounded theory', *Nursing Research*, 45 (2): 122–4.

Sperber-Richie, B., Fassinger, R., Geschmay-Linn, S., Johnson, J., Robinson, S. and Prosser, J. (1997) 'Persistence, connection, and passion: a qualitative study of the career development of highly achieving African-American black and white women', *Journal of Counselling Psychology*, 44 (2): 135–48.

Spiegelberg, H. (1982) *The Phenomenological Movement: A Historical Introduction*. The Hague: Martinus Nijhoff.

Spiggle, S. (1994) 'Analysis and interpretation of qualitative data in consumer research', *Journal of Consumer Research*, 21(3): 491–503.

Squire, S. (1994) 'The cultural values of literary tourism', *Annals of Tourism Research*, 21: 103–20.

Srubar, I. (1998) 'Phenomenological analysis and its contemporary significance', *Human Studies*, 21: 121–39.

Stapp, C.B. (1990) 'The "public" museum: a review of the literature', *Journal of Museum Education*, 11 (Fall): 4–10.

Stern, B. (1989) 'Literary criticism & consumer research: overview and illustrative analysis', *Journal of Consumer Research*, 16 (December): 322–34.

Stern, B. (1992) 'Historical and personal nostalgia in advertising text: the *fin de siecle* effect', *Journal of Advertising*, XXXI (4): 11–22.

Stern, B. (1994) 'Classical and vignette television advertising dramas: structural models, formal analysis and consumer effects', *Journal of Consumer Research*, 19: 601–15.

Stevens, R. (1996) 'Making sense of the person in a social world', in R. Stevens (ed.), *Understanding The Self*. London: Sage.

Stokols, S. (1976) 'The experience of crowding in primary and secondary environments', *Environment and Behaviour*, 8 (1): 49–86.

Strauss, A. (1987) '*Qualitative Analysis for Social Scientists*. New York: Cambridge University Press.

Strauss, A. and Corbin, J. (1990) *Basics of Qualitative Research: Grounded Theory Procedures and Techniques*. London: Sage.

Strauss, A. and Corbin, J. (1994) 'Grounded theory methodology: an overview', in N. Denzin and Y. Lincoln (eds), *Handbook of Qualitative Research*. Thousand Oaks, CA: Sage.

Szabo, V. and Strang, V.R. (1997) 'Secondary analysis of qualitative data', *Advances in Nursing Science*, 20 (2): 66–74.

Thomas, J. (1990) 'Archaeology and the notion of ideology', in, F. Baker and J. Thomas (eds), *Writing the Past in the Present*. Lampeter: University College.

Thompson, C.J. (1993) 'Modern truth and postmodern incredulity: a hermeneutic deconstruction of the metanarrative of "scientific truth" in marketing research', *International Journal of Marketing Research*, 10 (3): 325–38.

Thompson, C.J. (1997) 'Interpreting consumers: a hermeneutic framework for deriving marketing insights from the texts of consumers' consumption stories', *Journal of Marketing Research*, XXXIV (November): 438–55.

Thompson, C.J., and Hirschman, E.C. (1995) 'Understanding the socialised body: a poststructuralist analysis of consumers' self conceptions, body images, and self care practices', *Journal of Consumer Research*, 25 (2): 139–53.

Thompson, C.J., Locander, W.B. and Pollio, H.R. (1989) 'Putting consumer research back into consumer behaviour: the philosophy and method of existential phenomenology', *Journal of Consumer Research*, 16 (September): 133–46.

Thompson, C.J. Locander, W.B and Pollio, H.R. (1990) 'The lived meaning of free choice: an existential phenomenological description of everyday consumer experiences of contemporary married women', *Journal of Consumer Research*, 17 (December): 346–61.

Turner, B. (1981) 'Some practical aspects of qualitative data analysis: one way of organising the cognitive process associated with the generation of grounded theory', *Quality and Quantity*, 15: 225–47.

Turner, B. (1988) 'Connoisseurship in the study of organizational cultures', in A. Bryman (ed.), *Doing Research in Organizations*. London: Routledge.

Turner, B. (1993) 'Baudrillard for sociologists', in C. Rojek and B. Turner (eds), *Forget Baudrillard*. London: Routledge.

Turner, B. (1994) 'Patterns of crisis behaviour: a qualitative enquiry', in A. Bryman and R. Burgess (eds), *Analyzing Qualitative Data*. London: Routledge.

Turner, J.C. (1991) *Social Influence*. Milton Keynes: Open University Press.

Turner, V. and Turner, E. (1978) *Image and Pilgrimage in Christian Culture*. New York: Columbia University Press.

Valentine, V. and Evans, M. (1993) 'The dark side of the onion – rethinking the meanings of rational and emotional responses', *Journal of the Market Research Society*, 35 (2): 125–44.

Vattimo, G. (1992) *The Transparent Society*, trans. D. Webb Baltimore, MD: Johns Hopkins University Press.

Venkatesh, A. (1992) 'Postmodernism, consumer culture and the society of the spectacle', *Advances in Consumer Research*, 19: 199–202.

Wai-Chung Yeung, H. (1997) 'Critical realism and realist research in human geography: a method or a philosophy in search of a method?', *Progress in Human Geography*, 21 (1): 51–74.

Wallendorf, M. and Brucks, M. (1993) 'Introspection in consumer research: implementations and implications', *Journal of Consumer Research*, 21 (4): 719–22.

Walsh, K. (1992) *The Representation of the Past: Museums and Heritage in the Postmodern World*. London: Routledge.

Watson, T.J. (1994) *In Search of Management*. London: Routledge.

Watson, T.J. (1996) 'How do managers think? Identity, morality and pragmatism in managerial theory and practice', *Management Learning*, 3: 323–41.

Weiner, B. (1992) *Human Motivation: Metaphors, Theories and Research*. Thousand Oaks, CA: Sage.

Wells, K. (1995) 'The strategy of grounded theory: possibilities and problems', *Social Work Research*, 19 (1): 33–7.

Willis, P. (1990) *Common Culture*. Buckingham: Open University Press.

Yalom, I. D. (1980) *Existential Psychotherapy*. New York: Basic Books.

Yuen, H.K. and Richards, T.J. (1994) 'Knowledge representation for grounded theory construction in qualitative data analysis', *Journal of Mathematical Sociology*, 19 (4): 279–98.

Zukin, S. (1991) *Landscapes of Power: From Detroit to Disney World*. Berkeley, CA: University of California Press.

# Index